HISTORIC
ASHEVILLE

Bob Terrell

WORLDCOMM
a division of Creativity, Inc.

Publisher: Ralph Roberts

Vice President/Publishing: Pat Roberts

Cover Design: Brett Putnam

Editors: Barbara Blood, Gayle Graham, Susan Parker

Interior Design and Electronic Page Assembly: **WorldComm**®

Printed in the United States of America

10 9 8 7 6 5 4 3 2

Library of Congress Cataloging-in-Publication Data
Terrell, Bob
    Historic Asheville (1792-1930) / Bob Terrell
        p. cm.
    Includes bibliographical references.
    ISBN 1-56664-124-1 (hardcover : alk. paper) -- ISBN 1-56664-128-4
(trade paper : alk. paper)
        1. Asheville (N.C.)--History.   I. Title
    F264.A8T45 1997
    975.6'88--dc21   97-40958
                                                                 CIP

WorldComm®—a division of Creativity, Inc.–is a full-service publisher located at 65 Macedonia Road, Alexander NC 28701. Phone (704) 252-9515 or (704) 255-8719 fax.

WorldComm® is distributed to the trade by **Alexander Distributing**, 65 Macedonia Road, Alexander NC 28701. Phone (704) 252-9515 or (704) 255-8719 fax. For orders only: 1-800-472-0438. Visa and MasterCard accepted.

This book is also available on the internet in the **Publishers CyberMall™**. Set your browser to http://www.abooks.com and enjoy the many fine values available there.

CONTENTS

4

We hear the tread of pioneers,
Of nations yet to be,
The first low wash of waves where soon
Shall roll a human sea.

This book is respectfully dedicated to all those
who have waded or swum
in that human sea.

*All photos in this book courtesy
of North Carolina Collection,
Pack Memorial Public Library,
Asheville, North Carolina*

Other Books By Bob Terrell

* All Aboard! The Story of Charlie (Choo Choo) Justice
* Diamonds in the Dust
* Grandpa's Town
* Prison Bars to Shining Stars
* The Reluctant Lawman
* The Spiderweb Trail
* Trouble on his Trail
* The Will Harris Murders
* The Old Ball Yard – Home of Memories
J. D. Sumner – Gospel Music is my Life!
Fun is Where You Find It!
Holy Land: A Journey Into Time
A Touch of Terrell
Billy Graham in Hungary
Woody (with Barbara Shelton)
Old Gold
The Peace That Passeth Understanding (with Connie Hopper)
Disorder in the Court (with Marcellus Buchanan)
Billy Graham in the Soviet Union
Keep 'em Laughing
Papa Coke (with Sanders Rowland)
The Ralph Sexton Story
The Chuck Wagon Gang – A Legend Lives On
The Music Men
Plenty More in the Pot (with Udean Burke)
Elvis – His Love for Gospel Music (with J. D. Sumner)
Who Are These Iraqis?
A Nickel's Worth of Hope (with Andre Vandenberg)
McCormick Field – Home of Reality
The Legacy of Buck and Dottie Rambo
Givens Estates – A History
The Life and Times of J. D. Sumner

*Published by **WorldComm**® / **Alexander Books**™

INTRODUCTION

Asheville was always different. Instead of being organized in a patchwork of city squares, the town was carved out of a rolling wilderness and its streets followed the direction of deer trails.

There was no way to give the town a semblance of geographic order, so high were the hills and crooked the trails, and there still isn't all that much order to it, except West Asheville lies to the west and East Asheville to the east, and so on.

The town was chartered by the North Carolina Legislature without a decent wagon road connecting it with the rest of the state. Its people felt more akin to the State of Tennessee than to their own capital in Raleigh and probably would have backed any serious effort to create a State of Franklin.

So jumbled were the streets of Asheville before the interstates came in the late 1960s, a carload of confused tourists stopped a mountaineer on the street one afternoon and asked how to get to Grove Park Inn.

The old fellow scratched his chin and hemmed and hawed, trying to map out a route in his mind, and when he couldn't, he pointed toward the side of the mountain to the east and said, "Right there she is in plain view. Just head thataway as best you can and after while stop and ask somebody else."

Founded as a frontier town, landlocked by high mountains, Asheville continued to be extremely isolated for almost a century while the world passed it by. Its citizens were hard-crusted pioneers, ready for action and as quick on the trigger as they needed to be.

The coming of the railroads in October of 1880 changed the town. Iron rails opened Asheville and the entire mountain area of North Carolina to the world, and the world came knocking at the door, ready to play in this marvelous alpine wonderland, or seek relief from respiratory ailments, or simply to look for a good place to live and bring up a family.

While presenting the history of Asheville, this book will portray among other traits the iron will, perseverence, and sense of humor of the mountain people who lived here from the start. It will lean more toward being a history of the people than a history of the area, and that's the way it should be—for it is people, not shacks and houses or tall buildings and monuments, or paved streets and motor cars that make history. People do that, and here they did it in grand style.

I am indebted to the librarians at Pack Memorial Library and at the *Asheville Citizen-Times* for giving me tremendous help in researching facts, dates, and information. Several times in trying to pinpoint the date of an historic event, I came up with two or three conflicting dates, and the ladies at the libraries supplied me with information I needed to determine which date was correct. I am also indebted to Forster A. Sondley, Buncombe County's foremost historian, and to many other sources, like the files of the *Asheville Citizen-Times,* my employer for lo these many years, from which I drew heavily to put this story together.

I ask the reader not to look upon this work as the *history* of Asheville, because it is far from complete. It is as accurate as hard research can make it, but it is still simply the *story* of Asheville. It should be considered the story of *early* Asheville because I shut it off around 1930. To do the entire story of Asheville would require much more than one volume.

Bob Terrell
PO Box 66
Asheville NC 28802
August 5, 1997

I

FRONTIER

No white man had penetrated the wilderness as twenty-four-year-old Samuel Davidson was doing that day in the spring of 1784. When he crossed the barrier between civilization and the wild frontier he was all alone. In the vastness of the steep forest around him, there were no houses, no barns or cleared fields, nothing . . . but Indians? John Parris described the land as "an unexplored wilderness of white water and tall trees and wild game and brooding silence."

Davidson was a careful man who came prepared for trouble. Riding a stout horse, cradling a long rifle in the crook of his left arm, he allowed nothing around him to go unnoticed. His life depended on alertness, attention to detail, and readiness. His rifle was loaded, his powder horn filled, the powder was dry, and the skinning knife at his side was honed to such a razor's edge that he could shave with it of a morning. He was as much a backwoodsman as Daniel Boone. Some of the frontiersmen back at the fort had fought Indians with Dan'l, knew him well, in fact.

A half-mile from his starting point at the eastern foot of the mountains, from a blockhouse called Davidson's Fort,[1] he had entered the wilderness, and from that point he rode with care. There were no Cherokee settlements between the fort and his destination across the mountains; but these were Indian hunting grounds, and he risked the chance of encountering a hunting party.

At times he rode a buffalo path, and now and then when the going was rougher elsewhere, he took to an Indian trail up the forbidding mountain, but when the forest opened enough for passage, he left the

---

[1] Known today as Old Fort.

View of Asheville and the mountains in 1851.

trace and moved through the woods, riding when the going was easy, walking and leading his horse when the grade was steep.

The horse was burdened enough without his weight. Behind the saddle, it carried an axe and froe, a frying pan, and a couple of blankets. One saddle bag contained a tin cup, a coffee pot, a bag of coffee beans, part of a side of hogmeat, jerked beef, salt, and other staples, an extra buckskin shirt, a new pair of moccasins, a hunk of lead, a sack of gunpowder, and a bullet mold. He did not think he had forgotten anything. The other saddle bag was filled with grain for the horse.

He was prepared to stay over the mountain until he could clear a piece of land and build a rough cabin of logs. When he returned to the fort and brought his wife and infant child to their new home, he would build a bigger, better cabin.

Around him the woods were silent, except for the chirp of birds and the occasional chatter of a squirrel. Sunlight glistened off newborn foliage, forming slanted shafts of light through giant, virgin trees of oak, hickory, beech, poplar, chestnut, and evergreens. When possible, he clung to a route that carried him away from laurel hells[2] dotting the mountainside, for these were prime hiding places for savages up to no good and provided excellent cover for an ambush. With the forest in early leaf, he could see far enough through the trees so no one would come up on him unnoticed.

He made his way up the mountains, holding to hollows, creekbeds, and mountainsides, never skylining himself on a ridgetop. He rode

---

[2] A laurel hell is mountain vernacular for the thick patches of laurel that grow to many acres in the Western North Carolina mountains. People have disappeared in laurel hells and never found their way out.

with care and kept himself constantly alert. There was no dozing in his saddle on that ride.

His wariness paid off. When he camped for the night beside a trickle of pure water and staked his horse nearby, he had seen no other human being that day, and caught only glimpses of a few deer.

He strapped a feedbag on his horse's muzzle, rubbed it down, and patted its neck. "Well, Brownie, we've made it this far. Day after tomorrow we ought to be on t'other side of the mountains, and then we'll look for a place to live."

Savoring the meager supper as if he were devouring the finest steak, he ate quickly and put out the tiny fire over which he had brewed coffee and fried salt pork and corn balls, working the latter by mixing cornmeal and grease and frying it to a crisp. Darkness closed in quickly in the woods, and he rolled into his blankets and went to sleep, knowing his horse would alert him to any danger.

This was the life he loved. Hours spent in the forests where God's handiwork was so evident were his most satisfying times.

He had learned from occasional woodsmen that across the mountains were broad valleys of rich land and more mountains thickly covered with forest. There were wide rivers filled with jumping fish and whitewater creeks rushing down the hills and along the valley floor, creeks that carried cold water from bold springs high in the hills, and the forests held plenty of game for the table. Life would not be easy, not with the backbreaking work of carving out a homestead, clearing fields, and planting crops, but he did not mind that. The promise of a new and better life overshadowed the thought of strenuous labor, and the solitude appealed to him, regardless of the amount of toil.

History records that Davidson was the first white man to plant a homestead over the mountains, but he was not the first to explore west of the Blue Ridge. It is probable that DeSoto came through the Valley of the Tuckaseigee as early as 1540, and others intent upon scouting the country or wreaking havoc among the Cherokees had crossed through Swannanoa Gap since. The German explorer John Lederer came into the western mountains in 1669 or 1670 and probed the country. Englishmen James Needham and Gabriel Arthur poked about west of the Blue Ridge in 1673. Both of these parties came through Swannanoa Gap or Hickory Nut Gap.

A more recent expedition had been led by General Griffith Rutherford, who in 1776 brought 2,400 fighting men across

Swannanoa Gap and down along the river, passing through or near the site that would later become the town of Asheville, and moved on to the west to destroy Cherokee towns.

Two days later Samuel Davidson crossed the divide and descended into a broad, lush valley[3] divided by a small river.[4] Pausing to let his eyes roam the valley, he noticed pine- and hemlock-covered ridgelines, the thickness of the forest, and the location of ample water. A more beautiful sight had never passed before his eyes. The country fairly burst with natural resources, and the resources of a nation were for the benefit of all. He felt very good about entering this land, even if he was taking a grave chance, coming here all alone. All day he rode through the forest, encountering streams of varying width, and coming to a creek[5] that flowed from deep in the hills toward the river, he pulled his mount to a halt and surveyed the glade through which the creek rushed. He rode around it to a knoll from which he could see into the glade, and slowly a smile of satisfaction spread over his face.

"This is the place," he said to his horse. "This is where we'll build our home."

Enough said. He had seen aplenty, and Samuel Davidson never had trouble making up his mind. This was the place. He would go no farther.

Weeks later, under a warm sun, he removed his hat, wiped sweat off his brow, and surveyed the work he had done. He had cleared a small area of timber, pulled the stumps, and in the center of the clearing had grooved together a cabin. With froe and maul he had rived boards for the roof, and with rocks from the creek and good clay from its banks he had built a fireplace and chimney that drew well and would provide warmth on the coldest days.

On one side he had built a lean-to opening into the cabin, large enough for a small bed and table for the Negro servant girl his wife would bring with her. With no window, the lean-to would be warm

---

[3] The Swannanoa Valley.

[4] The Swannanoa River. There are various traditions concerning how the Swannanoa River got its name. Some said it was the Cherokee word for beautiful; others said it was intended as the Indian imitation of the sound made by the wings of the raven when flying rapidly, and was applied to this river because of the great number of these birds that congregated upon its banks. But to the historian Forster A. Sondley, Esq., it seemed more probable that this was just another way of spelling the name Shawano, a name for a tribe of Indians, some of whom lived in Ohio territory and others in northwestern South Carolina where their lands on the Savannah River adjoined the Cherokee territory. The word Savannah even appears to be a corruption of the name Shawano.

[5] Later Christian Creek.

in winter and cool in summer, and he figured the negress would fare well in there. He and his wife and daughter could easily make do in the main room. The cabin would have to be enlarged, perhaps this winter when there was no field work pressing him. He would clear land for crops and by next spring the homestead would still be raw but comfortable enough.

The horse lounged in a pole lot beside the place on which he would build a barn as soon as he could split the planks, and beside the horse lot was a garden plot with vegetable growth tall and healthy.

By carefully cutting the pieces and pegging together a rough bed, table, three chairs, and cupboard, and a bed and table for the servant's room he had furnished the cabin. On a rainy day he fashioned a cradle for their infant daughter.

Surveying the homestead and marveling at the work he had done, he turned his attention to the next task, that of returning to Davidson's Fort and bringing his family over the mountain.

At the fort a few days later, he made a sled of sturdy oak with runners cut from the crook of a sourwood tree, bought another horse, and headed again for the hills.

They made a caravan this time: two horses, one ridden by Samuel Davidson with his baby daughter strapped behind him, and another pulling the sled in which the Davidsons were moving their earthly possessions, including plow blades, hoe blades, other tools, a grinding stone, cooking pots, and seed corn for the fields. Davidson's wife drove the sled and the servant girl carried articles for the cabin.

They wove a careful though uneventful way up the mountain and a day or so later down into the valley to their new home. After supper that night, the Davidsons gave thanks to God for their bounty and good fortune, looking to the future with unbridled anticipation, and thus settled into the cabin to become the first white settlers west of the crest of the Blue Ridge Mountains.

Early fall arrived and Samuel Davidson made plans to clear more land for planting. He could clear as much farmland as he needed—and he had the jump on other settlers who would come over the hills later.

All day he studied the woods about him, pausing in his work to slowly run his eyes around the clearing in which he labored, taking in every detail. Had a rock been moved he would have known.

It was not a slackening of alertness that brought Davidson's end, but a small bell. At times he allowed one of his horses to graze freely and tied a small bell around its neck in case it wandered.

One morning in early autumn a small band of Cherokee hunters, seeking meat for the winter, moved into the valley and immediately saw wisps of white smoke drifting up from the woods. Investigating, they found the Davidson cabin. Moving nearer, they were attracted by the tinkling of the horse bell. Removing the bell, they led the horse to hiding in the woods, and returned to climb the forested hill beside the cabin, shaking the bell as they went along.

Samuel Davidson heard the bell and taking his rifle went to bring the horse back. He followed the sound up the hill and was gaining on the bell when a rifle ball knocked him from his feet and he saw a puff of smoke and heard the blast of a flintlock rifle from the trees. Other rifles boomed and Samuel Davidson felt the shock of lead balls striking his body, then heard no more as life slipped away.

In the cabin, Davidson's wife heard the crack of rifles and knew instinctively what had happened. Gathering her baby and the servant girl, she snatched wraps off pegs in a wall, and a handful of food, and pushing the girl ahead of her, fled into the forest. There they hid until dark. As soon as twilight settled, they made their way down the hill, around the cabin, and hurried toward the mountain they would have to cross to reach Davidson's Fort.

At the fort, a party of men including several members of the Davidson family saddled up within an hour after the arrival of Mrs. Davidson and headed for the mountains to avenge the death of Samuel Davidson. On the hill above Christian Creek they found the pioneer's scalped body and buried it on the spot. Trackers picked up the trail of the marauding Indians and brought the avengers in close to the Indian camp at the mouth of Rock House Creek, not far from the place of Davidson's death. Opening fire, they killed two Indians and the others fled into the blindness of the forest to the west.

In the valley, Colonel William Davidson, Samuel's twin brother, scooped up a handful of soil and let it sift through his fingers.

"That's good soil," he said, and a kinsman, standing beside him, caught the flowing dirt and felt it.

"Good, all right," he said, and his eyes glowed with interest.

The richness of the land and promise of the forest did not fail to register with members of the group, and soon a trickle of white men

came over the mountain from Davidson's Fort, entering through
Swannanoa Gap, and under the protection afforded by numbers
began building homesteads in the valley land along the Swannanoa
River, settling in a place they called Grey Eagle,[6] and others who
came settled along the length of the river to its confluence with a
greater river.[7]

First to come were the Davidsons, Alexanders, and Edmunsons.
Then came more Davidsons, the Smiths, and finally almost too
many to count. Samuel Davidson was killed before he could clear his
fields; thus, the first land cleared by a white man west of the Blue
Ridge was Edmunson land near the mouth of Bee Tree Creek and
was known for decades as the Edmunson Field.

Man has always been intrigued with the conquest of uncharted
lands, and suddenly the Valley of the Swannanoa was no longer a
part of the Cherokee hunting grounds but was commanded by a
growing number of fearless, well-armed whites who found the land
to be unbelievably lush and fertile. They loved the flat bottomland
which required little clearing and took easily to the plow, and they
recognized the presence of plentiful game in the forests and netted
fish in quantity from the streams. Wherever the river afforded a good
place to set a fish trap, someone quickly settled.

The stream of settlers grew into thousands, and soon all across
the land were scattered settlements of white homesteaders.

These frontiersmen had no idea they were hacking homesteads
out of an area to be called Buncombe County. When they settled they
were in Burke and Rutherford counties.

The Swannanoa River was the dividing line between Burke and
Rutherford, with Burke on the north side of the stream and Ruther-
ford on the south. Buncombe was carved out of them eight years after
Samuel Davidson was killed and scalped on Christian Creek.

In 1791, David Vance, who lived on upper Reems Creek, was
a member of the Legislature from Burke County, and Col. William
Davidson, who had settled on the south side of the Swannanoa at

---

[6] Black Mountain.
[7] The French Broad River. The usual account of the origin of the name French Broad is
that, as the settlements from the east advanced toward the mountains, the Broad River was
found and named. It rose on the east side of the Eastern Continental Divide and flowed
southeastward to dump its waters eventually in the Atlantic Ocean. When the larger river was
discovered on the western side of the same mountains, it was found that it flowed in a huge
arc which led to the Tennessee and then the Mississippi and at New Orleans, then claimed
by the French, emptied into the Gulf of Mexico. Thus, it was called the French Broad. It is
an unusual river, flowing south to north, and is one of the oldest rivers in the world, proven
by the fact that it flows northward through the Great Smoky Mountains which geologists say
are the oldest mountains in the world. Thus, the French Broad was in place before the
mountains were created.

Gum Spring, was the Rutherford representative in the State Senate. The two had raised petitions in December 1791, asking for the new county, and now they introduced legislation for the organization of a new county. It would be formed of the western portion of Burke and Rutherford counties with its western border fixed by the line of the territory North Carolina had ceded to the United States two or three years before, which afterward became the State of Tennessee. The legislature ratified the act creating the county on January 14, 1792. The bill was passed the same day it was received.

The county was named for Col. Edward Buncombe, a North Carolina soldier who commanded the 5th North Carolina Regiment, Contintental Troops, in the Revolution.

This, the legislature considered, was apt honor to give one who gave his life for the freedom of the new country. Buncombe was a patriot who led North Carolina forces under General George Washington's command in the northern phase of the war. Buncombe was severely wounded and captured at the Battle of Germantown in October 1777, and died in Philadelphia in May 1778, while a paroled prisoner in the hands of the British.

It is interesting that Col. Buncombe's final fame came not as the man for whom the mountain county was named, but for a phrase that coined a new word in the American language.

It was many years after formation of the county that the word "Buncombe" was given a new meaning by the Congress of the United States. The 16th Congress, which convened in 1819, debated the Missouri question; and after hours of rhetoric, the House, tired of speeches, wanted to come to a vote.

Felix Walker, representing Buncombe County in the lower house, was opposed to the bill. He secured the floor and apparently stalling for time, launched a long, windy, and rather meaningless address. Impatient members whispered to him to sit down and let the vote be taken, but he refused, saying, "I must make a speech for Buncombe," meaning for his constituents. Several members rose and left the hall in disgust at the threat of filibuster, and when Walker saw them go, he interrupted his ramblings to say to the remaining members, "You might go too, if you wish, for I am only speaking for Buncombe."

The phrase was caught up at once and the English vocabulary was enriched by a new term: "Buncombe," sometimes shortened to "bunk," which meant "empty talk" or "pointless ramblings." The word first appeared in Webster's dictionary in 1900 with the definitions of "insincere or foolish talk" and "nonsense."

2

THE CHEROKEES

Buncombe County held within its boundaries all the Cherokee land in Western North Carolina. There was more to the Cherokee Nation than that, however; much of the Indian territory lay in the northwestern part of South Carolina, northern Georgia, and some of Tennessee. The Cherokees[1] were a huge Indian nation.

Not any of the Cherokee towns appear to have been located in the Swannanoa Valley, nor even along the French Broad River. The hills neighboring the French Broad was something of a buffer zone between the mountain Cherokee and the Catawba tribe to the east of the Blue Ridge divide.

Cherokee hunting parties roamed this no-man's land, and probably Catawba parties did also, and large bands of Cherokee hunters camped often along the mountain rivers. Hunters would come in force, perhaps harvesting the coming winter's meat, and there is evidence of this—or used to be—at various places in Buncombe County.

Stone arrowheads by the bushels were found in certain places within the boundaries of Buncombe, and since most of them were defective or unfinished, historians conclude that these places were temporary hunting camps in which the Cherokees made their arrowheads, stone axes, and other weapons used in the hunting of meat.

There is a hill in Chunn's Cove in Asheville where hundreds of such unfinished stone implements were found. Traditionalists believe it was one of these great hunting camps. Another encampment apparently was

---

[1] In his *Sketches of Western North Carolina*, Dr. Hunter writes: "The Cherokee derive their name from Cheeta, or fire, which is their reputed lower heaven, and hence they call their magi Cheera-tah-gee, men possessed of the divine fire!"

located in a small valley near the northeastern corner of Riverside Cemetery in Asheville, and yet a third was found in the bottoms of the Swannanoa River near the point where it flows into the French Broad. Here, too, Sondley tells us, on the southern bank of the Swannanoa, just below the last branch above its mouth, once stood an Indian mound, and when it was opened sometime in the 19th century it was found to contain only some Indian relics of the common type.

Since no conceivable reason could be found for Indians carrying defective or broken arrowheads into these places, all evidence points to at least a temporary residence, or hunting camp or camps here in the heart of unsettled country teeming with game.

A tradition exists that Asheville was built upon the site of a great Indian battle, possibly between the Cherokees and Catawbas, who were inveterate enemies always on the prod, or between the Cherokees and the Shawano tribe. It was said that long before the white man came, the Shawano had a town on the banks of the Swannanoa, near its mouth. This town was abandoned about 1730. Whether the Shawanoes left in a free migration or if they were driven out by the Cherokee is pure speculation. There are fragmentary legends that tell of a terrible battle fought by the Cherokees on the site of Asheville, and some historians believe it was at this time that they drove out the Shawanoes. A belief also exists that the country along the French Broad and Swannanoa was once a neutral hunting ground for the Cherokee and Catawba tribes.

However, as pointed out by Sondley, "conjecture is always busy in accounting for physical appearances of a country, and what to one age is surmise to the next age becomes tradition." Or, stating it plainly, because the last ice age reached this far south, pushing into the mountains seeds from which sprang more flora than is located anywhere else in the United States, there could have been a tradition that the Cherokees and Catawbas once hunted polar bears in the rich valleys of the Swannanoa and French Broad.

These things give us no more than a glimpse into the distant past, and from these only can we draw anything of a picture of Buncombe County and Asheville before they were settled by Caucasians.

The Cherokees were then a powerful, savage civilization, constantly threatened by other tribes, always ready to defend themselves, and when threatened by the encroachment of white civilization, retaliation was the only route for them to take. The word "savage" would have been the white man's word. What to him would seem savage might seem common to others.

If the Cherokees were hostile to the white settlers, no one should doubt the reason. They looked upon the white man as an encroacher who wanted to take away their hunting lands and, who knows? perhaps all of their homelands in and around the Great Smoky Mountains.

Thus, when they made war with the whites, they considered themselves as doing no more than aggressively defending their own property.

Hostilities between the whites and Cherokees, except for scattered incidents, mostly between individuals, ended after the close of the American Revolution, and the Cherokees began to adopt the more civilized ways of their new brothers, noted in their apparel, residences, general demeanor, and lifestyles.

Dr. Ramsey, in his *Annals of Tennessee,* writes that the French Broad River was called by the Cherokees the Aguqua, and received on its northern bank the Swannanoa and the Nonachunheh (Nolichucky). Zeigler and Gossup refine this further in *The Heart of the Alleghanies,* writing that the French Broad was known as the Agiqua to the Erati or "over the mountain" Cherokees, and as the Tocheeostee to the Ottari or valley towns from its headwaters to Asheville, and above Asheville it took the name of Zillicoah.

Whatever its name, the Indians took fish from the river and game from the land and lived a good lifestyle of their own choosing (or within the limitations of their knowledge and environment) until the white man settled Buncombe and changed their ways forever.

It is recorded that the Cherokees, by then a thoroughly civilized tribe, stripped to their breechclouts, painted their bodies and faces, and, known as Thomas's Legion, wreaked havoc among Union troops in Western North Carolina during the Civil War. The Cherokees have fought on the American side in every war since the Revolution and distinguished themselves gallantly on many fields of combat.

3

THE REVOLUTION

The City of Asheville, though not founded and chartered until after the American Revolution, can nevertheless be proud of the part its state played in revolting against the Crown.

Sir Walter Raleigh was the man responsible for England's colonizing efforts on American soil, and it was most appropriate that North Carolina named its state capital after him. It was he who sent the first expedition to form a colony, and he who continued to send them—including the historically mysterious Lost Colony—until a colony finally took hold and Englishmen established themselves as forerunners in a great new land.

John Cabot discovered the continent of North America in 1497, and in 1498 his son Sebastian Cabot explored the coast from Nova Scotia to North Carolina.

In 1584 Sir Walter Raleigh sent an expedition under Philip Amidas and Arthur Barlow, who conducted trade with the Indians. The following year Raleigh dispatched the Ralph Lane expedition to colonize the new world. His efforts, conducted in North Carolina, met with failure. Two years after that, Raleigh sent out a third colonization effort which resulted in the Lost Colony.

But advances, despite the failures, were being made. It has been said that Lane's expedition introduced Indian corn, sassafras, Irish potatoes, and tobacco to the civilized world. That may have been, but in the 1970s when the mummy of Egyptian Pharoah Rameses II, who ruled Egypt from 1292 to 1225 B.C., was discovered to contain termites, it was sent to France for treatment, and Frenchmen discovered the mummy contained bits of tobacco. It is possible, one would think, that the Rameses mummy could have been treated with tobacco at some date in the not-too-distant past.

At any rate, upon North Carolina's shores a colony planted by Raleigh eventually survived, and from there spread the human tide that eventually populated the nation.

History led North Carolina to the formation of this new nation, and the first blood was spilled in the name of independence upon North Carolina's sandy soil on May 16, 1771, at the battle of Alamance, brought on by the famous Stamp Act. This was four years before the uprising became a full-scale revolution.

The British Parliament passed the Stamp Act in 1765, taxing paper and certain other articles the American colonies needed. North Carolinians cried "Taxation without representation" and rose up in anger, claiming that submission to the Stamp Act would have been a concession that they were not entitled to the same rights as other English free men. John Ashe, Esq., speaker of the North Carolina House, informed Governor Tryon that the law would be resisted to blood and death.

The governor did not allow the legislature to meet during the existence of the Stamp Act. He remained loyal to the Crown and made attempts to calm the leadership of North Carolina, but the people refused to be seduced by his undisguised attempts of appeasement.

A British sloop of war, the Dilligence, arrived in the Cape Fear River early in 1765 carrying a load of stamp paper for the colony's use, and Col. John Ashe of New Hanover County, for whose brother Samuel, Asheville would later be named, and Col. Waddell of Brunswick County marched at the head of North Carolina citizens to Brunswick where the Dilligence was anchored, threatened violence to the ship's captain if he attempted to land the paper, and seized the sloop's boat.

The citizens put the boat on a cart, fixed a mast, hoisted a flag, and marched in triumph to Wilmington, where they joined a celebration of the action. On the following day they marched to the governor's house to beard the lion. They demanded that the governor make no attempt to enforce the Stamp Act, and when the governor refused, they threatened to burn his mansion with him in it—and at that point he capitulated and agreed to the demands of the people. The people cheered.

Wrote Wheeler, the great historian, of this incident: "Here is an act of North Carolinians worthy of all Grecian or Roman fame." He continued: "Here is an act of the sons of the 'old North State,' not committed on the harmless carriers of the freight, or crew of a vessel; not done under any disguise or mask (references to the Boston Tea Party); but on the representative of royalty itself, occupying a palace, and in open day, by men of well known person and reputation; much more decided in its character, more daring in its action, more important in its results . . . ."

On May 20, 1775, the people of Mecklenburg County drew up the first declaration of independence from the Crown. The first open and public declaration for independence by any one colony was that made on April 12, 1776, by the Provincial Congress of North Carolina assembled at Halifax when on motion of Cornelius Harnett, resolved "That the delegates for this colony in the Continental Congress be impowered to concur with the Delegates of the other Colonies in declaring Independence and forming foreign alliances, reserving to this colony the sole and exclusive right of forming a constitution and laws for this colony."

The first battle for American independence was fought against British troops at Alamance on May 16, 1771, and there, on North Carolina soil, the first blood was spilled for independence in a battle between Royal forces and the Regulators.

Nine years later, the war had been waged with varying fortune, and it seemed at last that America's quest for freedom had about run its course. Cornwallis had plastered Gates with crushing defeat at Camden on August 16, 1780, and Gates's army was demoralized and licking its wounds. Two days after Tarleton had whipped Sumter at Fishing Creek, Georgia and South Carolina were thoroughly overrun by enemy forces, and it seemed that America's dream was about to expire. Cornwallis was set to begin his journey northward to whip North Carolina and Virginia, end the war, and knuckle the American upstarts under again.

American forces had been depleated by heavy losses suffered at Charleston in May and at Camden in August, and no one stood to oppose the advance of Major Patrick Ferguson and 1,100 Loyalist troops made up mostly of New York and South Carolina men who were loyal to the Crown.

As the crisis darkened with no American troops to oppose Ferguson, the woods suddenly opened up and hundreds of sharp-eyed squirrel hunters, over-mountain men, they called them, carrying long rifles and bags of provisions, came out of the hills and made a steady way toward Kings Mountain. More men moved southward from the Watauga settlement now in Tennessee, and from the hills of Virginia. These men had no idea of obtaining reward, other than earning the right to make their own decisions and mistakes. This was no part of the Continental Army, no part of any organized army, but backwoodsmen who were willing to die for freedom. Wearing buckskins and homemade woolens, slouch hats and coonskin caps, they moved steadily southeastward. They had no hope or thought of monetary reward, they furnished their own arms and courage, and they were men of different breeding and standing. But there was something similar about all: their rifles were oiled and well handled, their powder was dry, their knives were sharp, and the glint in their eyes was that of extreme determination.

They walked out of the mountains, over the foothills, across the rolling piedmont toward the high, sharp mountain west of Charlotte, and there they moved into battle in no military fashion or formation but with fingers on the triggers and eyes on the enemy. When they arrived at Kings Mountain, there were 2,000 of them. All they knew was that in front of their rifle muzzles waited Major Ferguson and the Loyalists who were trying to subdue them in the name of the Crown. They had come to stop the advance of the British into North Carolina.

Donald Culross Peattie dramatized this answering to arms by writing, "They swept quiet and swift and dark as a raven's shadow, over the ridges and hollows" to crush Ferguson's force that had thought it held an impregnable position atop Kings Mountain.

The date was October 7, 1780, and this band of straight-backed men, whom the British probably called rag-tag, surrounded the Loyalists who had taken positions on Kings Mountain. The backwoodsmen aimed true and reloaded quickly, and when the smoke cleared off the mountain, Major Ferguson was dead and the Loyalists were killed or captured.

And then these members of their own private army turned silently away and made their way back into the hills.

This victory turned the tide. It revived the all but lost cause of the Colonists and breathed new life and spirit into the rebellion. It was the first of a series of setbacks that eventually brought the collapse of English effort to hold North America.

It made possible the final triumph of freedom on the peninsula at Yorktown, Virginia, on October 19, 1781, when American and French forces cornered Cornwallis and forced his surrender, and after that, except for scattered naval battles, which ended in 1783, America breathed the sweet air of freedom. And liked it.

When the revolution began, settlement had reached the Blue Ridge Mountains and there it halted until freedom had been won. Only then did the pioneers top the ridges of a new world and walk into rich valleys to settle the verdant land along swift streams that gave promise of a new beginning and a new life.

4

PENETRATING THE WILDERNESS

W hile Samuel Davidson was the first white man to settle west of the Blue Ridge, Captain William Moore moved farther west and became the first white man to settle west of the French Broad River. Moore had actually preceded Davidson into the Indian lands by eight years, but he was not a settler at the time. He was a soldier.

A fifty-year-old captain in the Revolutionary army, Moore first saw the Valley of the Swannanoa when he crossed through Swannanoa Gap by horseback on October 19 or 20, 1776, six weeks behind General Rutherford. Moore was captain of a lighthorse cavalry company attached as support to the Rutherford Expedition against the Cherokees.

The Cherokees frequently descended from their mountain homes upon the white settlers in Georgia, South Carolina, North Carolina, Virginia, and what is now Tennessee, hoping to discourage them from further encroachment upon their hunting lands.

In 1763 King George III set the boundary for white settlers at the eastern slope of the Blue Ridge and obtained a promise from the Indians that if need arose they would aid the British against the Americans.

This was a logical move for the Cherokees, for it was Americans who were encroaching on their hunting lands. For the British it was an expeditious accomplishment, and at the same time it was welcomed by the Americans for it presented hidden possibilities. When war came between the colonies and the British, the Americans no longer recognized the British-Cherokee agreement of holding white settlers east of the Blue Ridge, and when the British and Indians lost the war, Americans, seeking new frontiers, claimed the lands west of the mountains as spoils of war to be occupied by those strong enough to populate them.

When the British saw that revolution of the American colonies was inevitable, they sent agents among the Cherokee, Alexander Cammeron and John Stuart, who persuaded the Indians to keep their promise and enter into the war against the colonies.

The Crown had begun making treaties with the Cherokee in 1730 and their treaties were no more binding than the later treaties made with the Western tribes in the 1800s. The 1730 treaty with Britain stipulated that the Cherokee would receive "striped duffles and white cloth to be dyed blue" in return for friendship, but offered "five hundred pounds weight of swan shot and five hundred pounds of bullets" for the Indians to keep their lands free of all white men save the English. The implication, of course, was that the Cherokee use the powder and lead upon any foreign intruders, including Americans.

Emboldened by this alliance and the unsettled state of affairs among the colonists, the Cherokees launched raids against the whites that reached out of the mountains into other areas and were more disastrous and bloody than ever before.

They raided South Carolina villages and ranged as far as the Catawba River into that part of North Carolina already settled by the whites. Their wrath reached into Tennessee and Virginia. On the day the British fleet attacked Charleston, the Cherokees made a daring raid on frontier settlements in South Carolina, killing, destroying, and plundering. At the same time, they murdered thirty-six colonists at the head of the Catawba.

Inevitably, the colonists struck back, launching military forces out of Georgia and Virginia, both acting independently, to subjugate the savages. They met with moderate success, the Virginians, under Col. William Christian, slightly moreso than the Georgians. The force that brought Indian depredations to an end, however, was the Rutherford Expedition from North Carolina, led by General Griffith Rutherford, who scorched the earth along a route through the Cherokee towns known afterward as the Rutherford Trace.

With a force of 2,400 fighting men, Rutherford crossed the Blue Ridge over Swannanoa Gap and drove through the entire Indian country of North Carolina and on into Tennesse, sacking and burning an estimated thirty-six Indian towns and villages, destroying crops, slaying men, women, and children, and driving the rest from their homes, much the same as the United States Cavalry chopped down Indian resistence on the Western plains a century later.

Rutherford struck such an effective blow, driving the remaining Indians deep into their Smoky Mountains sanctuary, that never afterwards did they venture in any considerable number or as an organized body to give trouble to white settlers.

So unsuspected and brutal was this thrust that Rutherford lost only three men while killing hundreds of Indians.

Little is known of General Rutherford's early life. He was Irish by birth, a brave and patriotic man, who lived in the Locke settlement west of Salisbury when the Revolution began. In 1775 he had represented Rowan County at New Bern and in 1776 was a member from that county of the Provincial Congress at Halifax. This congress convened on the fourth of April, and on the 22nd appointed Rutherford brigadier general of the Salisbury District.

After his Cherokee expedition he commanded a brigade of the American army in the ill-fated Battle of Camden, fought in August of 1780, and was taken prisoner by the British. His command was assumed by General William Davidson, who was killed on Feb. 1, 1781, at Cowan's Ford while attempting to prevent Lord Cornwallis from crossing his command over the Catawba.

When exchanged, Gen. Rutherford again took the field and commanded at Wilmington when that town was evacuated by the British. In 1786 he represented Rowan County in the Senate of North Carolina, but soon afterward moved to Tennessee, and there on Sept. 6, 1794, he was appointed president of the Legislative Council.

Near the beginning of the 19th century, Rutherford died in Tennessee. Both North Carolina and Tennessee commemorated his memory by giving his name to one of their counties.

Rutherford was a salty old campaigner who had earlier struck as much horror among his schoolteachers as he spread among the Indians. Verifying this was a letter he wrote early in the American Revolution to officials of Rowan County, North Carolina, in which he stated:

"TO THE GOLOR of the Gole of Salisbery District:
"Whereas, a certain John Auston, Late of Tryon County, is charged of being an Enemy To Ammerican Liberty & also Refuses to take the oath Proscribed by the Counsel of Safety

of this Provance. These are therefore to Command You to Take the sd. Auston Into youre Possession & him safely keep in youre Gole Till Furder Orders.

"Given Under my hand this 13 Day of July, 1776.
"GRIFFITH RUTHERFORD."

Unscholarly as he was, this distinguished general had few peers as an Indian fighter.[1]

Moore's company, which apparently acted independently but in support of the main Rutherford forces, marched down the Swannanoa, crossed the French Broad, and drove westward across the Balsam Mountains to the Tuckaseigee River, where it encountered various Indian towns and obliterated them.

Moore eventually was forced to turn back because of a lack of provisions, and on the return his troops captured three Indian men whom they sold into slavery for 242 pounds. Moore reported the total plunder they confiscated came to 1,100 pounds sterling which was divided among himself and his men.

Moore camped his troops on Hominy Creek on October 31, 1776, and immediately recognized the land as the place he would like to put down his belated permanent roots. Like Samuel Davidson, he loved solitude far more than the crowds who had moved into the Salisbury district where he then made his home, and the quiet forests along the Hominy beckoned to him hauntingly. Thick stands of virgin hardwoods were magnificent—especially the huge oaks, which still held some of their autumn color. From his campsite, Moore could look upward and see the towering peaks of mountains he thought would run upward of five- to six-thousand feet in height.

He liked the grassy fields and canebrakes along the Hominy.

This was a place in which he felt secure and felt it was here he stood a better chance of making a late fortune than anywhere he had seen.

Moore was an Irishman, born in Ulster County, Ireland, in 1726. He emigrated and settled near Salisbury in Rowan County and later married a sister of General Rutherford, he for whom Rutherford County was named. His home in Rowan County was on Shadracks Creek and South Muddy Creek, which are now in the southern tip of McDowell County.

---

[1] Other military expeditions came through the site of Asheville. In 1781 Col. John Sevier led an expedition against the Cherokee that at one point "went up Cane Creek and crossed the Ivy and the Swannanoa. This campaign lasted twenty-nine days and was carried on over a mountainous section of country never before traveled by any of the settlers and scarcely ever passed through even by traders and hunters." (Ramsey's Annals of Tennessee).

At the end of the expedition, Rutherford left Capt. Moore and a force of men in Hominy Valley with orders to build a string of blockhouses within bugle distance of each other. Moore built them across the main east-west Indian trails and with little apparent effort held the already subdued Cherokee west of the line to prevent further Indian depredations upon white settlements.

Moore's actions were furtive, unpublicized, and little talked about downstate, for fear, according to historian Owen Gudger, that the Moore troops would be pulled away from the defense of white civilization in the mountains to reinforce the defenders of the wealthy and politically-strong plantation owners in tidewater North Carolina.

There were other such forts strung out between the Cherokee and their downstate targets. A command under General John Sevier came out of Tennessee into what later became Madison County, North Carolina, and built four blockhouses to help hold the Indians in check. These stations were constructed at Hough's, at the Burnt Canebrake, at the Painted Rock (Paint Rock), and at the Warm Springs (Hot Springs). Scouts prowled regularly from these block-houses to a point where they met scouts from the Moore forts, and in that manner maintained a line of resistance against the Cherokee. These forts were manned by volunteer sharpshooters as outposts against Indian attack long after the end of the war.

Moore returned to Salisbury at the end of the Revolution in 1783, and soon thereafter the North Carolina General Assembly declared the western lands open for settlement. In 1784 Moore, then fifty-eight, moved his possessions over the mountains, across the French Broad River, and became the first white settler west of the river.

It has been noted that Captain Moore was the first to drive a wagon across the French Broad in 1784, but most historians credit two Asheville merchants, brothers Zebulon and Bedent Baird, who had opened a mercantile in the new town, with "carrying" a wagon over the mountains in the year 1793–historians claim it was "the first four-wheel wagon ever seen in Buncombe County"–and that was nine years after Capt. Moore was supposed to have brought a wagon across the French Broad. The Bairds brought their wagon from South Carolina over Saluda Gap, evidentally carrying it up the mountain, and reassembling it to drive through the southern part of the county and into town.

When Moore reached Hominy Valley, no matter how he transported his possessions, he expanded the headquarters fort of the string of outposts into a spacious log home of two stories. Then he surveyed 400 acres along the Hominy, but Gov. Richard Caswell granted him 450 acres for his service in the Revolution.

At the end of the Revolution, which began in 1775 and lasted until 1783, the fledgling United States had no money to pay its soldiers, so it paid them in land.

Capt. Moore's third wife, Margaret, bore him three sons. It is interesting to note that three of Captain Moore's grandsons, Walter, Charles, and Fred became superior court judges. The captain was married three times, to Ann Cathey, Margaret Rutherford, and Margaret Patton, whom he married in 1774.

Capt. Moore lived a long and fruitful life, dying November 11, 1812, at the age of eighty-six and was buried at the homesite. Mrs. Moore lived another year and a half and died on April 27, 1814, at the age of sixty-five. She was buried beside her husband.

5

FRONTIER TOWN

Even before it got its name, Asheville was rocked with controversy.

Creation of Buncombe County, ordered by the state legislature on January 14, 1792, was done in a barn at Gum Spring, which still flows into the Swannanoa, although it is now capped and runs underground. The spring lies about a hundred feet inside the present main gate to Biltmore Estate.

The barn belonged to Col. William Davidson, in whose house the first court of Buncombe County was scheduled to be held on April 16, 1792, but when so many people showed up for court that the crowd overflowed the house, proceedings were removed to the spacious Davidson barn, and all subsequent sessions of the court were held there until April of 1793 when the court moved to a new log courthouse on the town square of Morristown.

Herein lie two good tales concerning the location of the town center (or square) and the naming of the town, both of which generated a good deal of controversy under which Asheville came into being.

First, there is a tale about location which may be apocryphal but could easily have happened. It was said that two sites were under consideration for the town square, one in Biltmore where a steam sawmill was located and where later the Buncombe Turnpike ran, and another higher on the hills to the north, apparently near an old Indian graveyard located somewhere around Stony Hill (Battery Park Hill).

The Biltmore location, more thickly settled along the Swannanoa, was favored, but a tavern owner named Patton at the site farther north–his groggery was on the location that became South Main Street–invited the appointed commissioners to a meeting in his tavern and after a sufficient amount of popskull whiskey made the rounds, the commissioners voted unanimously to place the center of the town on that very spot. That bartender was probably a friend of John Burton.

What is known for sure is that the first set of commissioners appointed by that first court to locate the town, failed to agree and, hopelessly deadlocked, turned the matter back over to the court on December 31, 1792.

The court replaced the failed commissioners–Philip Hoodenpile, William Britain, William Whetson, James Brittain, and Lemuel Clayton–with a second set of commissioners, consisting of Joshua Inglish, Archibald Neill, James Wilson, Augustin Shote, George Baker, and John Dillard "of the county aforesaid," and William Morrison of Burke County. They were instructed to name the county seat.

The failure of the first set of commissioners was due to disagreement over the site rather than unwillingness to act. Morrison had been something of an at-large commissioner with the first group, and with the second he was appointed to settle the issue should the six commissioners deadlock on a three-three vote.

Actually, without William Morrison the second set of commissioners would have fared little better than the first. Half were from the north end of the county and half from the south end, and it is noteworthy that only those from the north side signed the report. Morrison, who had been appointed to the committee as a disinterested person, apparently had to make the decision to break a tie vote.

It is likely that Morrison's final reasoning to place the county seat where he did was because it would be of a more equal distance between Reems Creek and other settlements in the north of the county and those in the south along the Swannanoa.

Whatever the reasoning, the location was providential, for had the town been located in Biltmore, it surely would have been destroyed 123 years later in the Great Flood of 1916 when the Swannanoa River swelled to a mile's width in Biltmore and carried away everything in its path. Asheville's location several hundred feet higher saved the city from certain annihilation.

From time to time in the 200 years since, the elevation of Pack Square has been lowered. Where the square lies today, men of those days in the 1790s faced a hill so tall and steep that a man standing at the southwest corner of the public square could not see the top of a high covered wagon standing on Main Street on the far side of the square where College Street crosses it.

So, Morristown came into being, but it is not clear for whom the town was named. The name was officially given to the fledgling town at the April, 1793, term of court, and construction began immediately on a log courthouse where Biltmore Avenue and Broadway meet at the square today. They also constructed stocks and a jail, and the center of what was later to become Asheville came into being.

It is likely that the town was named either for William Morrison, or for Robert Morris, who financed the American Revolution and owned large tracts of land around Buncombe County. Sondley supported the Morrison theory, and John Preston Arthur, who wrote a history of Western North Carolina, believed the Morris story.

The town did not remain Morristown for long. In 1795 Samuel Ashe of New Hanover County was elected governor of North Carolina, and it was in his honor that the name of Morristown was changed to Asheville. By October 1795 the name Asheville had become so common among the people that the clerk of county court, forgetting for a moment that the town was still Morristown by law, began to write the name Asheville in the opening statement of his minutes, but he suddenly remembered that the town was still Morristown and finished writing it as Morristown.

He made the same mistake in the minutes of the opening of the April term of 1796, writing the full word Asheville, and then marking through it, wrote the name of Morristown beside it.

Finally, in one of the sessions of County Court in 1797, the name of the town was changed to Asheville.

The state legislature, which had yet to incorporate the town, apparently also thought Asheville a better name than Morristown, and when it incorporated the town in November, 1797, it specified that the town be named Asheville. John Jarrett, Samuel Chunn, William Welch, George Swain, and Zebulon Baird were appointed commissioners to carry into effect the plan of the town. However, the town did not begin its existence as a municipal corporate until the commissioners meeting of January 27, 1798.

James McConnell Smith was the first white child born west of the Blue Ridge in North Carolina. He came along on June 14, 1787, born to Col. Daniel Smith, a veteran of both the American Revolution and the Indian wars who was said to have killed more than one hundred

Indians, and Mary Smith, apparently a sister of Col. William
Davidson. Thus, James M. Smith was a nephew of Samuel Davidson,
the first white settler in Buncombe who was killed by Indians three
years earlier on Christian Creek.

Born in a two-story log house on a knoll overlooking the point
in the river where Carrier's Bridge was built later, James Smith grew
up and married Polly Patton, daughter of Col. John Patton, one of the
city's pioneers. On North Main Street he built the Buck Hotel that
was later replaced by the Langren Hotel and is now a parking garage,
and on the opposite side of the street he kept a store. He owned a
nearby tanyard and built Smith's Bridge in 1827, the first to span the
French Broad River. It was on the Buncombe Turnpike and he
operated it as a toll bridge.

Smith became one of the largest landholders and slavekeepers
in the area, owning several farms in Buncombe County as well as
farming property in Georgia.

When in 1840 he set out to build a home for his unmarried son,
John Patton Smith, he spared no ends, designing it to weather the
years. The house stands today as the Smith-McDowell Museum at
283 Victoria Road on the south side of Asheville.

Plans for the modified Colonial home were brought from
England and contained several unusual features. The brick walls
were eight to twenty inches thick. There were ten rooms in the house
and two large open porches across the front, one above the other. A
carriage entrance on one side had high steps for the convenience of
ladies. Above the door, a priceless fan window was installed, and
stairs leading to the upper floors were of an unusual design and
featured a small built-in pulpit. Heavy mahogany was used to make
the inner doors and mantels, some with built-in candle holders.
Numerous fireplaces were constructed to heat the home. A basement fireplace held five-foot logs.

Wealthy to the end, Smith died December 11, 1853, at the age
of sixty-six and was buried in Newton Academy graveyard beside
his wife, Polly, who had died in 1842.

His son lived in the house until he died in 1858, and then James
Smith's daughter, Sarah Lucinda McDowell, moved in with her
husband, Captain W. W. McDowell, and nine children.

The house was originally a farmhouse—a rather palatial one—
and was surrounded by several hundred acres of corn, flax, cane, and
other cash crops.

James Smith's father, Col. Daniel Smith, a native of New Jersey, moved to Asheville after years of fighting with the military. When he died on May 17, 1824, he was buried with military honors on the hill where he had settled, but about 1875 his body was removed to the Newton Academy graveyard where it now rests. The inscription on his tombstone is interesting. It reads:

"In memory of Col. Daniel Smith, who departed this life on the 17th May, 1824, aged 67. A native of New Jersey, an industrious citizen, an honest man, and a brave soldier. The soil which inurns his ashes is a part of the heritage wrested by his valour for his children and his country from a ruthless and savage foe."

6

FATHER OF THE TOWN

By trade John Burton was a miller who built the first grist mill in Buncombe County, but he was also an entrepreneur who knew a good thing when he saw it.

A veteran of the American Revolution, he petitioned the state for his pension of 400 acres to be divided into two 200-acre plots. The first of these, encompassing what later would become the city of Asheville, was granted July 7, 1794.

The northern boundary of this tract was formed by a line extending from a point at the intersection of the present Charlotte Street with Clayton Street westward along Orange Street to Broadway. Its southern boundary was formed by a line running from the eastern end of Atkin Street westerly to Ravenscroft. Its eastern boundary ran northward along Valley Street and the southern part of Charlotte Street, while the western side ran from Ravenscroft up through Pritchard Park.

This acreage was known as the Town Tract.

At the same time Burton obtained his second grant of 200 acres adjoining and immediately north of the Town Tract. This strip was known as the Gillihan Tract.

Early in 1793—a year and a half before these grants were issued—Burton, an optimistic man, marked out a townsite lying north to south upon twenty and one-half acres of the land he had petitioned for. This plot ran along the present Biltmore Avenue and Broadway from College Street on the north to Hilliard Avenue on the south. He divided this strip into forty-two lots, each consisting of one-half acre, except the lots on the southern end were a quarter-acre each. The larger lots had a frontage of five poles (82 1/2 feet) on a thirty-two-foot-wide street running north to south with half the lots on one side and half facing from the other side.

If all this is confusing, here in a nutshell is the way the town began:

January 14, 1792–An act establishing Buncombe County was ratified by the State Legislature. A committee was appointed to locate the county town.

December 31, 1792–A new committee was appointed to replace the old members who could not agree on location of the town.

Early 1793–John Burton surveyed and laid out the village of Morristown on land he did not yet own.

Third Tuesday of April, 1793–The town was located by the county court at Burton's site.

Late April, 1793–Courthouse erected on the square.

July 7, 1794–Burton received his grants of 400 acres, including the townsite he had marked off.

Morristown was sometimes called Morris Town or the Town of Morris, which leads one to believe it probably was named for Robert Morris[1], but was more generally spoken of as Buncombe Courthouse. The townsite had only one other street, the same width as the first and running east-west where Patton Avenue lies today. It ran an equal distance on each side of the north-south street, and was only as long as the lots were deep. South of the square, in the vicinity of the present Aston Street, a fifteen-foot-wide alley ran east to west, separating the lower five lots from the others.

Burton lost no time making his first sale. On July 28, 1794, he sold a lot to Thomas Burton, probably his brother, for twenty shillings.[2] Thomas bought lot No. 4 on the north side of the east-west alley.

No one knocked down Burton's door in a rush to buy lots. He made his second sale three months later on October 15, to Ann Gash who bought half of lot No. 2 for five pounds. It lay two lots below Thomas Burton's and only two lots from the south end of town. She built a house upon her lot and lived there many years.

Burton favored family members in his sale of lots. Thomas Foster, Burton's brother-in-law, paid twenty shillings for a lot on October 21, prompting Sondley a hundred years later to write: "Five dollars was not a high price for a half-acre lot near the center of the

[1] According to the Asheville City Directory for 1896-97, the town was named Morris in 1794, changed to Morristown in 1795, and then soon changed to Asheville. However, city directories are not the most reliable source of information such as this for historians.

[2] Twenty shillings were the equivalent of five American dollars at that time.

town and fronting 82 1/2 feet on the main street, although we are so often assured that real estate has always been ridiculously high in Asheville."

John Burton continued in the real estate business until he had either sold or contracted to sell thirty-one or thirty-two lots, and then he apparently grew tired of that business, or thought the lots were selling too slowly, and sold his remaining lots and his other property in and around the townsite to Zebulon and Bedent Baird for two hundred pounds. The sale included all his tracts of land "including"– in his own handwriting–"the Town, all except what lots is sold and maid over."

Some of the lots he had previously contracted to sell had not been paid for when he made this transaction with the Bairds, and it could be that he simply grew tired of waiting for his money.

Gleaned from the pages of history, here is a listing of the property John Burton sold and the price paid:

Date	Buyer	Lot No.	Price
July 28, 1794	Thomas Burton	4	20 shillings
Oct. 15, 1794	Ann Gash	1/2 of 2	5 pounds
Oct. 21, 1794	Thomas Foster	7	20 shillings
Oct. 21, 1794	Thomas Foster	11	4 pounds
Oct. 22, 1794	Sarah Hamilton	5	10 silver dollars
Oct. 22, 1794	William Wilson	24-25	10 pounds
Oct. 24, 1794	Thomas Foster	3	25 pounds
Oct. 24, 1794	Zebulon, Bedent Baird	x[3]	4 pounds
Jan. 19, 1795	John Hawkins	20	4 pounds
Jan. 21, 1795	Harris Hutchison	9	4 pounds
Jan. 22, 1795	John Street	6	5 pounds
Apr. 20, 1795	John Street	x[4]	4 pounds
Apr. 22, 1795	James Hughey	18	4 pounds
Apr. 22, 1795	John Craig	20	4 pounds
Apr. 22, 1795	Joseph Hughey	29-30	4 pounds
Apr. 22, 1795	William Forster	12	4 pounds
Apr. 23, 1795	Ephraim D. Harris	17	4 pounds
Apr. 23, 1795	Samuel Lusk	13	4 pounds
Apr. 23, 1795	Edward McFarling	1/2 of 27	2 pounds
Apr. 23, 1795	William Wilson	x[5]	10 pounds
Apr. 23, 1795	Robert Branks	39	4 pounds

[3] Lot unknown.
[4] Back lots, no frontage on street.
[5] A lot south of the Town Tract.

Date	Buyer	Lot No.	Price
Apr. 23, 1795	William Lax	8 1/2 acres[6]	40 pounds
Apr. 23, 1795	James Brittain	14	100 pounds
Apr. 24, 1795	Col. William Davidson	21	? pounds
Oct. 15, 1795	John Patton	15, 2, 10	20 pounds
Apr. 21, 1796	James Davidson	26	6 pounds
Apr. 24, 1796	Benjamin Hall	23	4 pounds
July 20, 1797	James Chambers	19	100 dollars
July 18, 1797	Hugh Tate	1/2 of 13	50 dollars
Mar. 15, 1805	Patton & Erwin	4	40 dollars

Zebulon and Bedent Baird opened the first store in the area in 1793. They went to Charleston, South Carolina, bought a wagonload of merchandise the new county needed, and somehow brought it over the tortuous grade of Saluda Mountain.

When they bought their downtown lot from John Burton in 1794 they constructed a large log building and moved their goods into it. They imported the first Jew's harps, which soon rivaled the gourd fiddles and cornstalk bows with which the early settlers made music.

Other log businesses sprang up. Everyone wore hats in those days and George Swain built a hatter's shop, Silas McDowell a tailor shop, and James Patton expanded his home into an inn and offered meals and lodging to travelers.

Burton built his grist mill on Glenn's Creek, about where it emptied into the French Broad River near the Woodfin end of Riverside Drive.

The fledgling town flourished on the hill.

There is confusion about the location of the first courthouse. Writing in *The Asheville Daily Citizen* in 1898, Sondley reported thusly:

> THIS LOT was very near what was then the most improved part of the town. The first courthouse, if we may credit tradition, was a log structure one story high, containing a single room. It was covered with boards held to their places by the weight of large pieces of timber laid horizontally across them.
>
> The courthouse is said to have stood about one hundred feet south of Sycamore street[7] on the eastern side of South

---

[6] Located outside the Town Tract.
[7] On the east side of South Main Street (Biltmore Avenue) near present Aston Street.

Main street, as this lot seems to have been left vacant for the purpose, but more probably it stood on the Public Square in the center of Main street. Apparently the lot opposite the vacant lot just mentioned was intended for "the Stocks and prison to be convenient to the courthouse."

This courthouse appears to have been used as such for many years.

The first school west of the Blue Ridge was opened in 1792 by Robert Henry, who named it Union Academy. It was located about a mile south of Burton's Town Tract. Five years later when the Reverend George Newton, a Presbyterian minister, took over the school, its name was changed to Newton Academy.

Robert Henry was glad to turn the school over to Dr. Newton. He thought it was time he found another line of work.

He was a learned scholar who had written an account of the Battle of Kings Mountain, in which he was wounded. His paper was used by a Professor Draper in a book called "Kings Mountain and Its Heroes."

Knowing Henry, however, one would assume that his gentlemanliness took precedence over his combativeness, judging from an incident that occured in his classroom in 1797 and no doubt hurried his departure to seek other employment.

He had occasion to punish one of his pupils, a rather large, well-grown girl. Calling her to the front of the classroom, Prof. Henry took up his ruler and reached for her hand with the intention of "ruling" it, but she seized his long cue of hair with both hands, leaped behind him, and swung him about the room by the hair.

Coming near the door, she turned him loose, and he flew into a corner. She disappeared out the door and never came back to school to receive her just dues. Robert Henry turned the school over to Dr. Newton and later became a member of the survey team that located the state line between North Carolina and Tennessee in 1799.

Born in Tryon (later Lincoln) County on February 10, 1765, in a rail pen, Robert Henry was the son of Thomas Henry, an emigrant from the north of Ireland. He was still a boy, only fifteen, when he fought on the American side at Kings Mountain and was wounded in the hand by a bayonet thrust. Later he was in the heat of the fight at Cowan's Ford and was very near Gen. William Davidson when the latter was killed.

Henry discovered several sulphur springs five miles west of Asheville and settled there. The Sulphur Springs Hotel was later built at the springs.

He also studied law and in January of 1806 was made solicitor of Buncombe County court.

In spite of his flight around the classroom in that old log schoolhouse, Henry still believed in education, even though he didn't want to teach. He provided a schoolhouse and teacher for those in his neighborhood in West Asheville, and many a person who rose to prominence in Asheville had been educated at Henry's School.

He died in Clay County January 6, 1863, at the age of ninety-eight years and was undoubtedly the last of the heroes of Kings Mountain.

In those early years of the town's existence, the county changed as more settlers moved in and claimed land, but the county was still primitive enough to support wild turkeys, which fed many a family with hearty meals, and deer, which not only provided food but also skins from which trousers and leggings and shirts were made for the men and skirts for the women.

Despite the store of the Baird brothers, this was still a country in which a family had to make its own way. There was no way the Bairds could haul enough goods over Saluda Mountain to clothe the county.

Farmers cleared land for more crops and pasture, and flocks of sheep and small herds of cattle grew and could be bartered for other necessities.

Tough farmers from Tennessee and Kentucky and a few midwestern states began driving occasional herds of cattle, horses, sheep, and swine through the hills, holding near the French Broad River, taking them down rugged Saluda Mountain to markets in South Carolina and Georgia. This led farmers to raise larger crops of corn to sell to drovers coming through and prompted them to petition the state capital for funds to build a real road to accommodate the drovers.

Roads were still almost nonexistent. Short corduroy roads were constructed on the north and south lanes leading away from town, made of logs laid side by side with dirt and gravel thrown on them to give better footing to animals in wet weather.

It would be another quarter-century before the first major road was constructed through Buncombe County—the Buncombe Turnpike, which opened in 1828. But the citizens of 1800 made do the best they could.

After he sold his properties to the Bairds, John Burton moved to Gap Creek on the road from Asheville to Fairview east of town and went into business again, but he suffered such losses that he eventually lost all of his property. There John Burton faded from history. No word exists of his life after that.

Ironically, information on Burton's wife survived. She was Jane Burton, better known as Jean or Aunt Jean, and was a sister of pioneer William Foster and an aunt of Thomas Foster. She was born April 13, 1746, and died January 28, 1824.

7

THE ASHE IN ASHEVILLE

Other than being governor of North Carolina so long ago, who was Samuel Ashe? For the most part, his name and service to his country have been lost in the memory of present-day Ashevilleans. Not one in a hundred could say what sort of man Samuel Ashe was. Probably no more than one in fifty could tell you that it was he for whom Asheville was named.

Samuel Ashe was more than a patriot. He was one of the rocks on which North Carolina—and therefore the nation—stood in their clamor for independence. He never had a doubt that the fight for independence would be the hardest thing the young colony had ever faced, but he also never had a doubt that the colonies would win. He also knew that this move not only would be met with harsh repercussions but that it would divide the state almost in half—and it would take good men willing to pay the price to gain independence and then to prove that independence would work and would be the best thing for the people.

Samuel Ashe's life spanned the American Revolution, and it was he perhaps more than any other figure, who stood in the forefront of North Carolina's every move toward independence.

His character was rugged enough in its integrity to match the everlasting hills in which he would find double honor for his actions. He was one of the most useful men in laying the foundation of the State of North Carolina and who gave direction to the people's thoughts in the early days of statehood.

If Asheville can today stand as a proud monument to Governor Ashe's fame, the city itself should feel great pride in having been named for a man worthy of so high an honor. No city in the state was named for a stronger or more faithful patriot. His peers in the State Legislature recognized the great deeds he had done for the state, the time he had put in both in preserving the state and in forming the new nation, but their knowledge of the western part of the state was limited.

In November of 1797, the legislature met in Raleigh with one of the items on its agenda being to pay a tribute to Samuel Ashe, who was then governor, for his remarkable accomplishments. They gave his name to the new frontier town in the far western mountains, but it is clear that members of the legislature had no idea how important that town would become as the hub of the whole of Western North Carolina.

So in the next assembly—that of 1798—probably thinking that the honor they had bestowed upon Governor Ashe was hardly enough to recognize him for his deeds, they created a new county in the hills and named it Ashe County in his honor.

Of the two, Asheville grew to be more widely known and became the highest honor paid Governor Ashe by that assembly.

Ashe sprang from good stock. For centuries his kinsmen had been held in high esteem in England. In the struggle between the Parliament and the Stuart Kings, John and Sam Ashe were members of the Parliament, and John was named as one of the judges to try the king, but he declined to serve.

The Ashes were stolid opponents of arbitrary power, and of this stock came John Baptista Ashe of South Carolina, grandson of the original Sam Ashe. John Baptista was chagrined by the tyrranous measures taken by the crown against South Carolina dissenters and felt so strongly that he decided in 1702 to go to London and seek relief from Parliament.

Many South Carolinians were angry and so on edge over the tyranny of the Crown against dissenters that they, thinking Ashe was trying to appease the oppressors, raised a riot that lasted several days, meaning to seize Ashe and exile him to an out-of-the-way island. Seeing that he was unable to leave Charleston by sea, John Baptiste set out for Albemarle through 300 miles of wilderness and eventually took shipping in Virginia.

His efforts in England came to naught, however, and he returned to Albemarle and made his home there, refusing to return to Charleston. In this case, South Carolina's loss was North Carolina's gain, for the Ashe descendants remained in the Old North State.

A son of this John Baptista Ashe, named for his father, also settled on the Albemarle. He inherited the fearlessness and liberty-loving characteristics of his ancestors and helped form the Popular party. His party opposed, first, the exactions of the Lord Proprietors, and later, the prerogatives claimed by the king and the Royal Governors after the king had purchased the province.

This John Baptista Ashe had two sons, John and Samuel, and it was this Samuel for whom Asheville was named. John, the elder son, became speaker of the North Carolina Assembly and was a leader in the Stamp Act problems. He is spoken of by the early historian Jones as "the most chivalric hero of the Revolution."[1]

Here, now, enters the Samuel Ashe for whom Asheville was named. Born in 1725 on the Albemarle, Samuel lost his parents early. His father died in 1734 and his mother earlier still. Young Sam was reared by his uncle and guardian, Sam Swann, who was head of the Popular party and for a quarter-century speaker of the Assembly and a most trusted representative of the people.

Samuel Ashe grew to manhood with kinsmen whose foremost trait was integrity. His family struggled mightily for the liberties and freedom of the people, which placed them against the authority of the crown.

Educated in the north, Samuel studied law under Sam Swann, married early, and devoted himself to planting in the rich Albemarle soil and to the practice of his profession.

He was described as "a man of large frame, strong physically as well as intellectually—self-reliant, independent in his views, sturdy in maintaining them, and of unbending integrity."

As the threatened rebellion became apparent, Samuel Ashe, without ever having occupied a public position, suddenly found himself at the forefront in public consideration. This was a time when good men of staunch character were sorely needed if the young colony and its counterparts were to gain independence from England and form their own nation.

When the Royal Governor Martin became a fugitive, all of his powers were invested by the Revolutionists in a committee of thirteen. Martin reported the uprising to the king, speaking disparagingly of eleven committee members, but admitting that "Mr. Samuel Ashe and Mr. Samuel Johnston (members of the committee) have the reputation of being men of integrity."

A giant step was taken in 1774 when Martin refused to convene the legislature at the request of the people, and to meet this emergency, some of the inhabitants of the Cape Fear counties met at

---

[1] *The Asheville Daily Citizen*, February 5, 1898.

Wilmington on July 21 and appointed a committee of eight, including Samuel Ashe, to prepare a message for the people of North Carolina, calling on each county to send delegates to the Johnston courthouse on August 20. This was the first Congress held in North Carolina and the first legislative body elected by the people of any colony.

According to an unnamed chronicler of Samuel Ashe's life, "It was then that the first great step in the Revolution was taken. In the succeeding January the inhabitants of New Hanover County organized a committee of safety, and Sam Ashe was chosen one of the members. He was now the soul of activity, not only at home, but in other counties, explaining to the people the grounds of the movement, allaying apprehensions, strengthening the wavering, persuading the doubtful and urging on the revolution to a successful issue."[2]

This was a difficult task for in every colony the number of those who opposed revolution was very large, and those who favored revolution had to work extremely hard to prevent a revolt from breaking out against the rebellion.

Samuel Ashe won a seat in the Congress in 1775 and immediately became a factor in its business. He was named to important committees, including one to map out a temporary plan of government for the nation. To insure that administration continued while Congress was not in session, supreme power to administer was vested in a safety committee of thirteen, and Samuel Ashe was one of the thirteen.

Things came to a head with the Congress of April 1776, which declared for independence, and a committee was raised to prepare a permanent state constitution. Yes, Samuel Ashe was on that committee, too. In the face of strong opposition from Sam Johnson, Ashe advocated that ultra democratic principles be incorporated in the constitution.

That issue produced one of the hardest party battles ever recorded in the annals of North Carolina, and the confrontations became so heated that when prudence and wisdom eventually surfaced, the issue was postponed. The cause of such extreme differences was laid aside when Congress came to realize that "we all must stand together or hang together."

A Council of Thirteen was appointed to govern North Carolina, and Ashe, who was appointed, was elected president of the body on August 26, 1776.

---

[2] *The Asheville Daily Citizen*, Feb. 5, 1898.

Thus, in the echelons of its government, North Carolina publicly disavowed any obedience to the crown and joined the rebellion which was already underway.

The first order of business was to raise and equip troops to oppose the Red Coats, and to do this the discontented citizens, who feared being trampled by the crown, had to be quieted and law and order preserved at home. The second order of business was to administer public affairs. In all of these movements, Samuel Ashe stood at the fore, a beacon to the people of the state.

That fall, 1776, the Congress of Halifax appointed Ashe to a committee to prepare business for the House. He relished this work because he was helping prepare bills to be put before the next legislature to insure the freedom of the people.

Samuel Ashe was afforded a double honor by the first session of the General Assembly of the State: He was elected speaker of the Senate and chosen presiding judge of the Supreme Court of the State.

Thus, Ashe played an all-important role in leading North Carolina up to and through the Revolutionary War. Then in the aftermath of war, when the young nation was pulling itself back together, beginning to build an economy within itself and a trade with other nations, Ashe continued to lead. He continued his judicial career until 1795 when, at the age of 70 he was elected governor of North Carolina. He held office for three years.

A thoughtful man who realized that education would become a prime factor in the success of the state, Ashe was one of the original trustees of the University of North Carolina.

He was a staunch backer of Thomas Jefferson for the presidency because he thought Jefferson adhered more closely to his own democratic ideals. He was deeply disturbed when John Adams defeated Jefferson in the 1796 election to succeed George Washington, but he was somewhat appeased when Adams named Jefferson vice president.

Ashe immediately began working toward Jefferson's election in 1800. He addressed a letter to New Hampshire, and then to all other states, urging friends of Jefferson to organize democratic societies to promote and insure Jefferson's election four years hence. That was the first movement toward an organized Democratic party in this country, and historians credit Ashe with the work that got it started.

In 1798 when Ashe's term as governor expired, he threw himself totally into the death struggle between Democracy and Federalism, still fighting for total liberty for the people. To him the supreme

compliment came in 1800 when he presided over the North Carolina Electoral College when Jefferson was elected and Federalism
was defeated. Federalism never rose again and in a few years became
a by-word of reproach.

That was Ashe's last act in public life. He had fulfilled his tasks
and the principles of freedom and self-government had triumphed.
He retired from political activity at the age of seventy-five and spent
his declining years in calm serenity on his plantation at Rocky Point.

There on the plantation Ashe died in 1813 at the age of eighty-
eight. Today his name lives on, incorporated in one of the mountain
counties and the largest city in the mountain area, two places of such
extreme beauty that they would have pleased him deeply, but he
never laid eyes on either of them.

8

LANDLOCKED

Asheville's first necessity was roads. The town was landlocked with not one good road leading in. For the most part, roads were crude trails, rude and rough, narrow and steep, hacked out and maintained by inhabitants under a public road law. They were of utmost importance since they were the only means of communication between the scattered settlers. All news had to be obtained by word of mouth. The roadbuilders were hunters and farmers, for the most part unlettered men, who knew nothing of civil engineering; therefore the roads were laid out and built according to the easiest grade. Too, there was no money to pay roadbuilders, and mountain men in those early days could scarcely spare time from the support, and particularly the protection, of their families.

Some of the roadbuilders made trails across their own lands. They were permitted by the court to charge tolls for passage and collected a penny for horse and rider and a few more cents for a wagon, of which there were still only a few.

Those who live in this modern day of four-lane superhighways and fast jet travel through the air cannot fathom the difficulty people had getting into and out of the mountains.

Roving bands of Indians harrassed the white settlers constantly, and often when the man of the house was absent, Indians would frighten the women and children into hiding in the woods and burn furniture and destroy bedding and other items in the house.

Before the Cherokees were tamed by General Rutherford's forces, history records that privations suffered by settlers at the hands of Indians were many, and the hardships some of the pioneers underwent at the hands of predatory savages were grave.

Still, men found time and ways to build roads, some of which were only slightly passable but with time were improved.

The first wagon road was built from Swannanoa Gap down through Swannanoa Valley to the point where the village of Best[1] would be built, and there it turned north along Valley, Oak, and Charlotte streets to Beaverdam Road and thence to Reem's Creek.

A road was built between William Davidson's farm at Gum Spring and Davidson's Creek (Davidson River) in what later became Transylvania County. Another connected Reems Creek with Cane River in Yancey County. One ran from the mouth of the Swannanoa at the French Broad River through Asheville to Beaverdam and Reems Creek. Another connected Buncombe Courthouse with what became known as Bull Mountain to the east after Joseph Rice shot the last buffalo in the Eastern United States there around the turn of the century.

Roads were improved from the courthouse to Haw Creek and to Hominy Creek, to Warm Springs, to Weaverville, and to Saluda Gap at the South Carolina state line, but these roads, lacking constant care, were quagmires in winter and heavily rutted the remainder of the year.

Wheeler wrote that the first wagon passed from North Carolina to Tennessee by the Warm Springs in 1795.

The period from the end of the Revolution to construction of the Buncombe Turnpike in 1827-1828 was one of almost total self-sufficiency for settlers in the mountains, who had no way to import goods into the hills in large enough quantity to satisfy the needs of the people.

To give an idea of how hard travel was, we turn to the best source of information for that period–the journals of Bishop Francis Asbury, first bishop of the Methodist Episcopal Church consecrated in the United States. From 1800 on he made a pilgrimage almost every year into Western North Carolina as a circuit-riding preacher.

He was a circuit-rider carrying the Word to people up the creek who had no other way of getting it, and when named bishop he required every Methodist preacher to travel a circuit, thus the term "Circuit Rider."

Asbury, who had come from England at the behest of John Wesley, grew to love America and favored independence. He remained in America when every other active preacher appointed by Wesley went back to England at the beginning of revolutionary hostilities.

---

[1] Later to become Biltmore.

An 1890s photo of the Daniel Killian house on Beaverdam where Bishop Asbury held Methodist meetings between 1800 and 1813.

How he ever found time to keep an extensive diary is a mystery. Riding the circuits, Asbury crossed the Alleghenies sixty times, and at his death in 1816 his odometer showed that he had traveled 270,000 miles by horseback in forty-five years, and had preached 18,000 times, averaging a little more than a sermon a day. The growth of the church was largely due to his efforts. When he arrived in America in 1771 there were only three Methodist meeting houses and about 300 communicants. At his death there were 412 Methodist societies with a membership of 214,235. There were 700 ordained Methodist ministers and eleven annual conferences. Bishop Asbury made his first journey to the mountain metropolis of 350 people in 1800 at the age of fifty-five. At his age, how he survived the ordeals of the next thirteen years is another mystery.

The mountains leading into and out of Asheville were not one of Asbury's favorite places. Once, after riding down Saluda Mountain into the open, flat country of South Carolina, Asbury wrote: "Once more I have escaped from the filth, fleas, rattlesnakes, hills, mountains, rocks, and rivers; farewell, western world, for a while!"

On another occasion when Bishop Asbury and the Rev. R. N. Price rode through Indian country with some companions, an alarm of Indian uprising was given, which proved to be false. When the scare was over, one of the preachers riding with Asbury asked him if he did not feel for his faith when he thought the Indians were upon him. "My faith?" Asbury exclaimed. "I felt for my gun!"

Here, to give an idea of how rugged travel was in the mountains at the turn of the 19th century, are excerpts from his journals:

Friday, Nov. 7, 1800

I PURSUED my journey and arrived at the Warm Springs, not however without an ugly accident. After we had crossed the Small and Great Paint mountain and had passed about thirty yards beyond the Paint Rock, my roan horse, led by Mr. O'Haven, reeled and fell over, taking the chaise[2] with him; I was called back, when I beheld the poor beast and carriage, bottom up, lodged and wedged against a sapling, which alone prevented them both being precipitated into the river. After a pretty heavy lift all was righted again, and we were pleased to find there was little damage done. Our feelings were excited more for others than ourselves. Not far off we saw clothing spread out, part of the loading of household furniture of a wagon which had overset and was thrown into the stream, and bed clothes, bedding, etc, were so wet that the poor people found it necessary to dry them on the spot. We passed the side fords of the French Broad, and came to Mr. Nelson's; our mountain march of twelve miles calmed us down for this day. My company was not agreeable here—there were too many subjects of the two great potentates of this Western World—whiskey and brandy. My mind was greatly distressed.

Saturday, Nov. 8, 1800

We started away. The cold was severe upon the fingers. We crossed the ferry, curiously contrived with a rope and pole, for half a mile along the banks of the river, to guide the boat by. . . .

Sabbath, Nov. 9, 1800

We came to Thomas Foster's and held a small meeting at his house. We must bid farewell to the chaise; this mode of conveyance by no means suits the roads of this wilderness.

---

[2] A lightweight carriage, often with a convertible top, consisting of 2 or 4 wheels, drawn by one horse.

We were obliged to keep one behind the carriage with a strap to hold by, and prevent accidents almost continually. I have health and hard labor, and a constant sense of the favor of God.

We had our horses shod by Philip Smith; this man, as is not infrequently the case in this country, makes wagons and works at carpentry, makes shoes for men and for horses; to which he adds, occasionally, the manufacture of saddles and hats.

Monday, Nov. 10, 1800

We took up our journey and came to Foster's upon Swannioo (Swannanoa). Company enough, and horses in a drove of thirty-three. Here we met Francis Poythress—sick of Carolina. . . . I, too, was sick (of it).

Wednesday, Oct. 7, 1801

We made a push for Buncomb Courthouse; man and beast felt the mighty hills.

Sabbath, Oct. 11, 1801

Yesterday and today held quarterly meeting at Daniel Killian's, near Buncombe Courthouse. . . . We had some quickenings.

Tuesday, Oct. 13, 1801

The French Broad, in its meanderings, is nearly two hundred miles long; the line of its course is semi-circular; its waters are pure, rapid, and its bed generally rocky. . . .

Wednesday, Nov. 3, 1802

We labored over the Ridge and the Paint Mountain. I held on awhile, but grew afraid of this mountain, and with the help of a pine sapling worked my way down the steepest and roughest parts. I could bless God for life and limbs. Eighteen miles this day contented us, and we stopped at William Nelson's, Warm Springs. About thirty travellers having dropped in, I expounded the scriptures to them, as found in the third chapter of Romans, as equally applicable to nominal Christians, Indians, Jews, and Gentiles.

Sunday, Nov. 7, 1802

The descent of Seleuda (Saluda) exceeds all I know, from the Province of Maine to Kentucky and Cumberland; I had dreaded it, fearing I should not be able to walk or ride such steeps; nevertheless, with time, patience, labor, two sticks and above all, a good Providence I came in about five o'clock to ancient John Douthat's, Greenville County, South Carolina.

Tuesday, Oct. 25, 1803

We reached Buncombe. The road is greatly mended by changing the direction, and throwing a bridge over Ivy.

Friday, Oct. 28, 1803

I walked down the mountain, after riding sixteen or eighteen miles before breakfast, and came in about twelve o'clock to Father John Douthat's; once more I have escaped from filth, fleas, rattlesnakes, hills, mountains, rocks, and rivers; farewell, western world–for a while.

Wednesday, Sept. 24, 1806

We came to Buncombe: we were lost within a mile of M'Killion's (Killian's), and were happy to get a school house to shelter us for the night. I had no fire, but a bed wherever I could find a bench; my aid, Moses Lawrence, had a bear skin and a dirt floor to spread it on.

Friday, Sept. 26, 1806

My affliction returned; considering the food, the labor, the lodging, the hardships I meet with and endure, it is not wonderful.

Wednesday, Oct. 1, 1806

Now I know what Mill's Gap is, between Buncombe and Rutherford. One of the descents is like the roof of a house, for nearly a mile: I rode, I walked, I sweat(ed), I trembled, and my old knees failed; here are gulleys and rocks, and precipices; nevertheless, the way is as good as the path over the Table Mountain–bad is the best.

Friday, Oct. 16, 1807

We reached Wamping's (Warm Springs). I suffered much today, but an hour's warm bath for my feet relieved me considerably.

Tuesday, Oct. 25, 1808

It has been a serious October to me. I have labored and suffered; but I have lived near to God.

October, 1809

Our way now lay over dreadful roads. I found old Mr. Barnett sick—the case was a dreadful one, and I gave him a grain of tartar and a few composing drops, which procured him a sound sleep. . . . Eight times within nine years I have crossed these Alps.

December, 1810

At Catahouche (Cataloochee), I walked over a log. But O, the mountains—height after height, and five miles over! After crossing other streams and losing ourselves in the woods, we came in, about nine o'clock at night, to Vater Shuck's. What an awful day! [3]

Monday, Dec. 30, 1812

Why should we climb over the desperate Spring and Paint Mountains when there is such a fine new road? We came on . . . a straight course to Barratt's (Barnett's), dining in the woods on our way.

Sabbath, Nov. 24, 1813

I preached in great weakness. I am at Killion's once more. Our ride of ninety miles to Staunton bridge on Saluda river was severely felt, and the necessity of lodging at taverns made it no better.

Friday, Nov. 29, 1813

On the peaceful banks of the Saluda I write my valedictory address to the presiding elders.

Born August 20, 1745, Bishop Asbury died March 31, 1816.

---

[3] He was 65 years old at this time.

9

EARLY CHURCHES

Buncombe County's first settlers were largely Baptists, Methodists, and Presbyterians, and for a long while the only preaching they heard was that which they did themselves or by a traveling preacher. Early church meetings were held in private homes, and perhaps the most famous of those was the Daniel Killian place on Beaverdam where Methodists gathered even before Bishop Asbury began his annual journeys into the mountains.

The earliest Methodist congregations also gathered at Salem Campground in Weaverville, and on a campmeeting ground on Turkey Creek.

Samuel Edney had ridden a circuit in Western North Carolina from 1788 on, and from 1792 for a few years it was said that he preached once a month at Newton Academy. Edney lived in what is now Henderson County and most of his efforts were in that area. Once, preaching a funeral sermon for a member of the Stepp family, Edney is said to have angered the family by shouting, "Yes! and after all these warnings from God, you will go on step by step (or did he mean Stepp by Stepp?), till you all go down to hell!"

Presbyterians had their first meetings at Swannanoa, once called Piney Grove, Reems Creek, Asheville, and Cane Creek.

Baptists first met in Asheville and at Green River and Ivy.

Robert Henry's school, which later became Newton Academy, may have been the first building in town put to a joint use of school and church.

On July 11, 1803, William Foster, Jr., brother of Thomas Foster and son of William, Sr., conveyed eight acres, including that on which Robert Henry's school stood, to Andrew Erwin, Daniel Smith,

The Methodist Church, built in 1837, was Asheville's first church building.

John Patton, Edmond Sams, James Blakely, William Foster, Sr., Thomas Foster, William Whitson, William Gudger, Samuel Murray, Joseph Henry, David Vance, William Brittain, George Davidson, John Davidson of Hominy, and the Reverend George Newton, as a gift "for the further maintenance of the gospel, and teaching a Latin and English school or either." These men were the trustees of Union Academy and therefore the trustees of the first building constructed with both school and church in mind.

Robert Henry's log school building stood on the grounds until 1809 when it was torn down and a brick house rebuilt on the site. That was the year that Union Academy's name was changed by the State Legislature to Newton Academy.

For many years this was the place where folks in Asheville went to hear preaching, where they sent their children to school, and where they reverently buried their dead.

From 1797 to 1814 the Rev. George Newton taught a classical school there which was famous throughout several states. Newton served Presyterian congregations on Cane Creek and Reems Creek, and after he retired from the school he continued to serve a congregation in Robert Patton's meeing house, an old log church used by the Baptists.

That old log church was constructed only for the purpose of worshipping God and was built in 1829, but its location, down by the river where West Haywood Street later ran, was too far out of town for the Asheville Baptists.

The first building in town constructed primarily for church use, was the Methodist Church in 1837 on property donated by James M. Alexander on Church Street, which has been occupied by the Methodist Church since that year. Today, it is the home of Central United Methodist Church.

Methodists shared the church with Presbyterian and Baptist congregations, who also met at times in the courthouse on the square. The church had classrooms in the basement for Sunday school and they were also used as a girls school. At the east end of the church was a saddle room. Most members rode horses to church, and this room was used to store saddles and riding skirts to keep them dry in wet weather.

The church was lighted by candles molded by Mrs. Jimmie Lusk. The first presiding elder was Uncle Joe Hasquew of Virginia, a circuit preacher, and the first pastor was Dr. McAnally who preached at the church every four weeks, and then every two weeks. The church was made a regular station entitled to a pastor in 1848 and the Rev. J. S. Burnett became pastor. At that time it had sixty-five white and fifty-nine black members.

Presbyterians had a meeting house in the Swannanoa settlements around the mouth of Bee Tree Creek by 1794. Later in that year, a congregation was formed to meet in Robert Henry's Union Academy. In 1841 James W. Patton and Samuel Chunn gave the land on which the present First Presbyterian Church stands, and the church's original building was erected across Church Street from the Methodist Church.

The area's first Baptists arrived about 1802. They built the log meeting house down by the river and had a congregation of twenty-nine members, seven of whom were men. They found the sledding tough and in thirty years gained only eighteen members. The reason for this was the church's distance from the town.

Baptists during those years met often in the courthouse, in the Methodist Church, and in the Presbyterian Church.

The log building, which sat on land the church never owned, was sold in 1850, and the church realized only twenty dollars for the building.

Until recent years the Baptist Church in Asheville struggled mightily. In 1861, the year war broke out between the states, the Baptists moved into the basement of a church they had begun building at the corner of Spruce and Woodfin streets. The war drained the resources of the church and the building was not completed until May 1871, six years after the war, and they finally moved into their own auditorium.

For years after that they struggled with indebtedness and the depression of 1892 set them back again. Finally, in 1927, the Baptists built a beautiful edifice, designed by Douglas Ellington, who also designed the art deco S&W Cafeteria building downtown. This church building, later expanded and refurbished, is used by the congregation today.

When this building opened, it was not the end of the road of struggling for the Baptists. Two years later, the stock market crashed and the nation was plunged into the Great Depression. It was not until 1951 that the church paid off its final indebtedness when Dr. Perry Crouch was pastor.

Trinity Episcopal Church, located just below the Methodist and Presbyterian churches on Church Street, was built in 1859 on land given by James W. Patton.

The Episcopal Church had its North Carolina beginnings with Bishop John Stark Ravenscroft, for whom Ravenscroft Drive was named just below the church. The drive at one time led to Ravenscroft School. Bishop Asbury would have liked Bishop Ravenscroft, whose voice was described as "the roaring of a lion."

The Rev. Robert Johnson Miller held together the early Episcopals of the mountains. From 1794 to 1834, he established and served Episcopal churches in Lincoln, Burke, and Caldwell counties.

More and more Episcopalians came to Asheville and in 1895 the Western North Carolina congregations were formed into the Missionary Jurisdiction of Asheville, and the church has enjoyed wide growth since that time.

Over the years, Asheville developed large communities and churches of Roman Catholic, Greek Orthodox, Hebrew, and other faiths, and in modern times some of the city's most beautiful buildings have been churches.

10

COMMUNITY LIFE

Early settlers in Asheville and Buncombe County were the epitome of sufficiency. In a day when a man had to be able to work at many tasks and a woman had to make do with what she had to run a household, they were surprisingly self-sufficient. In a land where no one expected shipments of goods from the outside world, a man who didn't know how to mend a coffee-grinder had to learn from someone else, and when next he needed that skill, he had it.

Some manufactured steel. Iron ore was found in several places in the county, and three forges sprang up, one on Hominy Creek, one on Reems Creek, and a third on Mills River, which later became a part of Henderson County. The mountain on which the latter forge was built has since been called Forge Mountain, and somewhere on its heights were the Boylston gold mines.

Folks made their own cow bells and by boring steel rods made their own guns.

They didn't have to send out for gunpowder, either. In 1796 Governor Ashe issued a proclamation that "in pursuance of an Act to provide for the public safety by granting encouragement to certain manufacturers, that Jacob Byler (or Boyler) of the county of Buncombe, has exhibited to me a sample of gunpowder manufactured by him in the year 1796, and also a certificate proving that he had made six hundred and sixty-three pounds of good, merchantable, rifle gun-powder, and therefore, he is entitled to the bounty under that Act."[1]

Later, after Jacob Boyler's death in October, 1804, the inventory of his property returned by his administrator mentioned "powder mill irons."

[1] Wheeler's *History of North Carolina*, 52.

The first consideration of these early settlers—because they brought their rifles, powder, and shot with them—was for a grist mill. Bread was indeed the staff of life. With long guns, these sharpshooters could put meat on the table: venison, bear, turkey, squirrel, rabbit . . . but they needed more than a pestle to grind enough corn to feed large families.

At the first session of County Court in April of 1792 an order was issued that "William Davidson have liberty to build a Grist mill on Swannanoa, near his saw mill, provided he builds said mill on his own land."

In January, 1793, the court ordered "that John Burton have liberty to build a Grist mill, on his own land, on a branch of French Broad River. . . below the mouth of Swannanoa."

Davidson apparently did not build his mill, but Burton did. He situated it on Glenn's Creek where it ran into the French Broad, and from the creek he flumed enough water to run his millwheel.

Sondley wrote that "the late James Gudger, who was brought in his early infancy to his father's residence on Swannanoa, just settled, and who, in 1830 and 1836 represented Buncombe County in the North Carolina Senate, told his grandson, Capt. J. M. Gudger, that when he was a very small boy it was the custom to send a number of boys with bags of grain to this mill to be ground and leave the grain there until a month later when the boys would return with other grain and carry back the meal ground from the first."

A man usually accompanied the boys to protect them from any Indians they chanced upon and to pick up the sacks of meal that slipped off the horses and put them back on.

Once, James Gudger, when just a lad, went to the mill with some boys his own age but without an adult. On the way home one of the sacks fell off the horse on Stony Hill, over which they had to pass. While they tried in vain to replace the sack, which was too big and too heavy for them to lift, a party of Indians came along and out of pure mischief told the boys they were going to hang them.

Gudger said the Indians actually began to go through the motions of hanging them and that the boys were badly frightened, but for a reason unknown the Indians went on their way, leaving the boys unharmed. That hill was afterwards known throughout the country as the hill where the boys were hung.

A man named Handlen, who was in charge of Burton's mill, cultivated a crop of corn on a mountainside on the western side of the French Broad, and once when he did not return from his field for a long while, his friends wondered if something had happened to him. A party went to his field and found him killed and scalped and his crop destroyed. That mountain became known as Handlen Mountain.

Before Burton built his mill, all settlers west of the Blue Ridge had to haul corn to the Old Fort, have it ground, and then haul the meal back across the mountains, a rough job that required several days.

These rugged people who either made their own or did without, raised sheep and from the wool manufactured cloth for garments. They cultivated flax and made a good grade of linen. They made their own floppy hats of straw or felt.

They sawed their own lumber, built their own homes, using rock from the fields for underpenning and fireplaces and chimneys, and constructed their furniture and other needed items. They made their own pottery and ironware, tanned leather, and from it fashioned shoes, harness, and saddles.

No one had trouble feeding his family. Game teemed in the woods. Capt. Thomas Foster, the brother-in-law of John Burton, said that when he and his wife set up housekeeping, he would turn his horse out at night to graze about the canebrakes at the mouth of the Swannanoa and next morning before breakfast would take his gun and go fetch the horse. On the way out he would shoot a deer, gut it, and leave it until he found the horse, and on his way home he would load the deer on the horse and return to the house in time for breakfast.

Fish were plentiful. The French Broad and its tributaries contained trout, and in some areas, bass and other fish. Those who came early to settle sought out places along the rivers that provided the best sites for fish traps, which greatly increased the value of the property in later years. Sometimes in a single night, a barrelful of fish would be taken at a good trap, well situated and strongly made.

Night fishing with gigs became great sport in the mountains, and in some cases profitable enterprises, so plentiful were the fish.

Since medicines were hard to come by, families treated sickness with herbs and brews and a liberal dose of corn whiskey. Nearly every prosperous man had a whiskey or brandy still, and no one looked askance at him.

Even some preachers of the gospel made whiskey and sold it. No one shunned a barroom. The court issued licenses to some who were prominent in church to manufacture and sell spirits.

There were some who did not drink strong liquor. Bishop Asbury noted in his journal on November 3, 1800, that "Francis

Alexander Ramsey pursued us to the ferry, franked us over, and took us to his excellent mansion, a stone house. It may not be amiss that our host has built his house and takes in his harvest without the aid of whiskey."

In the 1830s Buncombe raised only a little wheat. Most of the wheat or flour came from Tennessee. There was not a well-equipped flour mill in the county. Some mills ground wheat, but the flour would be turned down if offered in the market today.

The first post office was established January 1, 1801, located on the southwest corner of Public Square. Jeremiah Cleveland was the first postmaster. About 1805 a post-route was established on a newly built road through Buncombe County which soon became the thoroughfare for travel from the Carolinas and Georgia to the western states. In 1806 the Asheville Post Office became the distributing office for Georgia, Tennessee, and both Carolinas, and George Swain became postmaster.

It was said that during the years Swain held the job he never failed to hand out the mail personally. He knew everyone in the county. He knew that the Davidsons, Burgins, Alexanders, Stepps, Lytles, Shopes, Burnetts, and Doughertys lived in the Swannanoa section.

On Cane Creek and in the southern part of the county lived the Saleses, Toms, Ashworths, Powells, Lytles, Tweeds, Stroups, Garrens, Stephenses, Davidsons, Alexanders, Sumners, Lances, Murrays, Blakes, and a handful of others.

Living in the Hominy section were the Joneses, Morgans, Candlers, Woods, Starneses, Joyces, Carters, and Brysons, and in Leicester and Sandy Mush lived the Sluders, Robinsons, Plemmonses, Worleys, Laneys, Gudgers, Alexanders, Wellses, and Joneses.

In the northern part of the county, including the townships of Reems Creek, Flat Creek, and Ivy, were the Weavers, Penlands, Williamsons, Wagners, Ellers, Alexanders, Whites, Hunters, Blackstocks, Chamberses, Robertses, Morgans, McKinneys, Andersons, Carters, Dillinghams, Whitemores, Burlisons, Green-woods, and others.

One thing that Buncombe had from the start was law and order. Until officials could be elected or appointed, folks kept their own law, adherring strictly to the Ten Commandments. Joseph Hughey was elected the county's first sheriff at the court session of April 16, 1792, in Col. William Davidson's barn. His jurisdiction covered all of Buncombe County.

This was the session in which the work of county organization was done, and the machinery of government was put immediately into operation. The following extracts from the record of that day's proceedings, written in the clear hand of Col. David Vance, the first clerk of court, show the first officers and jurors elected in Buncombe County:

NORTH Carolina, Buncombe county, April 16th, A. D., 1792.

Agreeably to a commission to us directed, the county court of said county was begun, opened and held at the house of Col. William Davidson, Esq.

Present: James Davidson, David Vance, William Whitson, William Davidson, James Alexander, James Brittain, Philip Hoodenpile.

Took the oath of justices of the peace and the oaths for the qualification of public officers and took their seats as justices.

Silence being commanded and proclamation being made, the court was opened, in due and solemn form of law, by John Patton specially appointed for that purpose.

Lambert Clayton and William Brittain being duly commissioned as justices of said county, appeared and were qualified as such by taking the oaths for the qualification of public officers and the oath of office as justices of the peace for said county, and took their seats.

The court proceeded to the election of a sheriff for said county and did elect to that office Joseph Hughey, Esq., who was directed to find security, give bond, and qualify tomorrow at 10 o'clock.

The court then proceeded to elect the clerk of said county, and did elect thereto David Vance, Esq., who was directed to give bond with security tomorrow at 10 o'clock.

The court then proceeded to the election of entry officer of claims for lands in said county, and did elect thereto Thomas Davidson, Esq.

The court then elected, in order: John Patton, surveyor; John Davidson, register; John Dillard, ranger; Edmund Sams, coroner, and then adjourned until the next day at 10 o'clock, when it summoned the following jurors:

George Baker, Hickman Hensley, Will Treadway, Henry
Atkins, Thomas Patton, Matthew Patton, Samuel Forgee,
Robert Patton, Will Dever Sr., John Weaver, Will Gudger,
Benjamin Hawkins, William Greggory, Benjamin Odele,
Sr., Joshua English, Thomas May, James Stringfield, Sr.,
Nicholas Woodfin,
Benjamin Johnson, Elijah Williamson, John Craig, James
Wilson, John Ashworth, Henry Deweese, John Dillard,
James Cravens, Will Forster, Gabriel Ragsdale, James
Clemmons, Harmon Reid, James McMahan, Simon
Kuykendall, John Phillips, James Medlock, Adam Dunsmore,
Benjamin Yearly, Daniel Smith, Nat Smith.

All of those elected had stories to tell about frontier life, certainly,
but only Edmund Sams, the coroner, will be singled out here. His life
may not have been typical of every frontiersman, but it makes
interesting reading.

Edmund Sams was one of the early settlers of the Buncombe
section, coming here from the Watauga settlements as soon as the
land west of the Blue Ridge was opened. Sams lived on the west side
of the French Broad River, roughly a mile above the mouth of the
Swannanoa, so his home would have been southward from the
confluence of the rivers.

His daughter Orra married Thomas Foster, a long-time member
of the state legislature from Buncombe. It was Sams who built and
maintained the first ferry across the French Broad, and Foster who
constructed the first bridge over the Swannanoa on his farm where
Sweeten Creek flowed into the river.

In early life, Sams had been an Indian fighter for the army, or the
militia, whichever was the case. During that time he and a fellow
soldier and friend, in search of some Indian depredators, passed
through the woods with his long rifle over his shoulder when he
heard a gun fire very near, and turning he saw his friend down on the
ground with a bullet wound that took his life a few minutes later.

Sams quickly threw his rifle to his shoulder, knelt, and began
searching the forest for the culprit, calling out to his dying friend,
"Where is he? Where is he?"

"Why, Edmund," his companion managed to say, "it was
your gun."

Sams's gun had fired by accident and killed his friend behind
him. That incident saddened the remainder of Sams's life.

He fought on the American side during the Revolution and after serving as Buncombe's first coroner, he became a member of the county court and also served many years as a trustee of Newton Academy.

In the latter part of his life, he became an eccentric and highly excitable man who lived with his daughter, Orra, and Thomas Foster, whose farm was located on the banks of Sweeten Creek on the southern side of the Swannanoa River. His farm lay on the Rutherfordton Road, about two and a half miles from Asheville. It was on the Thomas farm about thirty years later that the Western North Carolina Railroad and the Asheville & Spartanburg Railroad came together.

Sams was exceedingly fond of music, especially of martial music, and he used to explain to one of his little granddaughters the emotions he betrayed when listening to a lively tune. "I tell you what, little daughter," he would say, "it just puts me on top of Buncombe!"

As he grew older, Sams looked forward each day to feeding Foster's cattle and would indulge them to such an extent that the cattle were many times in danger of being foundered. Capt. Foster would gently caution the old gentleman about overfeeding his livestock but without effect.

Some mornings when out earlier than usual, Foster would hear the old man talking to a pet cow while giving her an unreasonable quantity of food. "Hurry up, old lady," he would say, "Tommy's coming."

Foster was a Virginian by birth, born October 14, 1774. In 1786, when Thomas was twelve, his father, William Foster, moved his family to Buncombe and settled on the south side of the Swannanoa.

Foster was a Buncombe County member of the North Carolina House of Commons in the General Assembly in 1809 and 1812-14, and represented the county in the State Senate in 1817 and 1819.

He died on Christmas Eve, 1858, and is buried in Newton Academy cemetery. His date is erroneously listed on his tombstone as December 14, according to Sondley. Orra, his wife, had died five years earlier, on August 27, 1853, and he was buried beside her. This was the Thomas Foster of whom Bishop Asbury made frequent mention in his journals.

The first case tried in Buncombe County was that of the State against Richard Yardly, in the July session of that court in 1792, the trial taking place in the Davidson barn. Yardly was convicted of petit larceny and appealed to the Superior Court in Morganton.

The first civil suit was that of W. Avery against William Fletcher, which was tried by order of the court on the third Monday in April, 1795, by a jury summoned for that purpose.

The first pauper provided for by the court was Susannah Baker and her child.

The first processioning for unpaid taxes returned into court was "the processioning of a tract of two hundred acres of land on the east side of the French Broad about a mile and a quarter from Morristown, the place where James Henderson now lives," dated April 20th, 1796. This embraced property in the vicinity of Park Avenue.

The January term of court in 1799 produced an act of law enforcement that would be judged barbarious today. Court minutes read: "The jury find the defendant Edward Williams, guilty of the petit larceny, in manner and form as charged in bill of indictment. The court adjudge that the prisoner Edward Williams receive twenty-five lashes on his bare back, well laid on, at the public whipping post and that the sheriff of the county carry the judgment into execution. Appeal prayed."

This was the first infliction of such punishment in the county, and it is presumed that the sheriff laid on the licks well. Citizens and the court took a dim view of thievery.

One of those early punishments led to one of the strangest court cases ever recorded in Buncombe. Minutes of the October court session in 1793 read: "Ordered by court that Thomas Hopper, upon his own motion, have a certificate from the clerk, certifying that his right ear was bit off by Phillip Williams in a fight between said Hopper and Williams. Certificate issued."

In those days and for a long while afterwards, such crimes as forgery, perjury, and some others brought about punishment by cutting off a portion of the ear of the offender, commonly called "cropping." It is easy to understand why Hopper was so anxious that the truth of his misfortune be preserved in legal manner. The court, made up of sensible men, saw nothing unreasonable in the matter and gave a place on their records for the fact. Henceforth if any question arose concerning Hopper's missing ear he had only to refer the questioner to county court records.

There was no mention of prosecution of Williams by Hopper. The reason for this was likely man's propensity to fight. Good, old-fashioned fighting, without rocks, knives, pistols, or brass knucks, was one of the most common and popular amusements of the day. No other injury having been reported than the loss of an ear, and the fight in all probability having been a fair one, the court and those who kept the law felt no call to take further official notice of it.

There were additional ways of identifying criminals and other lawbreakers. Punishment for manslaughter was to burn a large "M" in the right hand of the culprit.

Farmers, whose work was from dawn till dark, had little time for recreation. They tied in their recreation—specifically hunting and fishing—with putting food on the table, and when the fish didn't bite or the dogs failed to get up a bear, they felt put out. They came to town only when in need of something they couldn't provide for themselves. They had no idea that one day man would reach into the air and pull down sounds which he could put in a box called a radio, or that soon after he would add pictures to it. This, like flying, was beyond their realm of imagination.

The main source of their recreation was court. County Court or Superior Court, particularly the latter, brought them to town, and they would sit attentively during a trial, soaking up the proceedings, taking sides, betting on the outcome, and, above all, forgetting for a while about their labors and the harshness of life.

They were fair-minded men in two ways. First, they rejoiced when the County Court during its term of July, 1799, ordered that two fairs be established in Asheville, "to wit, to commence the first Thursday and Friday in November next, and the first Thursday and Friday in June following, and to continue on said days annually, without said court should find it more convenient to make other alterations."

The county fairs were especially welcomed by women. While men crowded the courtroom to hear juicy trials, women were left at home to do chores and tend the family's needs, and fairs, of course, would provide recreation and competition for men, women, and children of all ages from all over the county.

Other acts of fair-mindedness were rendered almost daily by neighbor to neighbor, or even neighbor to stranger, and were epitomized by Squire Thomas Foster, one of the stalwarts of the community, who in 1799 petitioned the court to have his Negro man slave Jerry Smith emancipated and set free "for his meritorious services." The court agreed and adjudged that Jerry Smith would henceforth and forevermore be a freed man "with all the advantages and emoluments which it is in the power of this Court to grant, during his the said Jerry's natural life." As directed, the Clerk of Court issued a license to Jerry Smith, acknowledging his freedom as of that date.

County Court judged local matters well, but as town and county grew, the need for higher court became evident. For the first fourteen years of its existence, Buncombe County had to try its advanced cases in Superior Court at Morganton, distant by more than forty miles of hard travel.

But in 1806, the state legislature, after considering that "the delays and expenses inseparable from the present constitution of the courts of this State do often amount to a denial of justice, the ruin of suitors, and render a change in the same indespensibly necessary," enacted legislation to hold Superior Court at the courthouse in each county in the state twice in every year, and just like that, Buncombe County had its own Superior Court.

The state was divided into six circuits, the last consisting of the counties of Surry, Wilkes, Ashe, Buncombe, Rutherford, Burke, Lincoln, Iredell, Cabarrus, and Mecklenburg. Buncombe was directed to hold Superior Court on the first Monday after the fourth Monday in March and September.

Thus, in the spring of 1807 Buncombe's first Superior Court was held, and it was either at the fall term that year or the March term the following year, that the first murder trial was held. It attracted crowds from all over the county, most of whom stood on the streets hashing over reports from the courtroom, but all enjoying themselves immensely.

Randall Delk, who lived near the Forks of Ivy, was on trial for his life for murder. He and a neighbor named Groom had a quarrel and that night Groom was shot to death through a space between the logs of his cabin wall. Delk fled to the Indian Nation of the Cherokees and lived on the site of the present town of Franklin for a while, but he was followed, taken into custody, brought back to Asheville, and put on trial in Buncombe Superior Court. Found guilty, he was sentenced to be hanged. Sondley reported the execution was carried out where Commerce Street lies now, a bit east of Coxe Avenue.

Soon after that, a Negro named Christopher was hanged in the county for burning the barn of his master on Mud Creek, now in Henderson County. The most celebrated of these early capital trials was that of two Tennesseans, James Snead and James Henry, who in 1835 were charged with highway robbery, at that time a capital crime, committed against a man named Ben Holcombe of the Ivy Section.[2]

Insisting they had won in a gambling game the horse and other articles which Holcombe claimed they had robbed him of, they were

---

[2] Sondley recorded that the incident occurred "on the old Buncombe Turnpike road about a mile south of Swannanoa River," while information compiled in Asheville by a Federal Writers' project in 1937 concluded that the robbery was at Maple Springs on the Swannanoa road about a half mile east of the present Recreation Park.

convicted and on the 28th of May, 1835, were publicly executed by hanging on East Street, which today is Mt. Clare Avenue. The place of execution was near where Seney Street crossed East Street, which, according to retired postal worker George Roberts, a resident of Asheville for eighty-five years, was somewhere in the vicinity of the Wytchwood Acres development near Hillside Street. The section was previously known as the Doubleday section. The field in which the executions were held was known for years as the Gallows Field.

Immense excitement was created by the trial. Most of the populace believed the gambling story the defendents brought forth at the trial, and public opinion held that the executions had been little short of judicial murder.

Before their executions, the condemned men sent for Holcombe to visit them, but it was said that he refused to face them, and that his subsequent life was one of misfortune and suffering. Sondley made no mention of this, saying only that Holcombe was said to be "a man of good reputation."

Col. A.T. Davidson, a prominent lawyer who grew up on Jonathan Creek in Haywood County, was a 19-year-old boy in 1835. He and his brother-in-law, Paxton Cummins, a Methodist preacher, came to Asheville to witness "the great event." Late in the 19th century, Col. Davidson wrote of the Sneed-Henry hangings:

> "A BOY and I went to see the gallows field. We went down North Main Street by the old Sam Chunn tanyard about where Merrimon Avenue comes into North Main Street, near where the Woodfin stables used to be. The old road then ran directly over the hill to the branch. Then we went down the branch 200 or 300 yards and turned to the right in the gorge and there stood the gallows, grim and forbidding. The beams from which the ropes were to dangle were in place, and the trap door was there too, and the steps leading to the platform.
>
> There was a double grave half finished on the hill nearby . . . . Only the lowest vaulted place remained to be dug, and this is how it was explained to me that it had not been completed by the time we reached there: Some Negroes had been employed to dig in the evening before and while deep in the excavation they were suddenly confronted on the brink of the grave by what they took to be the devil himsself who sternly demanded to know what they meant by digging the

grave of men who were still alive? The Negroes ran and could not be induced to return. The devil was really George Owen, a harmless and inoffensive old wit and joker from Haywood County who had tarred his hair and beard and disfigured himself as much as possible for the purpose of having his fun with the grave diggers.

We examined everything and then went back to the Buck (hotel), where we got something to eat. The crowd still had not left the square. But at about 2 o'clock it started, but I had again gone ahead of it and was advantageously stationed on the slope of the hill about 60 paces from the gallows.

Here they came, thousands of eager and excited people and the prisoners seated on their coffins in a wagon surrounded by the military. They drew up at the foot of the gallows and several people mounted the scaffold with the prisoners. There were two long sermons, one by Rev. Joseph Haskew, then a young man, and the other by Rev. Thomas Stradley, followed by prayers, before the sentence was finally executed."

Col. Davidson wrote that 8,000 attended the double hangings; more, he said, than turned out for the 1898 visit here of William Jennings Bryan, Democratic candidate for president of the United States.

Soon after that, a man named Mason was convicted of wife-murder and was hung a little northwest of the western entrance of Beaucatcher Tunnel, probably on the west of where Interstate 240 emerges from the "open cut" through Beaucatcher.

Solemn as they were, the courts were not then without mirth.

The old Scotch-Irish men who settled the mountains were independent in thought, deed, and expression, and sometimes the Church thought they carried expression too far, causing George Newton, then moderator of the presbytery of Concord, to humbly petition the Buncombe court to carry into vigorous execution those laws enacted by the state to suppress evil and make daily life better for citizens.

"Gross immoralities," Dr. Newton wrote to the court here, "daily abound among the citizens of our state, of which intemperance in the use of ardent spirits, profane swearing, and breach of the holy sabbath are none of the least."

Not too many god-fearing mountaineers did a lot of breaching on the holy sabbath in those days, but if Dr. Newton had any idea that the courts could quell drinking and swearing among these people, he was barking up a flatland bush.

While practicing before the Buncombe bar, David L. Swain, later to be the youngest governor ever of North Carolina and long-time president of the University of North Carolina, was involved in a case in Buncombe court which also involved fellow attorneys James R. Dodge (a nephew of Washington Irving), Samuel Hillman, and Thomas Dews.

Dodge was addressing the jury when Swain chuckled and wrote on a piece of paper:

"Epitaph on James R. Dodge, Attorney at Law:

"Here lies a Dodge who dodged all good,

"And dodged a deal of evil.

"But after dodging all he could,

"He could not dodge the devil."

He passed the note among the other lawyers, in whom it created much mirth, and one handed it to Dodge when he sat back down. Dodge perceived that the handwriting was Swain's, and on the back of the note he wrote this reply and passed it back:

"Another Epitath to Three Attorneys:

"Here lies a Hillman and a Swain

"Their lot let no man choose.

"They lived in sin and died in pain,

"And the devil got his Dews."

11

THE DROVERS ROAD

From its infancy, Buncombe County and the town of Asheville struggled with the matter of roads. The community knew that the town and county's growth would be minimal until a suitable way was made to get into and out of the mountains.

Public conscription of manpower to work on the roads improved them. Under this system, every man of workable age was asked to work one day a month on public roads and more if the occasion demanded. Thus, better roads were cleared and graded, rivers and creeks bridged, and travelers found short stretches of easier travel on journeys into Asheville.

Sometime around the turn of the century, drovers from Tennessee and Kentucky began driving swine, a few cattle and horses, and sheep up the French Broad, making it as best they could over what roads there were. Through the forests paralleling the river where there were no roads, such trampling traffic as this helped beat down the forest floor and made a fairly passable track through the woods.

But everyone talked of a better road, a wide road of smooth bed suitable for wagons and easy horseback riding, and the answer to their prayers came from the animals that drovers moved along to South Carolina markets.

Reasoning that the entire area would benefit from the commerce, citizens approached the state legislature about constructing such a thoroughfare, and in 1824 the legislature incorporated the Buncombe Turnpike, a road that would become famous in the annals of Western North Carolina, for it finally opened the land to the rest of the world, albeit by a still tiresome method of travel.

A cry went up quickly from opponents of such an undertaking, and all attacks upon the legality of the act establishing the road were overruled by the Supreme Court of North Carolina.

The legislature directed James Patton, Samuel Chunn, and George Swain to receive subscriptions "for the purpose of laying out and making a Turnpike road from the Saluda Gap in the county of Buncombe, by way of Smith's, Maryville, Asheville, and the Warm Springs to the Tennessee line."

A similar road would be built by South Carolina up Saluda Mountain to the state line, and another by Tennessee to its border with Buncombe County, and in 1828 this road was completed and opened—and the land began to boom. The road paved the way, if you'll pardon the pun, for Western North Carolina to embark upon the first period of tremendous prosperity it had ever known.

It was a wide road that ran along the French Broad River all the way to Asheville where it deviated from the river bottoms and came up North Main Street and ran through the center of Asheville, across the public square, down South Main Street, and back to the river again. It followed this path because Col. John Patton had constructed a good road from the area of Newton Academy to his place and there crossed the river on a bridge Patton had constructed. At one point, the Turnpike ran through the land owned by Col. William Davidson, passing near the barnsite at Gum Spring where Buncombe's first court was held. After it crossed the river, the road ran its course to Saluda Gap where it joined the South Carolina road. At its completion the road ran from Greeneville (in Tennessee) to Greenville (in South Carolina.)

Seventy-five miles in length, the Turnpike was considered the finest road in North Carolina at the time of its completion.

In Asheville a spring of water rose from the earth where Pritchard Park is now located. This was turned into a hog wallow on the outskirts of the business district, and large animal pens were built to accommodate herds overnight. (Later this spring was capped and its water piped down Coxe Avenue, and a new post office was constructed where the hog wallow had been.)

Immediately, wealthy South Carolinians began coming up the road, seeking blessed relief in the wooded hills of Western North Carolina from the lowland heat. They built huge mansions for summer homes and populated Flat Rock with the affluent and genteel, whose descendents remain there.

Asheville merchants used the road to transport goods into the mountains from South Carolina, and citizens began immediately to see the great value of the road. They were able to obtain tools and clothing and goods that theretofore they had had to make for themselves.

Stagecoaches rolled along the Turnpike, carrying passengers south to South Carolina and north into Tennessee, and then bringing loads of travelers to Asheville on the return trips. Visitors became more prominent and Asheville showed signs of not only turning into a tourist town because of the marvelous scenery around, but also into a health center for those plagued by respiratory ailments who might be cured by the mountain air.

Too, the Turnpike gave new settlers an easy way to enter the beautiful woodland where they established homes and joined in the economic progression of the area.

But the greatest boon to the economy of the countryside came through the increased flow of animals along the Turnpike. Drovers from Tennessee, Kentucky, and even points in the Midwest, brought huge herds of cattle, horses, swine, and sheep, and flocks of turkeys along the road, bound for markets in South Carolina and Georgia. At times an almost steady stream of livestock moved on the road.

For the most part the Turnpike was a forest road, bordered by virgin timber which gave relief from summer heat. It was also flanked by the river, which helped cool things off in summer, but it could be almighty cold in the wintertime.

Way stations, most of them furnishing pens for holding animals overnight, sprang up along the road until drovers passed such a station every three or four miles along the route. At every nine miles, inns were constructed to overnight the drovers—nine miles being the maximum distance a hog or turkey could walk in a day.

Farmers prospered because more and more corn was needed to feed the great droves of livestock passing through.

Of course, not all the corn was sold by the bushel to drovers. That which was bottled, usually in clay jugs, brought a better price than corn sold by the bushel.

For the first time in many of their lives, residents of Buncombe could boast of having a few dollars in their pockets.

Close to 200,000 hogs came up the Turnpike every summer for many years, not counting other livestock, all of which consumed corn by the bushels.

Farmers sold their corn to stock stand operators, middle men who in turn sold it to the drovers. Considering that twenty-four bushels of corn were required daily for every thousand hogs, and that the amount for feeding cattle and horses was about the same, farmers extended their cornfields and reaped huge profits.

John Parris quoted Col. J. M. Ray, recalling the Turnpike in *The Lyceum* for December 1890, as saying that "In October, November, and December, there was an almost continuous string of hogs from Paint Rock (at the Tennessee line) to Asheville. I have known ten to twelve droves, containing from three hundred to one or two thousand stop overnight and feed at one of these stands or hotels. . . . Travel over this thoroughfare was the life of the country."

Between the Tennessee and South Carolina lines, hog drovers had to stop and pen up their droves at least eight nights, and a man driving a thousand hogs would buy almost two hundred bushels of corn to get through North Carolina.

Earlier in the century, Nicholas W. Woodfin had introduced orchard grass to Buncombe County and many large cattle-raising farms developed big herds. Cattle-raisers no longer wondered who they could sell their cattle to, and set out upon the Buncombe Turnpike, driving their own herds to market.

Buncombe Countians, always starved for news from the outside world, gathered at these stopping places to trade yarns and gather news of the world without.

Among such men, humor is of the first order. They would grasp anything to break the monotony of following so many cow's tails up the road, and most of the drovers were great jokers. They spun tales for entertainment; they would stop at strange houses to swap yarns.

There was once a drover from Kentucky who passed through the Turnpike with a herd of horses for the South Carolina markets. The fact that the drover was a stutterer did not keep him from having his fun. He was the sort who would do anything for a laugh, even to the extent of frightening the daylights out of a victim.

On the return trip by horseback, the drover, with his hired hands, came back across the Turnpike, and found a man named Sams working in a field a quarter of a mile below his house. He talked with Sams for a while and then rode on. Approaching the Sams' house he espied a younger Sams, a large, muscular fellow, standing in a doorway, and inquired if that was his father working in the field.

"Yes, sir, it is," replied young Sams.

"W-w-w-well you had b-b-b-better go and s-s-s-see about him: he's d-d-d-dead."

Scared out of his wits, Sams ran to his father's aid and found the latter working away in the field, sweat rolling, but sound as a dollar.

"That rascal," the younger Sams averred, his anger rising. Suddenly he boiled over, ran home, saddled his horse, and raced up the road in pursuit of the drovers, who were well-mounted and moving briskly along.

After several miles of hard riding, young Sams saw the drovers ahead and shouted to them to stop. They paid no heed until Sams closed the distance and shouted again.

The stutterer pulled up and inquired, "Wh-wh-wh-what do you w-w-want?"

"Get down," Sams said, sliding his horse to a stop. "I'm agonna whup you."

"Wh-wh-wh-what you going to wh-wh-whoop me fur?"

"Fer telling me that lie."

"Wh-wh-what lie did I t-t-tell you?"

"You said my father was dead."

"W-w-well, ain't he?"

"No, he is not dead. Get down off your horse."

"Well, you d-d-damned fool," said the drover, "why are you m-m-m-mad because your d-d-d-daddy ain't d-d-dead?"

Looking at it that way, and not being destitute of a sense of humor himself, young Sams saw the mirth in the situation and began to laugh. He was embarrassed that he had let his hasty temper put him into such an awkward position.

After taking a friendly swig from the drover's proffered jug, Sams shook hands with him, laughed heartily again, apologized for being so wrought up, and rode the several miles back home thinking how foolish he had been.

And the drover rode on toward Tennessee, looking along the way, no doubt, for his next victim.

By 1840 the stagecoach business was booming for Valentine Ripley, who lived in Henderson County where the town of Hendersonville would spring up seven years later. For a quarter century until 1865, Ripley's stagecoaches ran from Asheville in every direction.

One of his routes lay through Cumberland Gap to the north all the way to Mount Sterling, Kentucky, a 245-mile run. Two others connected Asheville with Greeneville, Tennessee, by way of Warm Springs, where the tourist business was growing because of the hot springs in the area, and Greenville, South Carolina, through Flat Rock and down Saluda Mountain. Each was sixty miles from

Asheville, and the coaches ran round trips of 120 miles, using the Buncombe Turnpike. In tourist season, special coaches often ran from Asheville to Warm Springs. Ripley's fourth route was a 140-mile run to Salisbury, and his fifth was the Hickory Nut Gap route that reached the North Carolina Railroad at Charlotte and came through Lincolnton, Shelby, Rutherford, and across Hickory Nut Gap to Asheville.

In Salisbury, Ripley's coaches connected with the North Carolina railhead from which passage could be made to any point in America that could be reached by rail. But the Asheville to Salisbury run required three twelve-hour days of hard riding.

All of these routes required four-horse hitches.

During normal operations, Ripley used 100 to 150 horses, fifteen or twenty coaches, and fifty men, but in the summer when tourists came to the mountains, his numbers increased to 300 to 400 horses, 100 to 150 men, and fifty to sixty coaches.

His was no small operation. He was not only concerned with rolling his stagecoaches through, but there were horse-changing stations, overnight inns, and daytime feeding places to be contracted along the routes.

Ripley retired in 1865 and sold his coaches to a firm called Blair & Hankins, which continued to run the South Carolina and Tennessee routes, but the Salisbury coaches only had to run to Morganton by that time because the railhead was then in that town.

In 1871 E. T. Clemmons bought the coach line and ran it one way to Greenville, and the other way to Wolf Creek, Tennessee, via Warm Springs. The eastern run only went to Old Fort which the railroad terminus had reached. Clemmons also put on a western run to Andrews via Waynesville.

By 1876 the railroad was coming up Swannanoa Mountain and Clemmons sold the stage lines to the firm of Weddin & Bradley, which continued all runs until 1883 when Asheville was connected by rail to Tennessee, and rails were being extended to the west on the Murphy Branch. After that, Weddin & Bradley had only one route left to Hendersonville, and when the Asheville & Spartanburg Railroad finally came through Hendersonville to Asheville, that line too went by the wayside and stagecoaches became a memory.

12

GROWING TOWN

Through the 1830s and 1840s there were only a few stores outside the town of Asheville, and almost all business of the county was transacted in or near town. It was not unusual for affluent men to own more than one business because this, as they saw it, was indeed the land of opportunity.

James Patton, and after him James W. Patton, were among the most enterprising people in Asheville. They, along with James M. Smith—remember him, the first white child born west of the Blue Ridge?—and Colonel Samuel Chunn, were enterprising men on a large scale.

James Patton had built the first frame house in Asheville in 1814 at the corner of South Main and Eagle streets. Born in County Derry, Ireland, in 1756, he came to America in 1783, to Buncombe in 1792, and finally moved to Asheville in 1814. His son, James W. Patton, later enlarged the frame house and turned it into the once-famous, three-story Eagle Hotel.

The elder Patton had formed an early-Asheville partnership with Andrew Erwin and for twenty years they were prosperous men and their holdings grew. Late in life, the two dissolved their holdings and settled the large estate in one day.

Around 1840, James W. Patton ran the Eagle Hotel and also had a large store, blacksmith shop, tailor shop, a harness and shoe shop, and a tannery with seventy-six vats that turned out huge quantities of leather.

He had some competition from James M. Smith who delved in much the same businesses but on a smaller scale—except for the Buck Hotel, which he still operated on the northeast corner of North Main and College streets.

The Eagle Hotel, established by James W. Patton on South Main Street in 1814.

The first bank in Asheville was the Asheville Branch of the Bank of Cape Fear, established sometime before the Civil War on the southwest corner of Public Square with a front on South Main Street. It was closed during the war and for many years after the war Asheville had no bank. A man named E. Shider loaned money and sold exchange until the establishment of the Bank of Asheville in 1879.

By 1844, not counting places of business, there were only two or three dozen homes in town. Most of the merchants lived outside town. That year there was only one building on College Street.

Stony Hill was good squirrel-hunting ground, and until 1872 boys of the village continued to shoot squirrels on that ridge, known after the war as Battery Porter Hill. Asheville by then was a town of 1,500 people.

Col. Chunn kept a hotel on the southwest corner of Public Square. He owned a store and had a tan yard on Glenn's Creek at the place where Merrimon Avenue crossed the creek. Leather goods were so prevalent in Asheville because of these tanneries and excellent leather workers that surplus leather goods were sold in Tennessee and South Carolina. Chunn was at times chairman of the Buncombe County court and jailer in Asheville. He was the original grantee of the greater part of Sunset Mountain, and the land on the east side of the mountain was named for him, Chunn's Cove. He died in 1855 and left a large estate in Buncombe and Madison counties to his children.

Enoch Cunningham was another entrepreneur. In addition to a public house, he had a downtown butcher shop and harness and saddle shop. Cunningham lived in the first brick house ever built in Asheville, the old Governor Swain mansion on South Main Street.

In 1845, Cunningham became the proud possessor of a tall silk hat, which was equipped on the interior with a mirror and a cigar.

Merchandise in Asheville was expensive in the early 1840s, even though there was a good road, the Buncombe Turnpike, connecting the town with other towns in Tennessee and South Carolina. Freight charges for the distance goods had to be hauled increased prices tremendously.

Any goods hauled from Augusta and Charleston cost from $1.75 to $2 per hundredweight. A 200-pound sack of salt, which cost $1.25 in Augusta, was hauled here at $1.50 per hundred, or $3 total freight, and Ashevilleans thought it was a bargain at $5.50 or $6.

To get a 200-pound sack of salt, a farmer would have to barter about eleven bushels of corn.

Those were the days of wagon trains when farmers made up trains of four or five wagons or more and hauled their produce to Charleston or Augusta. In Augusta, Irish potatoes brought $1.50 to $2 a bushel, bacon 6 cents a pound, hams 7 cents a pound. Corn averaged from 50 to 62.5 cents a bushel, while mountain-grown apples commanded $2 to $4 a bushel, depending on variety and condition. North Carolina tobacco brought 8 to 15 cents a pound, while Virginia tobacco commanded 15 to 50 cents. Ashevilleans had to pay 6 to 8 cents a pound for New Orleans sugar, 14 to 17 cents for refined sugar, 7 to 10 cents a pound for coffee, and $4.30 to $6.50 for a barrel of flour.

Wagon trains going to Charleston received a better return on their goods, but the trip was longer. There, corn brought 65 to 70 cents a bushel, oats 46 cents, peach brandy $1 a gallon, and Northern whiskey sold for 26 to 27 cents a gallon.

Three or four weeks would be consumed in these trips to southern markets. Farm families made such a trip an outing. The family—all who could be spared from the farm—traveled together, sometimes hauling two or three wagons of their own. They sold produce along the way, and South Carolinians in particular looked forward each summer to these laden wagons rolling down from the mountains.

Asheville had its own militia. Under state law, citizens mustered once a year, and General Newland, appointed by the state, was in command. The law compelled all white men between the ages of eighteen and forty-five to engage in the muster. Still living in the dark ages, Negroes were not allowed to drill. Parade grounds where the militia trained were located on flat land immediately northeast of the square.

Primarily because of its isolation, Asheville only had a population of 500 in 1840. The town's population in 1800 had been roughly 350 and grew by only 150 souls in the next forty years. There were only about fifteen private homes in the city in 1840. Most of the immigrants settled on farms in the county. Despite this influx of immigrants settling in the county, the county began to shrink. While it gained in population, it shrank in size. Four times in the first fifty years of the 19th century, other counties were carved off Buncombe's borders. Haywood County was taken out of Buncombe in 1808, and Haywood in turn spawned counties to the west of it. In 1833 the formation of Yancey County took some of Buncombe, in 1838 Henderson County was formed and took a bite from Buncombe, and in 1850 Madison County was cut off the north side of Buncombe.

In those years before the War Between the States, Uncle Alfred Walker, a Negro who was reared by James M. Smith, grew to manhood in Asheville. He served through the Civil War with Bartlett's Tennessee Regiment of the Union army, and at last, after the war, became a minister of the gospel, even though he could not read or write.

Born in 1826, he said people would ask him when he was an old man around the turn of the 20th century, how it was that he could preach although unable to read, and he would reply, "Who teached the fust man, Jesus Christ? Well, I've got religion; I know it; it keeps agrowin', and I'm richer than Vanderbilt, if he ain't got it."

He recalled that in his youth flax trousers and dresses were the height of fashion, and shoes for Negroes were an unknown quantity except on rare occasions. Also in his youth, flails for threshing wheat had not yet arrived, and the operation of separating the wheat berry from the stalk was done thusly, in Uncle Alfred's words, "The wheat was placed on the floor of the barn, several horses were rough shod and boys put on their backs to guide them around the room until the wheat had been tramped out."

He lived near Emma on the Murphy Branch of the Southern Railway, and at times he was engaged in peddling about town. When the Buck Hotel was built, the first one in town, he constructed a walk

The Buck Hotel, one of Asheville's first, at Broadway and College.

of cobblestones in front of the hotel, located on North Main Street, cutting the stones on Stony Hill and hauling them to the hotel in a sled. "That hotel," he said, "ain't nothing but a log house covered with planks, and it wouldn't fall down in a thousand years. They's millions o' rats in it; not thousands—millions!"

Late in the century, Uncle Alfred was quoted as saying, "If times were like they were then and my old master was back here, I'd rather be with him than to be free. He raised me to be truthful and honest, and I never had a mark on my back. Cause why? When he tole me to do anything I went right now and done it."

People then, white and black alike, were industrious and frugal and spent little for anything except the necessities of life. Even as late as 1840 there were not a dozen carriages and buggies in the county, and a piano was almost a curiosity.

Keeping city records was also a hit and miss proposition during that period; therefore there are no records known of the origination, say, of the Asheville Police Department.

In 1840 Asheville's town charter was amended to allow widening of North and South Main streets and the purchase of property to make more cross streets, but a more important point in the amendment allowed Asheville to establish a board of commissioners to oversee operation of the town government. This body was later renamed the board of aldermen.

Another important act was ratified by the legislature on March 8, 1883, upgrading Asheville's designation to that of a city.

Good transportation, 1890s.

With the Buncombe Turnpike still in use, the legislature in 1851 incorporated the "Asheville & Greenville Plank Road Company" with authority to build a plank road over the Turnpike road in an attempt to give better passage into Asheville. The plank road was constructed over the lower portion of the Turnpike, but never reached Asheville. It did help people negotiate part of the route leading to Asheville better.

By the end of the Civil War, the plank road had gone down, and in 1866 the charter of the plank road company was repealed. The Turnpike also fell into neglect after the war as talk grew of the railroad reaching Asheville.

Asheville's streets, however, and the roads leading into the city continued to be quagmires, fetlock deep during rainy spells, until the city began paving its streets in 1890.

But Christian Reed, in her charming descriptive novel, "The Land of the Sky," published in 1876, wrote: "It was less a town than a collection of country seats, scattered irregularly and picturesquely over innumerable hills . . . . There was an absence of the stagnation and depressing village air one knows so well."

13

LAND OF GIANTS

W hat would be the odds against two babies, born in the same house in the same year, of different parents, growing up to be United States Senators and governors of different states? In the year 1801 the odds would have been astronomical—yet it happened in Buncombe County.

On January 4, 1801, a baby boy was born to Caroline Lowry and George Swain, who lived in a double log cabin on Beaverdam Creek immediately northeast of Asheville. Caroline had been previously married to Capt. David Lowry, who was killed in an Indian fight. She married George Swain in 1788.

They named the baby, their second son, David Lowry Swain.

Later that year, on December 14, 1801, John and Elizabeth Street Lane became parents of a baby boy, born in the same cabin, whom they named Joseph Lane.

John Lane was Caroline Swain's brother, making the baby boys first cousins.

Joseph Lane was not long a North Carolinian. John Lane moved his family to the Kentucky frontier in 1804 and then on to Indiana. When twenty-one years old, Joseph Lane, who possessed a charming personality and was a fine public speaker even at that young age, was elected to the Indiana legislature. He served frequently in that house body until 1839 and was elected Indiana state senator in 1844 for a two-year term.

The United States went to war with Mexico in 1846, and the forty-five-year-old Lane volunteered to fight with an Indiana regiment. He entered the army as a private and so distinguished himself as a fighting man and leader of men—and his years of service as a representative of the people of Indiana didn't hurt him, either—that he was quickly elevated to the brevet rank of brigadier general. He led his brigade with such skill and bravery that he emerged as one of the true heroes of the war, and on October 7, 1847, was breveted major general. At that time, major general was the highest rank in the army.

In recognition of his fine service in the war, Lane was commissioned by President James K. Polk as governor of the Territory of Oregon in December of 1848. He resigned the governorship in June of 1850 to represent the Territory in the United States House of Representatives, a position he held four terms from 1851 to 1859. In the middle of these terms he was again appointed governor of Oregon Territory by President Franklin Pierce but resigned again to continue as a delegate to Congress.

Oregon gained statehood on St. Valentine's Day, February 14, 1859, and Lane became the state's first senator. However, early in that term, Lane was drafted as a running mate on the Democratic ticket of John Breckinridge for president of the United States in the 1860 campaign against Abraham Lincoln. When that election was lost, the fifty-nine-year-old Lane retired from public life to enjoy the last twenty-one years of his life. He died April 19, 1881.

His life was as distinguished as that of any child born in North Carolina.

Like Abraham Lincoln's, David Lowry Swain's early education was at his family's log-cabin fireside until he was fifteen. He enrolled in Newton Academy in Asheville that year and while still a teenager taught Latin in the academy. Later he became the first native lawyer of Buncombe County, a solicitor, and in his late twenties, judge of Superior Court.

Given such amiability of temperament, intellectual ability, and nobility of character, Swain attracted the eyes of North Carolina early-on. At twenty-three in 1824 he was elected Buncombe County's representative in the state legislature and was reelected in 1925. His star rose so rapidly that in 1832 he became the state's youngest governor ever at the age of thirty-one and served three gubernatorial terms.

Looking at David Lowry Swain, few would have suspected the intellect that lay within him. Sondley described him thusly: "His ungraceful carriage was such that he was described as a malformation in person, out of proportion in physical conformation, apparently thrown together in haste, and manufactured from the scattered debris of material that had been used in other work . . . gawky, lanky, with a nasal twang that proclaimed him an alien, and a pedal propulsion that often awakened derision." Despite such a description, Sondley recognized the genius that lay within David Swain.

So did others. At the expiration of his final term as governor in 1836, David Swain was elected president of the University of North Carolina. The story of the University of North Carolina for the next thirty-two years is the story of David Lowry Swain's life.

He lectured in the departments of constitutional and international law, moral science, and political economy, and it was said that he had no superior in the United States in these areas. His knowledge, especially in English literature, was encyclopedic. From his father he had inherited an exceedingly strong, tenacious, and utterly amazing memory.

Swain also established the North Carolina Historical Society in 1844.[1] Zebulon Vance, North Carolina's Civil War governor, told an interesting anecdote about David Swain's boyhood.

He said Swain saw his first wagon at his home as a young lad. It was brought up a washed-out channel of Beaverdam Creek, for there was no road in Buncombe County then wide enough to accommodate a wagon. Telling the story years later, Vance said, "The future governor of North Carolina stood in the orchard waiting its approach with wonder and awe, and finally, as its thunder reverberated in his ears as it rolled over the rocky channel of the creek, he incontinently took to his heels, and only rallied when safely entrenched behind his father's house. He enjoyed the relation of this to me exquisitely."

David Swain inherited his excellent memory from his father, George Swain, who lived an eventful life. Born in Roxboro, Massachusetts June 17, 1763, Swain became a hatter. In September of 1784, unsatisfied with business in Massachusetts, he invested what property he had accumulated in provisions and with his merchandise sailed from Providence, Rhode Island, for Charleston, South Carolina.

A vicious storm arose while Swain's boat was at sea, and it became necessary to throw overboard everything that could be spared. All of George Swain's goods were thrown into the sea and he arrived in Charleston with nothing. He lived at various places in Georgia, making hats, and finally moved to Asheville.

Business was good and in 1806 the post office in Asheville became the distributing office for Georgia, Tennessee, and the two Carolinas, and George Swain became postmaster. He held this office for more than twenty years, and in all that time he was not absent once when the mail arrived, and he always distributed the letters with his own hands.

He was a large man with no claim to good looks, but he possessed such a remarkable memory that it was said he could recite the entire

---

[1] Of this, Sondley paid David Swain high tribute: "To him more than any other man North Carolina is indebted for the preservation of her history and the defense of her fame."

Book of Genesis, and was so familiar with the Bible that on the first verse of any chapter being read he was ordinarily able to repeat the second.

He went insane before his death on Christmas Eve, 1829. His grave is in Newton Academy graveyard.

Zebulon and Bedent Baird were brothers who came from New Jersey to North Carolina in the latter part of the 18th century. Scotsmen by birth, they were the first merchants in Buncombe County. Both settled on farms north of Asheville.

These were the brothers who purchased the Morristown site from John Burton when he tired of selling real estate and went back into the milling business. Not much information has survived the two centuries on Bedent. He was apparently the quieter one, tending to business, letting Zebulon have the spotlight.

Zebulon Baird was the grandfather and namesake of Zeb Vance, the Civil War governor, but Zeb Baird was a fair country politician himself. He represented Buncombe County in the House of Commons from 1800 to 1803, and in the Senate of North Carolina in 1806, 1809, 1818, 1821, and 1822. He was one of the leaders in passing legislation to build the Buncombe Turnpike.

It has been written that Baird had difficulty in reconciling his constituents to his affirmative vote on the Turnpike measure. Hundreds of Buncombe citizens were against the expenditure of so much money to build the road. By way of apology, Baird said he hoped to live long enough to see the day when a stagecoach and four horses would gallop through the countryside, driven by a man with whip and tin bugle to announce his arrival from a bugle call away.

This vision was destined to become a realization, but Baird did not live to see it. He died in March of 1827, the year before the Turnpike opened. He was riding along Reems Creek road toward his home when his fatal illness struck him, and he fell dead off his horse. His home was about two and a half miles north of Asheville.

Of Zebulon Baird's dream, Sondley wrote some seventy-five years later: "No more exhilarating scene was ever witnessed than a handsome, newly painted stagecoach drawn by four fine horses as it bursts upon us around some bend in the mountain, dashing at full gallop along a road winding its way through mountain defiles. No more inspiring sound ever greeted human ears than that of the horn of the stagecoach rushing up to a mountain station while its reverberations penetrated the deep recesses and were tossed from hill to hill in wild and wierd musical cadences."

14

THE AMERICAN CIVIL WAR

North Carolina troops during the Civil War prided themselves that they were

First at Bethel
Farthest to the Front at Gettysburg and Chickamauga
Last at Appomattox.

Although there was a Battle of Asheville near the end of the Civil War, there was very little knuckles-and-skull fighting here. Some historians have scoffed at the Battle of Asheville as being something less than a skirmish, and they are right, if you wish to classify the battle. But real bullets flew from the rifles of both sides toward opposing troops.

It has often been written that Asheville escaped the war rather handily because the town was still landlocked. The railroads had not yet come and neither had hard-surfaced roads. Such roads as there were were mcadamized or still dirt and gravel. The city streets were quagmires in rainy weather and hard and deep-rutted thoroughfares in dry times. There was seldom a time when anyone could say that travel was easy in or around Asheville.

When the South went to war against the North, hundreds of men from Western North Carolina gathered at points of enlistment and rushed to get in the scrap. For the most part, they joined local Confederate companies raised by patriots from the mountains, but others who believed the nation should not be divided went to war with federal forces against the Confederacy. As has been written many times, brother was pitted against brother, or uncle, or cousin, or even father.

North Carolinians were not shirkers of military duty. This state entered the war only after great deliberation and soul-searching, but when the decision was made to fight for the South, North Carolina sent more men to war against the Union than any other state in the Confederacy, and suffered more casualties, too. It is to North Carolina's historic spirit of readiness for a good fight that she furnished fully one-fifth of the entire Confederate Army. Her troops were the first to repel the invasion of the South when on June 10, 1861, they fought and won the initial battle that passed into history as the Battle of Big Bethel[1] in Virginia.

The First North Carolina Volunteers took part in that opening battle, and in the Confederate victory the first man to die in action in the war was a North Carolina man, Private Henry L. Wyatt of Company 1, the Edgecombe Guards. That First regiment counted among its units the Buncombe Riflemen, commanded by Captain W. W. McDowell, and Company G of the Burke Rifles, under Captain C. M. Avery.

Throughout the war, North Carolinians distinguished themselves. There were fifteen North Carolina regiments in General George Pickett's famed charge up Cemetery Ridge at Gettysburg on July 3, 1863. Men of the 55th North Carolina Regiment, the command of Colonel John Kerr Connally of Asheville, penetrated Union lines to the deepest point in that ill-fated thrust. Connally, however, was not with his men that day. He had been severely wounded the preceding day in a skirmish at the town of Gettysburg.

Early on the morning of July 1, 1863, General Robert E. Lee had sent Col. Connally and the 55th, accompanied by two Mississippi regiments, into Gettysburg, not to harm the town but to buy shoes for barefoot Confererate troops. Approaching town they were blocked by federal troops who opened fire. General Joseph Davis, Confederate President Jefferson Davis's nephew, deployed his regiments into battle line and charged the enemy with the entire brigade. The 55th charged on the left flank.

As the battle lines came together, Connally directed his men to wheel to the right in a flanking assault that routed the Yankees. As the 55th charged, its line became ragged, and Connally, a stickler for

---

[1] Ironically that first battle was fought in the House of God. In original Hebrew, Beth meant House and El was a name for God: so, Beth El, House of God. Big Bethel, Big House of God.

order, seized the battle colors and rushed ahead of his troops, waving the flag to keep the regiment aligned for the assault. Federal sharpshooters zeroed in on Connally and shot him through the arm and hip. Going ahead, the 55th smashed the Union line to bits and routed the Yankees into full flight.

A Union captain, J. V. Pierce, whose troops had opposed the advance of the 55th, later described Connally's actions: "The Confederate regiment was pressing far to our right and rear and came over to the south side of the rail fence where their colors dropped to the front. An officer (Connally) corrected the alignment as if passing in review. It was the finest exhibition of discipline and drill I ever saw before or since on a battlefield."

Connally was taken to a nearby dwelling where it was presumed he would die from his wounds, but federal troops carried him from there to a Union hospital and skilled surgeons saved his life, amputating his arm in the process. He survived the war and lived well into the 20th century as an evangelistic preacher of the gospel.

Thus, the twenty-six-year-old Connally missed taking part in Pickett's Charge. He relinquished command of the 55th to Captain George Gilreath, who led the regiment in the charge. Again the Carolinians proved their mettle, reaching a point more advanced than that attained by any other of the assaulting columns.

At Chickamauga on Sunday, September 20, 1863, during one of the bloodiest battles of the war, the 60th North Carolina Regiment of infantry charged its way to military immortality. Commanded by Lt. Col. James M. Ray of Asheville, the regiment forced its way into a gap in the Federal lines, and although receiving enfilading fire, drove the enemy back into its breastworks.

The 60th suffered heavy casualties that day, including Col. Ray, and his command reverted to Captain James Thomas Weaver of Buncombe County.

The 60th had more Asheville and Buncombe County fighters than any other regiment in the state. Organized in 1862 as a battalion, so many local men joined that it had to be expanded into a regiment. It included these six companies: Hardy's Light Artillery of Asheville; a company from Madison County; a company from Asheville and vicinity; another company from Buncombe; a company from Haw Creek and the Swannanoa River area, and a company from Turkey Creek, Flat Creek, and Reems Creek in Buncombe County. A considerable number of Buncombe Riflemen who had been in the Battle of Bethel, hardboiled, seasoned veterans of the war, joined the

60th. Many were commissioned officers, giving the 60th excellent and experienced leadership.

Col. Ray, who survived his wounds, returned to Asheville and built a beautiful house that still stands on the southwest corner of East Street (Mt. Clare Avenue) and Hillside, and soon afterward Colonel Charles W. Woolsey, who had commanded a federal regiment in the war, built a mansion across the street from Col. Ray's home. The regiments of the two had faced each other on battlefields a number of times during the war, and Col. Ray won each battle. As neighbors in Asheville, they never spoke to each other.

According to historians, General William R. Cox's North Carolina brigade fired the last shots of the Army of Northern Virginia at Appomattox. The brigade included the Rough and Ready Guards from Buncombe, organized and commanded by Buncombe's Zebulon Baird Vance until he became a colonel of the 26th Regiment.

Mountain men of North Carolina played gallant roles at Bethel, Gettysburg, Chickamauga, Appomattox, and many other battles in what Sondley called "the greatest drama ever enacted on the North American continent."

The nickname of North Carolinians–Tar Heels–came from Robert E. Lee during the war. Carolina was divided in 1710, and the northern or older settlement was called North Carolina, or the "Old North State." The principal products of this state were tar, pitch, and turpentine from the great pine forests in the Piedmont and Coastal Plain.

It was during one of the fiercest battles of the Civil War that columns supporting the North Carolinians, who had successfully fought it out alone, were greeted by a regiment coming up from the rear with a question: "Any more tar down in the Old North State, boys?"

The answer came quickly, "No, not a bit; Jeff Davis has bought it all up."

"Is that so? What's he going to do with it?"

"He's gonna put it on you'ns heels to make you stick better in the next fight."

Hearing of the incident, General Lee comented, "God bless the tar heel boys."

The name stuck.

The brave military traditions traced to the mountain men at Kings Mountain have exhibited themselves in every war fought by the United States since. In the Spanish-American War they fought in

Cuba. In World War I they helped break the Hindenburg Line, they fought all over the world in World War II, and distinguished themselves again in both Korea and Vietnam.

Asheville bustled with Confederate activity, and townsmen hoped that before the war ended, because of its isolated location, Asheville would become the capital of the Confederacy.

Of course, that never came to be, but the Confederate presence here was large for a town of 1,200 citizens. There were two army camps, Camp Patton in the Chestnut Street area east of Charlotte Street, and Camp Jeter at the crossing of Flint and Cherry streets. In addition there were places in town where troops passing through could bivouac, one on Clingman Avenue and another on French Broad Avenue, and most of the time these were filled with army tents.

Trenches and breastworks had been dug all over town, and fortifications with batteries of cannon were erected at various commanding points around Asheville: on Beaucatcher Mountain overlooking the city and its approaches; on Stony Hill, which became Battery Porter Hill, named for the officer who commanded the artillery there; on Woodfin Street where the First Baptist Church now stands; on Montford Avenue near the present Highland Hall; on a hill at the end of Riverside Drive, overlooking North Main Street near the present town of Woodfin; and another across North Main on a ridge that is now on the campus of the University of North Carolina-Asheville.

At the North Main Street locations, on April 11, 1865, the Battle of Asheville was fought between Confederate troops at Asheville and a federal force that had come up the French Broad River from Tennessee.

The old Buck Hotel downtown on North Main Street was the Confederate post office. A Confederate commissary was located on the east side of North Main between Public Square and College Street, and a Confederate hospital treating war-wounded soldiers occupied the place on South Public Square where the Legal Building stands today.

But perhaps the most important military building in town was a Confederate Armory at the northeast corner of Valley and Eagle streets. Chief armories of the Confederate States were at Richmond, Virginia, and Fayetteville, North Carolina, but there were smaller armories at Asheville and Tallahassee, Alabama.

Rifles made in the Asheville Armory were at first inferior. The business was owned by Col. Ephraim Clayton, Col. R. W. Pulliam, and Dr. G. W. Whitson. In the fall of 1862 when the Confederates needed more rifles quickly, the government took over the Asheville Armory, brought in better machinery and superior iron from the mines at Cranberry, North Carolina, and began turning out Enfield rifles that were considered the best in the Southern armies.

To protect the armory, two light Napoleon guns were erected in front of the building and earthworks dug around it. Men from the armory organized and drilled themselves militarily to man the defenses in case of attack.[2]

Partially because Asheville was the mountain center of Rebel sentiment, it was on occasion victimized by deserters, bushwhackers, shirkers, and renegades who found refuge from the war deep in the hills. They used the war as cover for criminal acts, commiting dark and notorious deeds against the residents of Asheville and outlying villages and farms.

The most notorious of these was Colonel George W. Kirk, a Union officer who became the nemesis of the mountains by organizing guerilla forces and raiding, killing, plundering, and spreading destruction throughout Western North Carolina.

Kirk made one of his forays into Western North Carolina in 1862, coming from Tennessee by way of the Pigeon River, and then, instead of turning east toward Asheville, he went west toward Balsam Gap, which led into Jackson County.[3] Word reached Webster, the Jackson County seat, that Kirk and his Raiders were on the way, and a handful of old men and young boys walked from Webster to Balsam Gap to join a small Confederate force in an ambush of Kirk. Fifteen-year-old Thadius G. Bryson,[4] a member of the civilian force, related the story of this battle later.

At the gap the civilians joined Confederate Captain Andy Patton and his small force of Rebel troops. Patton had brought a wagonload of rifles and ammunition and quickly armed the sharpshooting squirrel hunters.

They felled trees to block the road and arrayed themselves in ambush along the ridgelines on both sides of the trail, each finding cover from which he had a good line of fire on the path.

Kirk came swinging along with his men yelling, stomping, and

---

[2] All of these buildings were burned by United States troops when they entered the town in the latter part of April 1865.

[3] Details written by the author in The Sylva Herald, centenniel edition, August 30, 1951.

[4] Great grandfather of the author.

laughing, rifles resting across their shoulders, most with arms hooked over their weapons.

When they came in sight of the barricade, they stopped in puzzlement on Kirk's command. Without warning the air was suddenly filled with flying musket balls.

Men dropped like flies, and those unhit, seeing none of the hidden attackers, ran in disaray into the woods. Before they could pull themselves together, the Rebels charged, firing on the run, and Kirk's force dropped their weapons and fled for their lives, crashing through the brush. Unencumbered by weaponry, the Raiders outdistanced the Rebels and got away. Kirk reformed what was left of his command and led his men through Indian country back to Tennessee. He returned later with replenished forces, slipped back into Jackson County, and set up his headquarters camp near Cullowhee in an area still known as Kirk's Camp.

As April of 1865 approached, the news reaching Asheville was anything but good. Lee was taking a pounding at Appomattox Courthouse, the flames of Atlanta were still dying out, and Johnston's army was retreating rapidly in front of the advance by Sherman through Georgia and South Carolina. To the east the fall of Fort Fisher at the mouth of the Cape Fear River on the North Carolina coast, blocked the import of supplies by sea and was virtually determining the fate of Lee's army in Virginia.

Federals closed in on Asheville. Kirk, one of the war's most brutal men, crossed the Smokies into Haywood County; Colonel Isaac M. Kirby marched with a strong force of 900 federal troops up the French Broad toward Asheville; and General George Stoneman was laying waste to Watauga County with sword and fire.

William Lewis Henry, son of Robert Henry, the pioneer Buncombe educator and lawyer, and William's wife, Cornelia Smith Henry, who lived on the west side of the French Broad River, chronicled in their journals the last days of the war.

On Thursday, April 6, 1865, three days before the surrender at Appomattox, Mrs. Henry wrote this entry:

MR. HENRY went to town this morning. About three o'clock we heard the Yankees were in town, but did not believe it till about four when George came up from the mill and said some men had come from town and said it was certainly so.... Sam said Mr. Henry had gone to the front and

sent me word not to be alarmed. . . . I am very uneasy about
Mr. Henry. I fear he will expose himself. . . . It has been
raining a little all the evening. . . . May a kind Heaven protect
my dear husband this night, and all our brave men, and turn
back our enemies. Oh! Lord, deliver us from our enemies,
I pray.

On April 3, Colonel Isaac M. Kirby of the 101st Ohio Infantry,
then based in Greeneville, Tennessee, was ordered to "scout in the
direction of Asheville."[5] Kirby came with 900 infantrymen, two
cannon, a train of wagons with supplies for seven days, and with
several Confederate deserters who knew the mountains toward
Asheville scouting to his front.

Kirby was a careful man. When he struck the Buncombe Turnpike he ordered scouts into the woods flanking the march because he
feared ambush by Confederate forces and their painted Cherokee
Indian allies–Colonel William H. Thomas's famed Thomas Legion–
who were fighting this time on the side of their American neighbors,
the Confederates.

Communications were so poor that Asheville was unaware of
Kirby's approach until it was almost too late. Kirby burned bridges
along the way, including one at Alexander, eleven miles out of
Asheville, and another at Craggy Station, four miles away.

Between the two bridges was Montrealla, home of Mrs. H. E.
Sondley, a widow, and her small son, Forster A. Sondley, later to
become Buncombe County's most famous historian.

Kirby's men took all the Sondley horses but one, which had been
hidden, and took a Shetland pony that belonged to young Forster,
who later wrote of the event: "As the invaders prosecuted their march
the stolen pony was unable to keep up, so they shot it to death in the
road." He never overcame his bitterness over this incident.

While the Yankee troops were passing, Mrs. Sondley sent a
Negro man into the woods to ride the hidden horse to Asheville to
warn the town that "The Yankees Are Coming!"

In a Reveresque rush, the man stuck to the woods in a roundabout
route and reached Asheville in time to spread the alarm. General
James C. Martin, the Confederate commander of the Western
Department with headquarters in Asheville, was away from town,
and in his absence, Colonel George Wesley Clayton, a West Point
graduate and son of Col. Ephraim Clayton, who had headed the

<hr>
[5] Some historians say Kirby was ordered to reach Asheville and join Stoneman, who
intended to take the town.

original company that manufactured Rebel rifles in Asheville, acted quickly, rounding up Confederate troops, old men, and boys too young for the army, armed them as best he could, and led them northward down North Main Street on the double.

About the time the Negro man arrived in town, so did Nicholas W. Woodfin, who owned a large farm in the area that came to be named for him on the northwest side of Asheville. Woodfin had fled the Yankees on horseback and Kirby's advance scouts had given chase, firing as they rode, but failed to hit Woodfin. After he helped spread the word, Woodfin retired to his home at 2 Woodfin Street, which later became a part of Asheville's YMCA, and from a crow's nest atop the house, from which he could survey his farm in the distance, watched the battle through a spyglass.

Arriving at the earthworks and cannon positions at the foot of South Main Street, Col. Clayton's Asheville force dug in and waited for the Federals to arrive. Cannon from the Confederate batteries on the right and left of the troops were trained on the road.

When the advance scouts who had fired on Woodfin reached the breastworks and saw that they were occupied by fighting men, they retired rapidly to report to Col. Kirby the presence of the enemy up the road.

While they were doing this, Clayton deployed sharpshooters along the ridge to his right and forward of the breastworks to give the defenders an enfilading fire.

At three o'clock that afternoon, the two sides came together. Wasting no time maneuvering for position, both sides opened up with long-range rifle fire. That of the Asheville riflemen was punctuated by their own cannon fire from ridges on both sides. Kirby rolled his cannons into position and fired. With sharpshooters on the ridge to their left, the Yankees dared not charge, and until about eight o'clock that evening the sides traded long-range rifleshots.

When at eight the Confederates increased their rate of fire, the Yankee troops retreated from the battlefield and raced back to Montrealla where they bivouacked, and before dawn they were on the march down the river toward their camp near Greeneville, Tennessee.

Along the road north of Montrealla they left discarded guns, bayonets, canteens, and anything else that might impede their progress toward Tennessee. Searching the battlefield the next morning, Rebel troops found all this paraphernalia and a man's leg, clad in blue, still in a boot.

The battle was remarkable in one respect: even though hundreds had been engaged in furious shooting for five hours, no lives were lost. Sondley reported that two federal troops lost legs to cannon shot. He added that no Confederate fighter was hurt, which was at slight variance with Mrs. Henry's journal in which she wrote that two Confederates were slightly wounded.

Her journal entry for the following day, April 7, was:

> MR. HENRY came back about eleven o'clock. I was glad to see him. . . . Mr. Henry said we repulsed them handsomely. I am very glad of it. He thinks they will fight again today. It nearly killed me this morning to tell him goodbye. He went to town this morning, and came back about twelve o'clock and said the Yankees left last night. I believe the Lord heard my heartfelt prayer. They took some prisoners at Rankin's tanyard, some four or five. We had two men slightly wounded. We do not know the enemy's loss as they were some six hundred yards apart. (Sondley said they fought at 'close range.') They left one leg in a boot. Our men acted well. The artillery played on them all the time. The Negroes here heard it, but I was upstairs where Matt was weaving, so could not hear it. They fought down about Nick Woodfin's farm. I do hope they may never come back again.

However far apart the opposing forces were, rough and wooded terrain may have been responsible for the low casualty count.

From their flanking positions the Confederates commanded the entire Turnpike approach to Asheville, and that may have been the reason Kirby was so reluctant to attack in force. In his report, Col. Kirby said he had positive orders not to sacrifice the life of one man for the town. That is likely true, for Asheville was not of great strategic value to the Federals, who expected the war to end at any moment.

Two days after the Battle of Asheville, on April 9, 1865, Lee surrendered the Confederacy to Grant at Appomattox Courthouse.

The Federal troops who moved into Asheville in late April did not remain long, but they were in town long enough to burn all the Confederate buildings and to "perpetrate a serious outrage near Weaverville," according to Sondley. He wrote that a Negro garrison was kept in Asheville for some time in 1865, and that some of these troops perpetrated the outrage. Eight or ten of them were court-martialed by a Union army court and condemned to be shot. The mass execution was conducted on Broadway at its junction with East and Chestnut streets—the place called "Five Points" today—and the bodies were buried on the spot. Their bones were uncovered thirty-five years later by workmen at the mouth of East Street.

Much of Western North Carolina was left in despair, homes wrecked, tools destroyed, livestock gone, no money, and many families were reduced to the state of those who first came into this wilderness in 1784. They had to make do with what they had.

The wounds of war, physical and mental, slowly healed, but for decades men on both sides verbally fought the war all over again. Here in the South, folks took defeat so hard that at least twenty years after the end of the war, mountaineers still shot verbal arrows at the Damnyankees.

The story was told that at the second battle of Bull Run a cannonball carried off a poor Yankee soldier's leg.

"Carry me to the rear!" he cried to a tall companion who had been fighting at his side. "They've shot off my leg!"

The soldier caught up his wounded companion, and as he put him across his shoulders, another cannon ball carried away the poor fellow's head. His companion, in the confusion, did not notice this, and proceeded with his burden toward the rear.

"What are you carrying that thing for?" cried an officer.

"Thing!" exclaimed the soldier. "This thing is a man with his leg shot off. I'm taking him to the hospital."

"Why, he hasn't any head," the officer said.

The soldier looked at his load and saw that what the officer had said was true. Throwing down the body, he thundered, "Confound him! He told me it was his leg!"

More than fifty years later, at the conclusion of the first World War, someone asked Mayor J. E. Rankin, a veteran of the Civil War, how the city would organize celebrations for returning veterans.

"There are no precedents here for general celebrations in honor of returning soldiers," he said. "The programs to be carried out for the boys who broke the Hindenburg Line will be unique in our local history."

He explained how he returned from the Civil War.

"When I came back from Tennessee at the close of the war between the states," he said, "I crawled over Smith's bridge at midnight, slipped to my home and like a thief in the night climbed through the kitchen window. As a reception for me and other

Illustration in Harper's Magazine of Negro registration to vote in Asheville in 1867.

returning soldiers, we were arrested soon after our return by the notorious Colonel Kirk.

"There seemed to be no indication as to when order would be restored and when such men as Kirk would be stopped from their operations, so with a few companions I started for Mexico. We planned to go to that country and start life over again. We went as far as Franklin, where we ran into Kirk's men and were arrested again. This enforced delay put an end to our plans for taking up residence in Mexico. We spent several days in Franklin under rather loose and comfortable arrest and after talking over the situation with friends in Franklin we decided to come back home.

"I happened to know some of Kirk's men; I am sorry to say that a few of them were former friends and neighbors who had deserted from the Confederate armies. Through their recommendation I was allowed to select a small mule from the large number of animals collected by Kirk's command as they journeyed through the country, and on this beast I made the trip back home."

15

ZEB VANCE

Zebulon Baird Vance of Asheville had led the state through the Civil War as a two-term governor (he was later elected to a third term). He was the people's man, born of pioneer stock in a log house on Reems Creek, and even he despaired at the condition of the state at the end of the war.

Vance was deeply crushed not as much over the defeat of the Confederacy as by the condition the people of North Carolina were left in at the end of the war.

In compassion and despair, Vance poured out his heart to one of his closest friends, John Evans Brown, who at that time was living in Australia. He was a native Pennsylvanian who had moved to Asheville, then on to the California gold fields, and finally across the Pacific to Australia, later returning to Asheville to build a famous castlelike home on Beaucatcher Mountain which he called "Zealandia." Vance, then incarcerated in a federal prison in Washington, D. C., wrote to Brown:

> OF COURSE I cannot give you much criticism upon the war, or the causes of our failure: nor can I attempt to do justice to the heroism of our troops or of the great men developed by the contest. This is the business of the historian and when he traces the lines which are to render immortal the deeds of this revolution, if truth and candor guide his pen, neither our generals nor our soldiers will be found inferior to any who have fought and bled within a century.
>
> . . . the States have been reduced to the condition of territory, their executive and judicial (and all other) officers

appointed by the Federal Govt. and are denied all law except that of the military. Our currency . . . is gone and with it went the banks and bonds of the state and with them went to ruin thousands of widows, orphans and helpless persons whose funds were invested therein . . . their railroads destroyed, towns and villages burned to ashes, fields and farms laid desolate, homes and homesteads, palaces and cabins only marked to the owners eye by blackened chimneys looming out on the landscape like the mile marks on the great highway of desolation . . . the stock all driven off and destroyed, mills and agricultural implements especially ruined . . . this is but a faint picture of the ruin of the country which years ago you left blooming like the Garden of Eden . . . alas, alas!

To travel from New Bern to Buncombe now would cause you many tears, John, unless your heart is harder than I think it is . . . yet charity and brotherly love doth . . . abound. A feeling of common suffering has united the hearts of our people and they help one another. Our people do not uselessly repine over their ruined hopes . . . Major Generals, Brigadiers, Congressmen and high functionaries hold the plough and sweat for their bread . . . a beam of hope begins again to reanimate our long tried and suffering people.

Our loss in men was very great. Seven-tenths of the spirited, educated young men of North Carolina fell in this struggle. Many old friends are almost extinct in the male line. I will instance the Averys and the Pattons. Of the former, Molton Waightstill (Avery) and Isaac (Avery) fell in battle, the father dying of grip. Alfonso is a fugitive (God knows where). Of the latter, Jas. W. Patton, Sr., Jas. A., Augustus, and Thos. T. are dead, leaving young Tom the sole representative of those two brothers in the male line . . . Of the bar in our town (Asheville) there are hardly any left. Yr Brother William, Jno. Woodfin, P. W. Roberts, Jordan, Edney, Davis, all fell in the contest. None remain except Nick (Nicholas) Woodfin, Coleman and Merrimon and Erwin.

After the surrender . . . I was arrested and sent to Washington City and lodged in prison . . . Mrs. Vance during my confinement was seized with hemhorrage of the lungs and came near dying. She is now, however, after much suffering, mental and bodily, restored to her usual health. We are living very poorly and quietly, as I can do no business until I am pardoned or released from my parole. We have four little boys, Charles (10 years old), David (8), Zebby (3), and Thomas (3) . . . trouble and anxiety have left their marks on me. I am getting very gray.

Vance's real purpose in writing Brown in Australia grew out of his despair for the future. He wrote:

THE POST-WAR radical-abolitionist proposals will revive an already half-formed determination in me to leave the U. S. forever. Where shall I go? Many thoughts have I directed towards the distant Orient where you are. The idea is so possible at the least I would be thankful to you for any information germane to the matter. Climate, soil, water, water courses, government, population . . . what could I do there? . . . What could I do when set down at the wharf in Sidney with a wife, four children, and perhaps "nary red?"

When released from my bonds, I think of going to Washington, N. C., to practice law if I don't leave the country. The mountains were much torn and distracted by the war, being almost the only part of the State which was not thoroughly united. The State of Society there is not pleasant, and I don't think I shall ever return there to live . . . .

Writing in the *Asheville Citizen-Times* ninety-five years later, Doug Reed added this note to a story on Vance: "Thoughts of a ravaged land, a stricken people, fallen comrades, of his own family, of his native section, of all the misery, death, and desolation: these accompanied Vance along on that birthday trip (his 35th birthday) to prison on charges not then, or at any time since, enumerated."

That was the same Zebulon Baird Vance in whose honor the granite obelisk was erected on Asheville's Court Square in 1898.

Born on Reems Creek May 13, 1830, to David and Margaret Vance, he came along with a lot of mountain backbone and a great sense of humor and that failed him only that once in the despair of a dark prison cell.

Earlier in this volume, reference was made to General Griffith Rutherford striking terror in the hearts of his teachers with home-made grammar. This was not a trait of the general's alone or else he passed it along in some way, for Zeb Vance probably struck a bit of horror in his teacher also with the first composition he ever wrote in school.

It was first printed in *The Charlotte Observer* and later, on October 28, 1899, in *The Asheville Daily Citizen*, and it read:

TOADS

You told me tell what I knowed about toads. Well toads is like frogs, but more dignity, and when you come think of it frogs is wetter. The warts wich toads is noted for cant be cured for they is cronick but if I couldent get well I'd stay in the house. My Grandfather knew a toad that some lady had trained till it was like folks, wen its master whissled it would come for flies. They catches 'em with their tong which is some like a long red worm butt more like litenin only litenin hasint got no gum onto it. The fli will be standing a rubbin its hind legs together and a thinking what a fine fat fli it is and the toad a sitten some distance away like it was asleep. While you see this fli as plane as you ever see anything, all at once it aint there—then the toad looks up at you solum out of his eyes like he said, What become of that fli? but you know he et it. Thats what I know about toads.

Z. B. Vance

To his credit, Zeb Vance outgrew his grammatical frailties and went on to distinguish himself enough in school to read for the law and pass the bar. He studied for a year at the University of North Carolina also, which was a great boon to the country education he received during his growing-up years. He didn't have the money to attend UNC but applied in 1851 for an educational loan to ex-governor David Lowery Swain, an Asheville man who was at that time president of the university at Chapel Hill. After a year at the university, Vance returned to Asheville and got his license to practice before the Buncombe County court.

But his heart lay more in politicking than in the law. He also tried a bit of newspapering. At the age of twenty-three in 1853, Vance took over Asheville's first newspaper, *The Highland Messenger*, and it was he who wrote the story in 1857 of the search for and discovery of the body of Dr. Elisha Mitchell on the peak that bears his name, Mt. Mitchell.

Vance apparently didn't acquire the newspaper to do stories like that, however good a story it was. He knew that the newspaper would be a handsome tool in his run for Congress in 1857, and he won election to both the 35th and 36th Congresses, serving his people in the House of Representatives from December 7, 1858, to March 3, 1861. His Congressional career was characterized by support of the Union and opposition to the rebelling sentiments then arising in the South.

He was elected to the 37th Congress but was prevented from taking his seat by the secession of North Carolina from the Union. Until that time he held onto his loyalties to the Union of States. He held that Lincoln's election was not a cause for secession when other states pulled out of the Union because of it.

At that point in 1861 came a dramatic turn in Zeb Vance's life. He was campaigning against secession, and in his own words here is what happened:

"I was canvassing for the Union with all my strength. I was addressing a large excited crowd, large numbers of whom were armed, and I literally had my arm extended upward pleading for peace and the Union of our fathers when the telegraphic news was announced of the firing on Fort Sumter and President Lincoln's call for 75,000 volunteers.

"When my arm came down from that impassioned gesticulation it fell slowly and sadly by the side of a secessionist. With altered voice and manner I called upon the assembled multitude to volunteer, not to fight against, but for South Carolina. I said if war must come, I preferred to be with my own people and to shed Northern rather than Southern blood. If we had to slay, I had rather slay strangers than my own kindred and neighbors."

On May 20, a state convention called by the legislature adopted an ordinance of secession, but Zeb Vance had beaten them to war. On May 4 he had organized a company of "Rough and Ready Guards" at Asheville and had been elected the company's captain. The guard became part of the 14th North Carolina Regiment under Colonel W. D. Pender.

Weeping and shouting crowds of men, women, and children filled Public Square and lined South Main Street toward Best when the company marched off to war. To the strains of "Dixie," the guards swung down that long avenue, marched to Best, and turned eastward along the banks of the Swannanoa.

The Rough and Ready Guards fought gallantly through the war, but Vance did not remain with them. He held command through that summer of 1861 with the guards on active duty along the North Carolina coast, but in August he was elected colonel of the 26th North

Carolina Regiment. Some of the North Carolina graduates of the Military Academy at West Point took a rather dim view of Vance's promotion, but the troops on the line cheered it heartily, for Zeb Vance was a people's man. He appealed to the masses of common men. He was never considered a military strategist or even an accomplished soldier, but he got the job done because his men respected him and would go through fire to fight for him.

His second in command, Lieutenant Colonel Harry Burgwyn, who was killed later leading the 26th in Pickett's Charge at Gettysburg, admonished Vance one day for his disregard of military conformity.

"Colonel," Burgwyn protested, "you simply can't have the men shoulder arms right after they have presented them!"

And Vance replied, "By gravy, I've already done it!"

Vance led the 26th through gallant action in the campaign against General Burnside at New Bern and in the Seven Day's Battle near Richmond.

Long after Vance had left it, the 26th distinguished itself in the Battle of Gettysburg in 1863, and the Rough and Ready Guards took part in the fighting at Appomattox Courthouse in the last great battle of the war in 1865.

Vance was called home in the summer of 1862 by the people of North Carolina, who elected him governor at the age of thirty-two. He was inaugurated September 8, 1862.

Vance held the state together as well as anyone could have through the Civil War. He remained loyal to the South to the end, and after the war was over he was arrested and imprisoned in Washington, D. C., by federal powers that never stipulated charges against him. But he was paroled June 6, 1865, seven weeks after his arrest, and pardoned March 11, 1867.

He won election to the United States Senate in 1870 and again in 1879, the year after his wife's death, and it was on the floor of the Senate that he made not the greatest speech of his political career, but certainly the most amusing.

Speaking against a proposed bill to build a bridge across a certain small stream near Asheville, he protested: "Mr. Speaker, that stream has a good ford and is not large enough to bridge. Why, Mr. Speaker, it is so small that I could pee halfway across it."

Against a roar of laughter from Vance's colleagues, the speaker banged his gavel, and railed, "Senator Vance, Senator Vance, you are out of order, sir!" to which Vance quickly replied, "I know it, Mr. Speaker. If I was in order I could pee *all* the way across it."

He filled the North Carolina governor's office twice more, and in his third term, beginning January 1, 1877, his administration, according to the *Asheville Citizen-Times,* "was distinguished by a revival of railroad enterprises; a stimulus to agriculture and industry, the enlargement and improvement of public schools and charitable institutions for both races, repudiation of the fraudulent Reconstruction state bonds, and adjustment of the state's legal debt on a basis acceptable to its creditors."

His accomplishments for North Carolina were by no means small.

In 1879, halfway through his third term as governor, he was elected to the United States Senate and was re-elected in 1885 and 1891. He served in the Senate until his death in Washington on April 14, 1894, a month before his sixty-fourth birthday.

16

DAYLIGHT ENTERS BUNCOMBE

Two occurrences within a six-year period in the decade of the 1880s accomplished the opening of Asheville to the world. First was the coming of the railroads in 1880, and the other was construction of the Battery Park Hotel on Stony Hill in 1886. The railroads gave people, especially the wealthy, a way to get to Asheville, and the Battery Park Hotel gave them a first-class place to stay. When the wealthy came, they brought money with them to boost the Asheville economy—and several of the truly wealthy loved the mountains so much they invested huge amounts of money and some made their homes here.

These were the stimuli the city had needed for so long . . . .

For fifteen years after the Civil War, Asheville, Buncombe County, and, indeed, all of North Carolina wallowed in the throes of carpetbagging government imposed by the Union victors in the Civil War. Even so, all eyes in Western North Carolina, particularly those in Asheville, looked eastward for salvation, not to Raleigh for help, because Raleigh was also under the control of Union scalawags, but eastward toward slowly moving railroad crews laying iron rails toward the mountains.

Asheville's leadership knew, and told the people, that the only thing that would unlock the isolation of the vast mountain area was transportation. Roads in Buncombe County were still primitive, especially those leading out of the county. The only means of travel was by stagecoach, private horse-drawn vehicles, horseback, or on foot. The Buncombe Turnpike had fallen victim to the Civil War and was in a state of fairly rapid decay. Asheville's deliverance from its

Asheville's buildings were still scattered around 1890. Note the Battery Park Hotel (center) on the highest hill.

geographic stranglehold lay to the east, not to the north and south, and the railroad was to be the answer.

The city's growth had not kept pace with that of the county, and as late as 1870 Asheville's population was only 1,450 in a county of 15,412 citizens. In the decade after that, through the 1870s, the city gained only 1,110 souls for a population of 2,610.

First came the railroad. Not only did it connect Western North Carolina with the downstate area and thereby with the world, it also gave all of North Carolina a direct route to the midwest and the west—and all of that traffic and all of those people had to come through Asheville to get there.

The railroad was a long time coming. It headed west from Salisbury in the middle 1850s, but it was twenty-five years before it reached Asheville in October of 1880.

The roadbed west was rockier than any of its dreamers and planners had imagined. The railroad company was beset by poverty, politics, malfeasance, ravages of the Civil War, and the insolence of a post-war carpetbag government.

In all that while of waiting, goods coming into the mountains were hauled by wagon trains that labored up the grades only in fair weather. Otherwise, all of Western North Carolina was dependent on itself.

Strong men were required to push iron rails over the mountains, and free men, slaves, and convicts sweated to dig the grade and lay the tracks. Many died in the effort.

John Motley Morehead, for whom the Morehead Scholarships at the University of North Carolina are named, was considered the Father of the North Carolina Railroad. A native Virginian reared in North Carolina, Morehead became successful in business, the law, politics, and building railroads. He was twice elected governor of North Carolina. In 1840 he was the first man to be elected to the governorship by popular vote.

Asheville knew that completion of the railroad would develop the mountains—if ever it got here—just as it had done for the Piedmont.

The North Carolina Legislature authorized construction of the Western North Carolina Railroad in its 1850-51 session, and according to historian O. K. Morgan, money to fund a survey of the line was to come from the sale of Cherokee Indian lands.

In 1856 construction began, and Ashevilleans anticipated seeing trains arriving in Biltmore within three or four years. Knowing how completion of the downstate railroad to Salisbury had developed the Piedmont, they believed it would do the same for the mountains.

Yet, more than a year later, only nineteen miles of roadbed had been graded from Salisbury to Statesville, and it was ready for track. Six more miles were soon graded west of Statesville, reaching the Catawba River. Progress slowed more, and by August 1860 the line was completed to Connelly Springs, thirteen miles from Morganton, and there construction ceased in April 1861 when Fort Sumter was fired on and the War Between the States began.

The war ravaged the unfinished road. Materials deteriorated from rot, wear and tear, and downright destruction by Union raiders. Enough work was done to extend the rails to within three miles of Morganton, but the cease-fire in April of 1865 found the railway in poor condition. Rails were worn, crossties rotten, ditches filled with debris, and shop and rolling stock worn and damaged. In addition, finances were low, and new money would have to be found to get the job moving again.

Fortunately, men of means knew what value a railroad into the mountains would be to the entire state and enough money was raised to get the job moving again. Frank Coxe of Rutherfordton, who would later build the Battery Park Hotel in Asheville, invested in the company and used his influence to get others to invest.

Asheville's hopes of being connected by rail to the rest of the state suffered setbacks and disillusionments, for progress was slow. From Morganton, only fifty-four miles away, fifteen years were required to get the high iron into Asheville.

For a while, laborers moved the tracks along very well. Contracts were let for the thirty-three and a half miles from Morganton to Old Fort, and this leg was completed by 1869.

But six years later, rails had been laid only three miles west of Old Fort and engineers and laborers stood looking in awe at the bulk of stair-stepped mountains rising to Swannanoa Gap—1,100 vertical feet in three miles—but they were ready and eager for the challenge. As the crow flies, it was only six miles from Old Fort to Ridgecrest on the west side of the gap, but those were terrifying miles of building a five percent grade, a rise of five feet for every hundred feet, switching back from ridge to ridge, trestling here, tunneling there, and then in 1872 the money ran out and the project slowed and finally languished for a year or more during which the weather virtually erased what progress had been made. Tunnels caved in and cuts and fills were ruined by slides. Encouraged by heavy rainfall and deep snows, mountain vegetation obliterated much of the work that hard labor had accomplished.

Fresh financing and an act of the legislature authorizing the use of convicts as laborers set the road in motion again in March of 1875, and under the guidance of Major James W. Wilson, whose company had contracted to build the road up the Blue Ridge, the grade was mastered. Wilson was an able man, thoroughly honest, and in 1877 he was elected president, superintendent, and chief engineer of the railroad company.

As the grade was completed toward the head of Swannanoa Mountain, a telegraph line was run up the mountain and into Asheville in 1877, giving the town and the railroad engineers communication with every place along the line. Newspapers reported that the telegraph reached the city "through the enterprise of Captain C. M. McLoud."

During the heaviest construction, 1,455 men and 403 boys worked to clear the grade up the steep heights of the Blue Ridge. More than a thousand horses, oxen, and mules were put to work. The bulk of the work force was five hundred convicts, mostly blacks, from Eastern North Carolina.

The state legislature had provided that "the Warden of the Penitentiary shall, from time to time, as the Governor may direct, send to the President of said company all convicts who have not been farmed out . . . to labor on said railroad, provided the convicts assigned shall be at least five hundred, and the number so assigned shall not exceed five hundred."

All supplies such as guarding, feeding, clothing, and doctor's bills and the pay for each convict by the company ("not less than fifty dollars each per annum") was to be furnished by the pentitentiary superintendent. The feeding allowance for each convict was 6 1/4 cents a day. Many of the convicts had to work shackled with thirteen-inch leg-irons.

The task of tunneling through several mountains was the toughest job railroad builders ever tackled in North Carolina. To cut tunneling time in half, crews would dig from both sides of the mountain and meet in the center, usually on line.

Tunneling depended heavily on how much black blasting powder could be found to shoot the hole through the mountain. There was still a shortage of powder because of the late war, and it appeared the project would be slowed again, but an enterprising powderman named Cambar came up with a method of making explosives by mixing nitroglycerine with sawdust and corn meal, and put the project back on track. He stirred a mixture of his blasting agent in a large tub until it became a thick mash, then poured it into rolled oil paper cartridges, making sticks of explosives. The sticks were powerful. A dozen or so plugged into hand-drilled holes in a large rock would break it into pieces that could be hauled away.

With Cambar's new explosive came one of the strangest and wildest tales of those construction days.

A man named Sandlin worked on the grade near High Ridge Tunnel east of the Blue Ridge crest and kept his six-year-old son, Will, and Will's younger brother, with him. Will grew up in a line shack among railroad workers as the road moved across (or through) the Blue Ridge and into Asheville and beyond. He was a bright boy who learned so much about railroad construction that he became a grade foreman before his eighteenth birthday and stayed with the construction forces until the road was completed to Murphy.

Will got his first job with the railroad at the age of six, and no one saw anything wrong with that since there were no school laws to force education upon him. He and his younger brother had been trading apples and chestnuts to the rail workers for tobacco and when not hanging around the work crews they were in the woods gathering nuts. Cambar, who was not the hardest worker in camp, noticed the way Will dogged the heels of the track gang and one day asked Will's father if he could hire the boy to stir his explosive mixture. There was no danger since the mixture had to be detonated with fire and blasting caps and Will, of course, had no idea how to do that.

But Cambar did not account for Will's quick mind and learning ability.

Will went to work the next day, stirring each tub of goo for half a day, helping make the blasting compound that eventually blasted several holes through the mountains.

Will watched Cambar work with more than passing interest, because he, being an enterprising young man, had figured a way to gather more chestnuts and perhaps trade them for a little money in addition to the tobacco he received.

Instead of climbing trees to gather chestnuts, Will reasoned, they could blow the trees down and pick the chestnuts off the ground. Cambar could not tell if a small amount of dough was missing from the huge tub.

So Will learned how to explode a charge of nitroglycerine by watching Cambar.

Each day he swiped a few handfuls of explosive and put it in a five-pound lard bucket hidden in the woods. When the bucket was filled, he and his brother carried it deeper into the woods to a selected chestnut tree—the largest they could find.

They dug a hole under the tree and poured in the five pounds of explosive. Just as he had seen Cambar do, Will inserted a blasting cap, which he had pilfered from Cambar's supply, and ran a line of dry leaves away from the charge.

Will set fire to the leaves and he and his brother raced for cover. The younger lad ran about seventy-five yards and hid behind a tree, plugging his ears with his fingers. But Will, who had watched hundreds of blasts, stopped at half that distance and waited.

Seconds later, the five pounds of nitroglycerine went off with a thunderous boom. The mountain seemed to shift under Will's feet, and a cloud of dirt sprayed upward in all directions. Rocks, soil, tree limbs, everything around the chestnut tree, hurtled through the air and crashed to the ground.

Will was buried to his neck and had to be dug out of the ground. When he was freed he surveyed the damage. Where the chestnut tree had stood, a hole in the ground was large enough to hide a six-room house. The tree had vanished and a section of trees had gone down like ten-pins in all directions. The blast had remodeled the landscape for many yards around.

That night Will's father exercised his authority and talent with a razor strop, and either the blast or the strop cured Will of any further desire to stir dynamite for Cambar.

Another major problem cropped up before the Swannanoa Tunnel was completed into Buncombe County. The railroad contract stipulated that a locomotive had to reach the "capital of Buncombe County" by a certain date in order to fulfill the contract, and it became apparent that the railroad could not reach Asheville on time.

But the contract did not stipulate "rails" reaching Asheville, only a "locomotive."

Captain Aldridge, engineer of the locomotive "Little Salisbury," solved the problem with a shenanigan that matched anything done on the road— short of Will Sandlin's new method of gathering chestnuts. On the stagecoach road over the mountain, he had a work crew lay a section of temporary track and brought the Salisbury over the mountain and into Asheville in time to fulfill the contract.

Laborers picked up ties and track behind the locomotive as it was pulled forward by oxen and mules, relaid them in front of the engine, and the struggling brutes strained to pull the engine forward again, and in that manner reached Asheville in time to fulfill the contract.

With Cambar's devastating blasting agent and Major Wilson's encouragement and guidance, the 1,832-foot Swannanoa Tunnel was finally completed on March 11, 1879, and Major Wilson telegraphed Governor Zeb Vance dramatically: "Daylight entered Buncombe County today through the Swannanoa Tunnel. Grade and centers met exactly."

When one considers how the railroad was built into Asheville, he realizes what a monumental task it was. All work was done by hand with picks and shovels, carts and oxen, and mule-drawn scrapes. Wagons and horses were the means of making cuts and fills. Rock in cuts and tunnels was hand-drilled and the explosive was black powder and Cambar's dynamite. All masonry was handcut. Concrete was hardly known. Trestles were built of heavy timber. The principal food of the laborers was white navy beans and cornbread with a biscuit on Sunday morning and an occasional vegetable thrown in. The convicts were taken to a creek once a week, usually on Saturday, and allowed to bathe in the cold waters.

The cost of spanning the Blue Ridge mountains was monumental in human life. Cold, wet winter weather in the mountains sent waves of pneumonia sweeping through the convicts, who were poorly clothed and poorly fed, and years ago a mountain old-timer said he knew where 400 unmarked graves lay just east of the last tunnel coming west. No one knew how many solitary graves lay along the track up the mountain. Drilling of the Swannanoa Tunnel was delayed several times by slides which cost more than a half million dollars and 120 lives.

A year and a half after Wilson wired the governor of daylight entering Buncombe County, the rails were finally laid into Asheville. They reached Biltmore on Sunday morning, October 2, 1880, and Asheville celebrated, realizing it had become a real part of the world.

Exuberance also oozed from the editorial columns of the Asheville newspaper, which editorialized:

THE NEWS that Major Wilson on Monday morning completed the laying of track through Swannanoa tunnel will be hailed with delight by the people of Western Carolina. For the last two decades these people have been anxiously looking for this result—have been waiting for the snorting of the iron horse through the bowels of the Blue Ridge—and now that this great feat has been accomplished, they feel that the strong barrier between them and the outside world has at least been pulled down, and that they may soon be reckoned in truth as "a part of the State of North Carolina."[1]

The celebration in the railroad camp on the west end of the tunnel was brief. Soon after Major Wilson sent the telegram to Governor Vance, a final cave-in occurred in the tunnel, crushing twenty-one laborers to death.

When the rails reached Asheville, Colonel A. B. Andrews became president and chief engineer of the railroad and pushed the rails down the French Broad River to the Tennessee state line where in 1882 they connected with the Cincinnati, Cumberland Gap and

---

[1] Quoted by Wilma Dykeman in *The French Broad.*

Charleston rail line, giving Asheville connections to the Ohio and Mississippi valleys and the far west.

Next, in December 1885, the Asheville & Spartanburg Railroad joined track with the Western North Carolina Railroad where Sweeten Creek pours into the Swannanoa River, opening a through line from Charleston via Asheville to Cincinnati and Louisville, completing a project that had been the dream of antebellum railroad builders of Charleston.

Thirty-two miles from Asheville, Saluda Mountain, like Swannanoa, was a great obstacle. It is much like a huge western mesa. From the plateau of the Land of the Sky, the land suddenly drops away steeply into South Carolina. The railroad's grade, at one point 5.03 percent, is the steepest standard gauge main line railway in the United States. Convict labor helped build this line, too, and numerous delays, mostly financial, put the road behind schedule. It reached Tryon in 1877, and two years later on June 21, 1879, the remainder of the mountain was conquered and rails laid into Hendersonville.

Only twenty-two miles of track remained to be built into Asheville, but because of financial delays and finally a receivership action against the line, construction was halted. The company was sold under foreclosure, and it was six and a half years before the rails joined with the Western North Carolina Railroad in Biltmore.

For many years there were probably more wrecks on Saluda Mountain than on any other stretch of railroad in the country. Runaways were frequent and devastating. In the late 1890s, an engineer named Pitt Ballew, who narrowly missed death by jumping from the cab of a runaway locomotive seconds before it left the tracks and plunged down the side of a mountain, devised a system of safety tracks leading off the main line. These tracks were always to be left open and were switched back to the main line only when an engineer coming down the mountain signalled the switchtender that his train was under control. If it were a runaway, it would switch onto the next safety track and would be stopped by an extremely steep grade. This system was completed in 1904 and reduced wreckage enormously on the mountain.

The Saluda Mountain rails pass through interestingly-named places, for example, Tuxedo, which is Cherokee for "the place of bears." Saluda itself was a Cherokee word meaning "Corn River."

Finally, Colonel Andrews of the WNC line turned his attention westward and drove the rails through Canton and Waynesville, over Balsam Mountain, down through Sylva to Bryson City and on to

Murphy, arriving there in 1890 to make connection with the rail line to Ducktown, Tennessee, where vast copper mines were then developed and the ore shipped out by rail.

The Murphy Branch took its toll in human life also. Twenty shackled convicts were being ferried across the Tuckaseigee River below Dillsboro to work in the Cowee Tunnel when the flat boat suddenly took water at the rear and when the convicts ran to the front, the raft capsized and threw all twenty and their guard into the river in a panic. Nineteen convicts were drowned, and only one convict and the guard survived.

As railroads opened up the Piedmont, so they opened Western North Carolina. The mountains were no longer the tremendous barrier they once had been. Railroads pulled all of Western North Carolina together with an iron link, and made Asheville famous as a health and recreation center, and eventually as location for considerable industry. Nothing in the annals of the mountains ever produced such results as the coming of the railroads, and importance of the railroads was never more pronounced than in July 1916 when the Swannanoa and French Broad rivers flooded tremendously, washing out roads and railroad tracks to the north, east, and south. The Murphy Branch, which escaped most of the deluge, became a lifeline for thousands in the Land of the Sky. Trains were able to supply these people with essentials until the rail damage elsewhere had been repaired.

17

THE COXE CONNECTION

"From records found in (his) possession at the time of his death it appears that he served in the Union and Confederate armies at the same time, giving additional proof of the old saying that truth is stranger than fiction. Aside from serving in both armies at the same time, he fought against himself in many battles, ran away from himself on more than one occasion, was twice shot to death, and lived to a ripe old age, haunted always by the fear that he had killed himself."[1]

As preposterous as that description sounds, Colonel Frank Coxe was nobody's fool. He was a man of sound mind and large build–six-feet-four and 265 pounds at the age of sixteen–who probably did more than any other person or groups of persons in making Asheville a tourist town.

Perhaps the description should be explained first. Colonel Coxe was a true Southerner, born in Rutherfordton November 2, 1839. He attended Furman College before enrolling in the University of Pennsylvania from which he was graduated in 1858 at age eighteen with a degree in civil engineering.

He really was a colonel in the Confederate Army at the start of the War Between The States. Already in the coal-mining business, he and his brother having inherited valuable interests in the anthracite coal region around Wilkes-Barre, Pennsylvania. Their grandfather Tench Coxe, one-time Secretary of the United States Treasury, left the mines to them. Coxe worked as an engineer in the coal fields until the outbreak of civil war in 1861.

The young Coxe enlisted in Company B, Butler's Guards, Kershaw's Brigade, of the South Carolina Volunteers. He joined in

[1] From The Asheville Citizen, July 9, 1939.

Greenville, South Carolina, just in time to take part in the first Battle of Bull Run.

Then only twenty-one, Coxe was soon elevated to the rank of colonel, but he didn't have time to enjoy his field-grade rank. Learning that his large Pennsylvania coal holdings were in danger of being confiscated by the United States government, he was released from duty by Confederate President Jefferson Davis, who gave him permission to go north on an indefinite leave of absence.

Being totally sympathetic with the secessionist cause and the Civil War being the last conflict in which a man could hire a replacement to fight for him, Colonel Coxe hired a young southern fellow to take his place in Kershaw's Brigade.

North he went to Pennsylvania where he played a dangerous cloak-and-dagger role of Union sympathizer. But because of his youth, Coxe soon found himself the target of Union recruiters, and to escape conscription by the federal army, he had to hire another substitute to fight for him on the Union side. Although he could well afford it, he thought it was more than strange that, in a way, he was fighting on both sides. Not only that, but he was fighting against himself.

Soon thereafter, he came to odds with the Confederate government, for reasons now lost in history, and left the United States to live in Paris for a while.

Returning to the states after hostilities ceased, Col. Coxe was appalled to learn that his alter egos had been killed on the same day in the same battle—one of the last of the war—and that their regiments had been pitted against each other on the day of their deaths.

Ever afterward, Col. Coxe considered himself to be responsible for their deaths. In later years, he fancied that his substitutes might have shot each other, and he died with the conviction firm in his mind that each of his hired fighters had indeed killed the other.

He threw himself into business, however, and formed the firm of Coxe Brothers and Company, Coal Dealers, in Philadelphia. It soon became the largest coal company in the United States. His financial fortunes increased by leaps and bounds.

Then fixed financially for life, and with no hostilities to prevent his return to Southern soil, Col. Coxe returned to North Carolina where he maintained residence until his death in 1903.

He invested heavily in the Western North Carolina Railroad, becoming its vice president under Colonel A. B. Andrews, the road's president, and after that railroad reached Asheville in 1880 he invested further in the Asheville & Spartanburg Railroad. His ties with Asheville, which he had visited from time to time, became stronger. Continuing his railroad interests, he later became president of the Charleston, Cincinnati & Chicago Railroad.

There is an old wive's tale that Col. Coxe once came to Asheville and found his hotel reservation had not been kept for him, and in his anger decided to build a hotel himself. So he bought Battery Porter Hill and built the Battery Park Hotel. He changed Porter to Park in the hill's name to fit the development of the hill around the hotel into a manicured park with walking paths and benches for his hotel guests and also for the people of Asheville to enjoy.

The more likely story, considering Col. Coxe's business acumen, is that he realized the potential of such an elegant hotel in Asheville when railroads gave the world access to the city. Certainly he was impressed with the advantages of Asheville as a health resort, but he also visioned the city as a haven of escape from the rigors of northern winters. Asheville's climatic advantages, he was convinced, would also be attractive to residents of the southern states who sought refuge from summer's heat. In his active mind, he saw a third portion of the people ganging into Asheville: those who wanted a lovely, quiet place to vacation away from the city's rush. Who wouldn't be attracted to the high, green mountains, the tumbling waterfalls, great hiking and horseback trails, excellent hunting and fishing, and swimming in primitive pools of pristine water?

There seems little doubt that his plans for this crowning achievement of his life were well advanced when he joined Col. Andrews in the railroad venture. Perhaps that is *why* he invested in the railroad, knowing that tourists, particularly the elite, would require a good place to stay while enjoying the mountain scenery and helping build railroads was a way to attract them.

There was nothing cheap about the colonel. He believed in traveling in style. Not only did he have his own private railroad car, a plush car in which he could ride in red-velvet comfort, he also had his own private, custom-built stagecoach. The railroad car was so badly damaged in a train wreck on Old Fort Mountain in 1895 that he never repaired it.

Without question, Col. Coxe incorporated the finest and most recent facilities and improvements in his hotel. The Battery Park, the first modern hotel in North Carolina, was also the largest and as the first resort hotel with such facilities in the South, it was considered the third finest resort accommodations in the Southeast.

A brochure advertising the opening of the hotel on July 26, 1886, stipulated that each room had its own fireplace, steam radiator, and light bulb. The Edison Lighting System, "the most perfect medium of artificial illumination," was installed, providing 275 electric lamps, most of which were eight candlepower, giving off almost enough light to read by. But they were electric lights, and few hotels of that day had them. The Murray Hill Hotel in New York had 950 lamps; the St. George in Brooklyn, 650; the Powers Hotel in Rochester, 500; the Lindell Hotel in St. Louis, 330, the Hotel Royal in New Orleans, 320; and the Battery Park, 275.

The hotel was equipped with a hydraulic elevator built by Otis Brothers & Co. An elaborately uniformed elevator boy ran the machine, a cage decorated in ebony and gold. When a guest walked into the elevator, the boy closed the door and pulled a cable. The guest could hear water come into the hydraulic mechanism. It slowly pushed the elevator upward. To come back down, the elevator boy reversed the process, and as the water ran out, the elevator lowered.

Folks came from miles around to see the lights go on and the elevator rise and fall in the Battery Park Hotel.

The hotel became an important factor in the growth and development of the city and section. Completion of the railroad made Asheville accessible, and wealthy tourists flocked to the new hotel. Many names high in the financial, industrial, and professional circles of the country were signed on its registers. Among them was the name of George W. Vanderbilt, and the moment of his signing the guest register was providential for Asheville.

Legendary or not, the story was that Vanderbilt stood on the hotel's south verandah and got his first view of the matchless panorama of scenic grandeur that rolled away from the hotel into the blue haze of distant mountains, and he was so entranced that he made up his mind then and there to purchase the land on which he built one of the world's great showplaces: Biltmore House.

Col. Coxe died June 2, 1903, at his home on Green River and was buried at Rutherford Memorial Episcopal Church, which he built in 1895 in memory of his mother. He left behind a large family, which he had begun with his wife, Mary Matilda Mills, daughter of Dr. Otis P. Mills, a linear descendant of Col. Joseph McDowell of Revolutionary War fame.

18

PEARSON'S PARADISE

Other giants walked these magnificent hills, and some like Richmond Pearson are still remembered here if in no other way than by the things they built and left. Pearson moved here in 1879 and bought 300 acres of land overlooking Asheville from the west bank of the French Broad River. He is remembered for Pearson Drive, running from Montford Avenue down the hill, across the river, and up the other side to his home on Richmond Hill, and for Pearson's Bridge, which he built across the French Broad. The Great Flood of 1916 washed the bridge away.

Pearson's bridge spans the French Broad around 1900.

He was a single man of wealth who had already begun a career in foreign service when he came to Asheville, purchased his land, and named it Richmond Hill, the same as his father's land where he had been born in Yadkin County.

An 1872 honors graduate of Princeton, valedictorian of his class, Pearson was admitted to the North Carolina Bar in 1874 and was appointed that same year by President Ulysses S. Grant as U. S. consul at Verviers and Liege, Belgium, a position he held until 1877 when he returned to his Yadkin County home.

For a long time his family had served in the high ranks of the military, foreign service, and politics. His father was Richmond Mumford Pearson, chief justice of the North Carolina Supreme Court (1858-1878). His mother was Mrs. Margaret Williams Pearson, whose father was John Williams of Knoxville, U. S. senator from Tennessee and U. S. minister to Guatemala by appointment of President John Quincy Adams in 1825.

Richmond Pearson's eldest sister, Ellen Brent, married Daniel G. Fowle, governor of North Carolina from 1888 to 1891, and his sister Sally married J. M. Hobson of Alabama. Their son, Captain (later Admiral) Richmond Pearson Hobson, achieved fame in the Spanish-American War by sinking the Merrimac, a collier, in the harbor of Santiago, Cuba, in June 1898. One of his wife's aunts married Dr. J. L. M. Curry of Alabama, U. S. minister to Spain in the first Cleveland administration.

So the Pearson family had power and wealth, and Richmond was a level-headed young man who used his shares wisely.

On March 30, 1882, Pearson married Gabrielle Thomas, daughter of a Richmond tobacco merchant, and in 1889 moved her into the house he had built that year on Richmond Hill. The hill was also called Pearson's View for the magnificent vistas seen from the farm.

Like George W. Vanderbilt, who followed him to Asheville a decade later, Pearson spent considerable money building up his farm. When he bought the land and built his house, he said his farmland was so poor that the jackrabbits had to carry their food in knapsacks when crossing it.

His major stroke was the hiring of James E. Alexander, an outstanding farmer and businessman who turned the land into a sparkling jewel on the high hill overlooking the river. Wherever Pearson was in the world—and he was in some faraway places—he stayed in touch with Alexander and often issued orders to him through the mails.

Turnout for Richmond Pearson's offer of a dollar a man for an hour's work building a road on his estate July 4, 1890, followed by a barbecue for all participants and their families.

Pearson was a Republican member of the North Carolina Legislature from 1885 to 1889, and of the lower house of Congress from 1895 to 1901 when President Roosevelt appointed him U. S. consul at Genoa, Italy, in December. The president next appointed him U. S. minister to Persia (1902-07), and he handled that assignment so well that Roosevelt named him Envoy Extraordinary and Minister Menipotentiary to Greece and Montenegro (1907-09). He retired from government service then to live as the country gentleman he was with his wife and three children on his beloved farm in Asheville.

An outstanding chess player, Pearson sought excitement, and in June 1897 as a member of Congress, he headed a House team in a chess match with a House of Commons team in London. After two evenings of playing by international cable, the game was declared a draw.

On the Fourth of July 1890, Pearson got the attention of everyone in Western North Carolina when he pitched a holiday barbeque with food and fireworks for a thousand people on Richmond Hill. He let it be known that every man who wanted to come was welcome, and that all should bring work tools because he intended to build one mile of finished road in one hour on his farm. He offered to pay a thousand men one dollar each for an hour's work in building the road. They began the job at eleven a.m. and finished at noon, and the road was done. Then everyone repaired to the barbeque tables.

The *Asheville Daily Citizen* editorialized: "Would that there were many such public spirited gentlemen in our midst and Asheville's boom would not be equaled anywhere. When the laboring classes are protected and encouraged, prosperity will be the result."

All his life, Richmond Pearson spent time caring for others. The poet and musician Sidney Lanier, who developed tuberculosis in a northern prison during the Civil War, was told by his physician early in 1881 that his only hope was to seek "tent life in a pure, high climate." At Pearson's invitation he came to Richmond Hill even before the mansion was built, and camped for several months in the open air before his death later that year at the age of thirty-nine.

Lanier faced death squarely. Not long before he died, he wrote a bit of verse welcoming death:

> "Look out Death; I am coming.
> Art thou not glad? What talks we'll have,
> What memories of old battles.
> Come, bring the bowl, Death; I am thirsty."

Lanier wrote to his wife of Pearson: "The Mr. Pearson who owns the land is a young man, son of Judge Pearson—a prominent lawyer of this state—who, after having practised law a while and after travelling extensively in Europe and in the West, has bought this beautiful tract of land lying almost entirely enclosed by the Swannanoa and French Broad Rivers, and is devoting much money—with which he seems to be abundantly supplied—to making it a sort of mountain Eden."

Pearson died September 12, 1923, at his home on Richmond Hill and was buried in the family plot in Riverside Cemetery. Mrs. Pearson survived him by a little more than a year and was buried beside him.

19

EXPANSION

With the arrival of the railroad, which brought to Asheville a couple of thousand visitors in 1882, the town's economy began to grow daily. Flexing its muscles with business and expansion in mind, the city put together and printed its first city directory, "The Asheville City Directory and Gazetteer of Buncombe County for 1883-84," and from that time on, historians have been able to glean a lot of information about the annual change in population, business, manufacturing, city officials, and almost anything else they sought.

In 1883, for example, the city's population (it had been a city for a year by decree of the state legislature) was 3,874, of which 2,408 were white and 1,466 were black. Total value of the city's real estate and personal property was roughly $1.5 million. Colonel Virgil S. Lusk was mayor and Herschel S. Harkins, chief of police.

Around Public Square were five general merchandise stores, and most of the town's commerce was conducted there. James C. Sawyer, a busy man, owned one of the stores. He was also president of the only bank in town, the Bank of Asheville, and chief of the Volunteer Fire Department.

Attorneys outnumbered physicians two to one. There were twenty-one law firms containing twenty-six attorneys, and only eleven doctors, one of whom was a woman, Dr. Amie M. Hale. She reminded folks that the first woman physician in the United States, Dr. Elizabeth Blackwell, had studied and taught in Asheville with two brothers, Drs. John and S. H. Dickson, who conducted a young ladies seminary in the Johnston House on the southeast corner of Patton Avenue and Church Street. Blackwell had continued her medical studies at Medical College, Geneva, New York, which she entered in November 1847, and had practiced medicine in the North. It was a coincidence that when Dr. Hale set up practice in Asheville, the location was only a few yards from where Elizabeth Blackwell had studied.

There were strange occupations listed in the directory. One man listed himself as a dealer in Florida curiosities and another as a gentleman of leisure.

Asheville had six hotels, nine churches (three of them colored), two newspapers, *The North Carolina Citizen* and *The Asheville News,* four "spacious" brick tobacco warehouses and eighteen firms of leaf dealers.

No street lights, no electricity, no gas works, no sewer system; it had thirty-eight streets, not any of them paved.

The editor of the directory wrote, "Asheville at present is lighted with the old-fashioned kerosene lamp; but the march of progress demands its speedy abolition. Gas or the electric light must inevitably take its place, ere long, in our growing city.

"An ice factory[1] is a much needed enterprise in our midst," the editor continued. He suggested that the city also needed a street railway, a coal and wood yard, a telephone exchange, an extensive carriage and wagon factory, and a national bank.

Educational institutions were growing in the city. Listed were the Asheville Female College, Asheville Male Academy, Newton Academy, Ravenscroft Diocesan Training School, and the private school of Miss Mary Sawyer. Two more schools were added late in 1883, the Asheville Grammar and High School and the Oak Hill Seminary for young ladies.

Besides a fledgling police department, the Asheville Light Infantry was the local militia, consisting of about fifty young men commanded by Captain W. T. Weaver. The editor wrote, "It is well equipped with arms and presents a brilliant and warlike appearance on parade."

He described activities of tourists in Asheville: "Carriage and horseback riding seem to be the principal, and, indeed, almost the only open-air pleasure indulged in by our summer visitors. They seldom fish; they never hunt, and the bare thought of a pedestrian tour through the mountains would strike a chill of horror to the heart of many a gallant 'carpet knight.'"

---

[2] Soon thereafter, Richmond Pearson built an ice factory.

Hauling wagonloads of lumber to Asheville lumberyard in 1890s.

Biltmore was then known as Best. It did not become Biltmore until George Vanderbilt constructed the Biltmore House in the vicinity. The directors pointed out that the post office knew the village as Best, the railroad called it Asheville Junction, and almost everyone else knew it as Swannanoa Bridge.

The book mentioned extensive improvements at Best, especially the filling up of Blowgun Gulch, a long-time dangerous pitfall for drunks.

Prominent names were listed as residents in the directory. One was Forster A. Sondley, the historian. Others were Thomas L. Clingman, attorney, scholar, scientist, who had claimed to have invented an electric light superior to that of Edison; Locke Craig, who would become governor of North Carolina thirty years later; Solomon Lipinsky, clerk in the store of S. Whitlock; J. H. Lange, who would build the Langren Hotel a block off the square; and W. C. Carmichael, who had a drug store on South Main Street, later on Pack Square, that became a hangout for author Thomas Wolfe and friends.

The Board of Trade, forerunner of the Asheville Area Chamber of Commerce, and the Volunteer Hook and Ladder Fire Company had been organized in 1882. The Swannanoa Hotel on South Main was the largest hotel in the city, and was used until the late 1940s.

The city marked more growth in the decade of the 1880s than in any other previous ten years. This was due, of course, to the railroad, upon which the first train rolled into Best Station on October 2, 1880.

Asheville's growth spurt turned into a boom in the next few years. The population swelled, all public facilities were taxed as quickly as they came into use, and more hostelry went up to satisfy the demands of tourists. Minimal waterworks and the city's first hospital, the Flower Mission on South Main at Hilliard, were opened in 1884, the Battery Park Hotel opened in 1886, Sulphur Springs Hotel in 1887, artificial gas was installed in 1887, the Asheville Street Railway cranked up in 1888, and the city leaped from 2,610 population in 1880 to 10,235 in 1890, a growth of 7,627 in ten years.

Asheville was a nice place, cultured yet blue collar, progressive but hesitant, and those who were farseeing, when they looked at the beautiful mountains, the rolling farmland, the rivers and creeks, could see great things about to happen.

Indeed, the city was on the verge of blooming like a rose.

The county had 35,266 residents, all of whom depended on Asheville for goods.

People liked the prosperity. Business grew tremendously. Now, instead of two newspapers, there were eight, including the two dailies, a weekly devoted to interests of the Republican Party and another to the cause of temperance.

Seven new churches had been built, giving the city sixteen. It also had a public library, three clubhouses, a YMCA, two fire companies, and a street car system.

There were then 144 business houses and fifteen manufacturing and lumber establishments, three tobacco warehouses with an annual volume of four million pounds, and a tobacco works making chewing and smoking tobacco.

More than 40,000 visitors had enjoyed vacations or business stays in Asheville the previous year, 1889, and eight hotels and twenty-seven boarding houses took them in. George S. Powell, president of the Board of Trade, in his annual report, stated: ". . . to the charms of climate and scenery we add unsurpassed inducements to the investor, the manufacturer, the artisan, the merchant, and all seeking homes, either for pleasure or profit. Word was going out all over the country of the wonderful opportunities Asheville offered.

Educationally, there were three graded schools for white children and one for black with a total enrollment of 1,200. For older students, the city offered two male academies, two female colleges, one female high school, and one theological school.

William Randolph School on Montford Avenue occupies the site of Asheville's first public school, which opened in 1888. Montford was known then as Academy Street and the public school was housed in the old Asheville Male Academy building for which the street was named.

In June 1887 the state legislature passed a measure it had had before it for nine years, authorizing public schools in Asheville. The first school opened in January 1888. The first superintendent of city schools was Philander P. Claxton of Tennessee, who later became the United States commissioner of education. J. R. Monroe was principal of the school on Academy Street, with nine teachers who were paid $30 a month.

The school's first term, having started in midwinter, ran for ninety-two days and 464 students were enrolled. Due to a lack of teachers, the school included only the first through fifth grades.

The first public school for Negro children opened that fall on Beaumont Street with 300 students enrolled. The 1888-89 school year began with another white school added on Orange Street with eight grades, the seventh and eighth classified as high school.

Over the years then, Park Avenue School for whites and Hill Street School for blacks opened in 1901. Livingston Street and Mountain Street schools were built before 1909, and Asheville High School opened on the corner of Oak and College streets in 1908 on the site of the old Asheville Female College.

Between 1920 and 1930, seven more schools were started: Claxton, Newton, Vance, Stephens-Lee, Hall Fletcher, Eugene Rankin, and Asheville Senior High School, later to be known as Lee H. Edwards High School.

20

ICE IN SUMMER

Affluent farmers and many merchants built ice houses in bygone days to preserve winter's ice for summer's use. There were merchants in Asheville who stowed away enough ice in winter to sell all summer.

Cold, rough winters were more often the norm than not. There seems to be no question but that winters have gotten warmer for decades.

Americans live today with so many modern conveniences—like refrigeration and electricity—that it is hard to imagine what our forefathers went through here in the hills.

At night the more common people used ignited pine knots for lights, while the more prosperous used candles made of beef tallow and, in rare cases, crude lamps consisting of an iron cup with handles. In the cup was hog's lard and projecting from the cup, a wick saturated with lard lighted at the outer end.

Petroleum and coal oil and their by-products had not been applied to useful purposes, and electricity lay somewhere in the future. Here in Asheville in the 1880s, natural gas preceded electricity for illumination.

Wood was the only fuel known until the railroads came in 1880 and began hauling coal from Kentucky mines.

Winters were more severe in the old days. Williamson's History of North Carolina reported that in the year 1703 Albemarle Sound was frozen over.

Winters in Asheville and all over Western North Carolina were extremely cold. Sondley recorded that in one winter in the second quarter of the nineteenth century a wagon carrying a full load of hay and drawn by four horses was driven across the French Broad River

Ice skating on French Broad River, 1890s.

on the ice at what is now known as Alexander.

Sondley also wrote that in the first week of January 1879 the Swannanoa River, then much larger than now, was frozen over throughout its length with ice so thick that it easily supported loaded wagons, and that the continuously freezing ice, heaped up three feet or more above the surface, cracked with noises as loud as the discharges of a cannon.

Throughout the months of January and February, 1918, the ground was covered so with ice that travel of any kind was difficult and dangerous.

In 1866 three feet of snow fell in Buncombe County and remained on the ground for nearly two weeks. The snow covered a sow and litter of pigs on the Samuel W. Davidson farm on Swannanoa River, and when the snow melted away the mother and pigs were happy and unharmed.

Some early settlers moved to the mountains from the Shenandoah Valley in Virginia where snows were so deep that trees cut for firewood during heavy snows sometimes left stumps higher than a man's head when the snow melted.

John Parris described in detail the ice houses that wealthy people and commercial establishments constructed with rooms in the ground to depths of fifteen or more feet. An ice house's heavily insulated roof came to the ground, and a door was built in one end on the surface of the ground.

Inside, workers descended ladders to fill the house in winter with large ice blocks sawed from the river and stored with layers of straw which preserved the ice for summer use.

Contrasted to those, present winters are relatively mild, and even if ice houses still existed, it's been a long time since they could have been filled with nature-frozen ice.

21

CARRIER'S GENIUS

One man who brought tremendous progress to Asheville was a lumber baron from Michigan who had made a flash fortune and was looking for wise ways to invest it. His name was Edwin George Carrier. He became one of Asheville's outstanding builders of the decades of the eighties and nineties.

Born in Summerville, Pennsylvania, in 1829, Carrier began in the lumber business when just a boy, and in 1874 moved to Michigan at the age of forty-five and struck it rich in the lumber fields. By 1885, he was looking for different pastures. Not greener pastures: he had enough money already. What he wanted now was to enjoy his money, to put it to work for himself and others, to build things he had dreamed of. Indeed, he was a public-spirited man. Shrewd, yes, but always public minded.

On his way to Florida in 1885, Carrier stopped in Asheville to break up the long train ride from Michigan, and when he beheld the mountain splendor and saw the little jewel of a city sitting on top of the plateau, with a wide sweep of sky around it, he found himself captivated. His was a case of love at first sight, and he was not one to dilly dally when there were things he wanted to do. He stayed in Asheville and eventually purchased 1,200 acres of good land to the west of the French Broad River. This land was largely undeveloped and he thought it had tremendous potential.

He liked the idea of catering to visitors in a monumental way, and, though he was then fifty-six years old, he began by forming a West Asheville Improvement Company and intended to make it exactly what its name implied. His first move was to buy the sulphur springs that Robert Henry had discovered at the beginning of the

19th century with the thought of building a fine hotel, not on the scope of the magnificent Battery Park, but something that would give people a comfortable and attractive place to stay when he turned the remainder of his plans into reality, plans that had been forming in his head for years. He built a three-story, brick hotel and called it the Sulphur Springs Hotel. It became an immediate success as one of the area's most popular tourist resorts. It was out in the country where peace and quiet prevailed, and people visited and passed the word to others. Soon he changed the name of his hotel to Carrier's Springs, and later, still not entirely satisfied with it, he changed it again to The Belmont.

More people began to settle west of the river and Carrier had plans to develop facilities that would be of use to everyone while making his hotel even more attractive.

Early in 1889 he built the area's first hydroelectric plant on Lower Hominy Creek, about three miles from the heart of Asheville near what is now Brevard Road, and began generating electricity. His plant was equipped with a 60-horsepower turbine and a 40-kilowatt generator. At the same time, he constructed a new three-story wing on the hotel and installed the first practical system of electric lights through the entire hotel. Then he put the first electric passenger elevator in the South in his hotel. It operated faster than the Battery Park's hydraulic lift.

His plant generated so much electric power that it supplied lights to illuminate West Asheville streets, an accomplishment that pleased the citizens no end, but he wasn't finished yet.

Late that year he constructed a tall, 250-foot steel bridge across the French Broad River near the mouth of the Swannanoa and called it Carrier Bridge. Firmly anchored on solid stancheons, the bridge was strong enough to support tremendous weights. Ashevilleans were puzzled when they saw work crews laying rails from the area of the Asheville Railroad Depot over the bridge and along a roadbed that generally followed the present Amboy Road and ended at the Belmont Hotel. Carrier brought in two electric street cars and put them in operation, and his hydroelectric plant became the first in the world to furnish power for a private commercial trolley line. That was in August of 1891.

Now, visitors who came to Asheville no longer had to employ hacks or ride the hotel's carriages to the Belmont. They simply switched from the railroad to the street car line and rode to the hotel. For a fare, citizens of West Asheville could ride these rails to downtown Asheville after Carrier's crews extended his line from the

Workers blast ice in the frozen French Broad River near Weaver Power Plant in 1905.

depot to the center of Asheville. Its terminus was at the corner of West College and North Main streets. It ran from the depot up Bartlett Street, South French Broad Avenue, and on into town.

This electric plant preceded by thirteen years W. T. Weaver's harnessing of the French Broad River to build the area's first sizeable hydroelectric development, the forerunner of Carolina Power & Light Company.

Folks in Asheville probably laughed behind their hands at Carrier's folly. How could one hotel and a handful of West Asheville citizens support a private railway? Operating expenses would soon be so high as to endanger the existence of the hotel.

But Carrier's genius had not totally surfaced. Early in 1892, his workmen built a half-mile horse racing track in the bottomland beside the French Broad River. He said the track was primarily for the entertainment of the guests of his hotel, who could step on a trolley, ride to the race track, and watch the races.

Training and racing horses had long been his favorite hobby, and he went into that with a fervor. But public-spirited man that he was, he made his large, flat field available to the city and county as a fairground, baseball field, a place for bicycle races, trotting races, and tournaments of various order. For decades this field was known as Carrier Field, later became the Doc Owens Flying Field, and now is occupied by the Asheville Motor Speedway.

Carrier knew his folly would turn into a bonanza. The opening horse races were held on July 13, 1892, and a crowd of 3,000 rode Carrier's street cars and a few private rigs to the track to enjoy the races.

Later, the French Broad Racing Association was formed and held three-day racing meets with more than $1,000 offered in prize money. The meets drew the leading southern thoroughbreds and stables to the half-mile track. For years, average daily attendance for the races was in the neighborhood of 1,500 people. Many tourists staying at the Hot Springs resort in Madison County rode the train to Asheville and took Carrier's trolley to the track.

Carrier also introduced to Asheville a scientific method of cattle-raising and dairy-farming, importing purebred Hereford and Jersey cattle from Lexington, Kentucky, to his West Asheville farm, giving the countryside a more pastoral setting for guests of the Belmont Hotel, and at the same time showing local farmers how to raise better beef and produce more milk.

Two disasters turned Carrier's interests back to lumbering. His Belmont Hotel burned, and his orange groves in Florida were destroyed by a severe freeze. He obtained extensive logging rights near Wilmington, North Carolina, and rebuilt much of his fortune timbering the cypress swamps.

Carrier spent his last twenty years in the quiet of homes in Asheville, Florida, and Georgia. In March 1927 he died in Albany, Georgia, and at his request his body was returned to Asheville and interred in Riverside Cemetery.

22

LET THERE BE LIGHT

On the night of October 21, 1886, three months after Col. Frank Coxe opened the electrically-lighted Battery Park Hotel, Asheville's streets were lighted with the same medium.

Huge lights shone from four steel towers, 125 feet high with four globes on each tower. One of the towers was located in front of the courthouse on Public Square, another at the junction of Woodfin and Locust Streets, a third at the junction of Haywood and Academy streets, where the Three Brothers Restaurant is located today, and the fourth on Merrimon Avenue. There were also smaller droplights on various downtown streets.

The Rev. B. E. Atkins, president of Asheville Female College, wrote in his personal dairy that evening: "The light is brilliant and gives general satisfaction."

Street lights, which few people in Asheville had ever seen and some had never dreamed of, did indeed give general satisfaction to most, but they were a matter of consternation to some.

One night about midnight, a distraught man, a guest at the Hotel Berkeley, appeared at the head of the stairs and shouted, "What in thunder can a fellow do with that doggoned light in my room? I've tried to fan it with my hat, and I've blowed on it till I'm dizzy, and the derned thing is aburnin' on!"

The amused hotel clerk went straight to the man's room and switched off the light, and the fellow went to bed, but next morning he appeared at the desk with his satchel packed. "I say doggone a light that won't snuff out nor won't blow out. I'm amovin' over to the Grand Central with its taller candles."

The Grand Central Hotel was located on Patton Avenue near Lexington, which was then Water Street because of good water springs located on its banks. The Grand Central had built an annex across the avenue and had adjoined the hotel and the annex with an elevated walkway over Patton Avenue.

A little later, Col. V. S. Lusk said Asheville's street lights had been seen thirty miles away in Madison County. *The Asheville Citizen* printed that it was "a Republican trap to be used against Democracy in the municipal campaign."

"I can prove it," replied Col. Lusk, "and by a Madison County Democrat at that!" He produced a mountaineer from Spring Creek in Madison County, Van Brown, who said that more than a score of times he had "distinctly seen my shadow outlined while walking on the mountainside at night."

The Citizen issued an apology to Lusk "because a Madison County Democrat says so."

On February 1, 1888, electricity from overhead wires powered a trolley car from Court Square to the Southern Depot at the Asheville Junction. As the car rolled out of sight, T. M. Byers expressed what most of the onlookers were thinking: "Well, it's gone!" he said in a tone of shock, "–but I don't believe it!"

So many people came to town to see electricity that the city played games for them. On the same day that electricity drove that trolley to the Asheville Junction, a contest was held between electric power and horsepower. Two trolley cars were stopped at the foot of South Main Street, one to be driven up the hill to the square by electric power and the other to be pulled by a six-horse hitch. The public gaped in awe as the electric car left the horsedrawn vehicle far behind.

Asheville's Street Railway was the first in North Carolina—some say first in the nation—and the city was proud of it. An editor of *The Citizen* commented in print: "No happier community than ours is to be found in America."

Despite their instant popularity, the electric cars drew some criticism. A man from Rutherford County rode his mule to town one day, and as the pair turned into Patton Avenue, a streetcar bore down on them.

Laying back his long ears, the frightened mule bolted and collided with a telephone pole, spilling its rider into the street.

"Me scared?" the man said to someone who asked. "That's a powerful small word for it. We had just got into town when here come that thing without even blowing a horn or ringing a bell."

He refused offers to help him, saying, "No, turn the mule loose and I'll follow. I'm agoin' back where we don't have nothing like them buses, and you can drive all over the country without getting every bone in your body broke."

Asheville enjoyed its streetcars for forty-eight years. They trundled along for the last time on September 6, 1934, and gave way to city buses.

When a new brick courthouse was built on the square in 1876, the name of the square, called Public Square until then, was changed to Court Square. This courthouse was razed in 1903 and a new courthouse built on College Street east of the square on land donated by George W. Pack. This one was used until 1928 when county offices were moved into the high-rise courthouse in City-County Plaza that is still in use today.

Buncombe County's first courthouse was indeed a one-room log cabin built in 1793 on the square at about the location of the present Vance Monument. The town apparently outgrew it in three years and in 1796 built a larger courthouse of logs on the same site.

This courthouse lasted until 1830 when a new two-story brick courthouse was constructed just east of the first two. It was a rather primitive structure and was destroyed by fire in 1848. By 1850 it had been replaced with another brick building which served the county until January 26, 1865, when it, too, was destroyed by fire. It was replaced with a small one-story courthouse built with the bricks from the 1850 structure destroyed by fire.

That courthouse was torn down in 1876 and a new courthouse built on the east side of Public Square, facing west. This was the one with arched doorways and a bell tower, which was added later for fire watch. On third floor was an opera hall that could seat 400 people.

The first courthouse not built on the square was the 1903 structure erected on four acres of land donated by George W. Pack. The building faced College Street very near the present location of the courthouse. This one was domed and a huge clock was mounted on the dome. That one stood until 1928 when the present courthouse was built at a cost of two million dollars. It is seventeen stories high with a brick and limestone classical skin. The lobby is ornamented with polychrome classical plaster work and marble balustrades, and some say that on the mezzanine can be seen the fossil of a 200 million-year-old lizard.

City records are scarce for the period before 1850, and it is possible that they were stored in the courthouse that burned in 1848.

The Crystal Fountain on Court Square in 1887.

Actual paving of Asheville's streets began in 1890. A section of South Main Street from the square was first to be paved, and for most of the citizens it wasn't a minute too soon. Old photos show South Main a sea of mud during a rainy spell in 1887.

It was during the reign of Charles D. Blanton, mayor of Asheville from 1889 to 1893, that paving was begun.

Asheville's mud was so bad in the fall and winter that dozens of wagon loads of tobacco came to a standstill and mired up on the west side of Smith's Bridge, remaining there two weeks before they could be driven across town to the warehouses.

At the present site of Pritchard Park, a cluster of mudholes made a perfect hog wallow for fifty hogs or so.

When Court Square was paved in 1890, it became the center of Asheville's business. One newspaper report read that after a winter and spring of constant rain, Asheville was "all mud and tourists." They made full use of stepping stones at street crossings. A favorite recreation for tourists was horseback riding, but in rainy spells when mud oozed ankle deep in the streets, the city's poor streets and roads leading away prevented horseback riders from galloping into the countryside.

Asheville thrived on vacationists' dollars, and tourist discontent more than the inconvenience of city residents led Asheville to quickly do something about its streets. The city was granted authority by the State

Legislature in March 1890 for a bond issue of $600,000 to pave principal streets and extend water and sewage lines. "Paving" was not an accomplishment with asphalt, as paving is done today, but with cobble-stones and large bricks baked in kilns at Fletcher. The square was paved with bricks, and so were other streets leading from the square: South Main, Patton Avenue, Haywood Street, and Clingman Avenue to the passenger and freight depots.

Market Street, running between College and Walnut off the northeast corner of the square, is still a street of bricks today, and the bricks are those put down in 1890. A short side street running to the west from Market near College Street is still paved with the original stones, which may have been laid before Market Street was paved with brick.

Much opposition arose to these "extravagances" and Mayor Blanton was the victim. His political career was ruined and repeated attempts to regain the mayor's office were futile.

Sondley reported that some paving was done before 1890. "Paving with rock obtained from the site of the new reservoir on Beaucatcher Mountain and crushed stone was put upon some of the streets near the city's center and near the passenger depot beginning about 1884. Soon other streets were paved with stone blocks. In 1890, a paving system was adopted. The system paved with large bricks."

Asheville's sidewalks were short and few until about 1876 when some merchants had walkways constructed of small round stones in packed sand in front of their businesses. Next came some sidewalks of thick planks in pairs running lengthwise along the side of the streets. Flagstones proved better and were put to wider use, and this was when stepping stones were placed about a foot apart across streets at crossings.

The electric streetcar line was the city's pride and joy. Cars trundled in every direction every quarter-hour. Down Patton Avenue they went, turned left on Asheland, crossed on Phillips Street to South French Broad, rumbled through Mud Cut and down the hollow to Lyman Street, and on to the depot. After discharging passengers there and loading up with new arrivals, the cars moved along Depot to Southside to South Main and back up the hill to the square, completing a large circle.

Other cars rolled out East Street to Spears, down Merrimon Avenue to Grace, from the square to Best, and up Haywood Street from Patton Avenue.

But for sheer power and excitement, Ashevilleans stood in awe of the huge, coal-burning 1400s that pulled loaded passenger trains and laden freight cars in all four directions from Asheville.

City residents drank at home from the waterworks that piped water by gravity from Beaucatcher Mountain. This system was installed in 1882 for $20,000, and by 1888 a sewer system was built, but folks waited until they were sure it would work before knocking down those little brown shacks out back.

The waterworks originated with several good springs on Beaucatcher Mountain. A million-gallon reservoir was built on the mountain about 250 feet higher than the elevation of the square. Terra cotta pipes carried water from the springs to the reservoir, ten-inch iron mains piped it two miles to the square, and from there it went through six-inch lines in all directions, watering the entire city population.

Folks complained about having to pay for water, however, and when the city raised water rates by 33 1/3 percent in 1899, a poetic expression of opposition arose:

> "Let me help you stand up, stranger,
> "You are drunk and in some danger.
> "Are you not a mountain ranger?"
>   "No, I'm not!
> "I've bin drink'n ale an' porter,
> "Coz they raised the tax on water
> "In a way they hadn't orter,
>   "And that's what!"

The city had certainly grown up from the chinquapin thicket it had once been. It was perhaps the most attractive town in North Carolina and folks in all of Buncombe loved it.

23

FAIRY TALE

George Washington Vanderbilt's arrival in Asheville and the decision he made here would have been a fairy tale in any town in the United States. And in truth, after more than a century, it is still a fairy tale in the Land of the Sky.

The year was 1887 when Vanderbilt, an unmarried man of twenty-five, and his mother, Mrs. William Henry Vanderbilt, arrived for a vacation in Asheville and checked into the year-old Battery Park Hotel. His father had died two years earlier. Grandson of Commodore Cornelius Vanderbilt, George Vanderbilt was a young man of genius and vision whose wealth was estimated at fifty-million dollars from a family fortune of more than one hundred million compiled by his grandfather in the steamship and railroad industries.

Encyclopaedia Brittanica called George Vanderbilt "an agriculturist and forester." Immediately upon his arrival in Asheville, he was apparently deeply impressed by the beauty of most of the forested country.

It is said that he first surveyed the vast, empty land to the south and southwest of Asheville from the south verandah of the Battery Park, but he was not entirely pleased with what he saw. Years of uncontrolled timber-cutting had left the woodlands ragged, almost naked in places, and heavily eroded. In the distance he admired Mount Pisgah and the Rat and other high peaks of the Pisgah Range, and at that moment he must have envisioned what he with his wealth and desire could do for a decimated forest such as that. His vision is still alive and working today for the benefit of thousands who profit from the influx of tourists drawn by the unparalleled beauty of Biltmore Estate.

After that first sight of the vast acreage of timber, Vanderbilt was far from satisfied rocking away the summer on the verandahs of the Battery Park Hotel. Rather, he turned to the hotel's stables as a means of escape, taking horses for long rides in the woodlands he had seen. What magnificent country, despite the damage and neglect he had seen from the hotel verandah!

He would trot on horseback down the Greenville Road, ford the French Broad, and ride up the valleys and over the mountains of this vast land, envisioning the beauty that would return with a controlled forestry program. This was exactly what he had been searching for.

Atop one mountain stood a scrubby pine tree of considerable size. It was surrounded by desolation created by the woodcutter's axe. He called this hill Lone Pine Mountain, and it was to become the focal point of his tremendous investment.

Returning to New York that fall, Vanderbilt took a kinsman, New York attorney Charles McNamee, into his confidence and commissioned him to go to Asheville and begin buying acreage in that wilderness. McNamee began purchasing sections of the forest in 1889 and Vanderbilt's holdings eventually reached 130,000 acres. His estate stretched forty miles to the high mountains he had originally seen, and included Mount Pisgah.

By 1890 Vanderbilt owned enough of the land that he could put the remainder of his dream into motion, and work began on the mammoth French Renaissance chateau that today is called Biltmore House, built on the side of Lone Pine Mountain. It was a house of such enormous proportions and scope that for the next five years Vanderbilt employed a thousand men to construct the building.

The scope of Vanderbilt's intentions astonished Ashevilleans. Most found out about the plans through gossip, but now and then reports printed in New York papers were reprinted in Asheville papers, and local residents found the entire project staggering.

In October 1889, *The Citizen* printed that a model of the home Vanderbilt planned to build on his "five thousand acres" had been put on display at the *New York Tribune* building. The model was five feet long and three feet high, and it was magnificent. After seeing the model, the *New York Sun* commented editorially: "Mr. Vanderbilt is apparently to have plenty of room for himself and a caller or two . . . ."

But more than that, Vanderbilt was building the mansion to house the priceless treasures he had collected, mostly in Europe. Vanderbilt was a man of scholarship and intellect and even while the

Locomotive takes workers and materials to Biltmore House site.

house was under construction he sent buyers abroad looking for treasures for the house.

Vanderbilt imported Richard M. Hunt, a famous architect, Frederick Law Olmsted, one of America's foremost landscape architects, and a corps of engineers to plan and oversee the work. Rebuilding the estate's forests occupied much of Vanderbilt's thoughts, and in this he listened to Olmsted who insisted that a trained forester was needed to accomplish the job. Never one to put up with second best, Vanderbilt in 1893 employed the only schooled forester in the United States, Gifford Pinchot, a great conservation pioneer who later became governor of Pennsylvania, to supervise the forests. He was succeeded in 1898 by Dr. Carl A. Schenck, a noted German forester.

The first task in construction called for flattening the land around the house, and hundreds of men using picks and shovels, mules and dragpans literally moved mountains to fill valleys and ravines and cover over the erosion of years of neglect.

From the start, Vanderbilt called his estate Biltmore, for the Dutch village of his ancestors named Bildt, and "more," an English word for rolling hillsides. Olmsted laid out plans for a village at Best to house workmen on the estate and their families, and called the village Biltmore. Soon Best was no more and the entirety of Asheville Junction was known as Biltmore.

As landscapers rearranged the face of the land, laborers constructed a three-mile spur line from the railroad in Best to the heart of the estate where the house would be constructed. Materials to construct the house would be hauled over this line.

Rock quarrying began and construction of a plant to make brick and tile was begun. The brickworks eventually turned out eleven million bricks used in construction of the house, and an enormous amount of tile used in twenty bathrooms, toilet rooms, hallways, fireplaces, the swimming "tank," and various other tiled surfaces.

The railroad spur line was completed by May 23, 1890, and a tram road three-quarters of a mile long was laid from the rock quarries to the head of the spur line.

So much woodwork would be needed for the house that Vanderbilt contracted for most of the output of the Asheville Woodworking Company, and in 1893 purchased the company outright. For the next two years its entire production was for Biltmore House.

Hundreds of local carpenters, masons, and laborers found five years of work at Biltmore Estate. The job was so vast and called for so much stonework that Vanderbilt brought in stone masons from various parts of the world. These artisans cut and fitted the Indiana limestone blocks and chiseled elaborate stone carvings that decorate the house.

Richard Sharp Smith was architect in charge of construction. When he completed his excellent work at Biltmore, he designed other things in Asheville, including the granite obelisk on Pack Square in memory of Zebulon B. Vance, patterning it after the Washington Monument, which in turn was built on the same lines as the obelisks of ancient Egypt.

Masons laid 20,000 feet of face rock in the house, which measured 375 by 150 feet, and one stone weighing more than three tons was laid in a 333-foot-long retaining wall. The wall's base varied from seventeen and a half feet in thickness at the bottom of the wall to two feet at the top.

Workmen constructed a thirty-foot impounding dam 125 feet long and built a reservoir at the top of Lone Pine Mountain which fed water by gravity to the house.

Vanderbilt would occasionally take time off to roam Europe buying canvasses, statuary, porcelains, tapestries, and relics for the mansion's 250 rooms. He also increased his holdings by purchasing additional acreage during the construction period. In 1893 he bought half of Mount Pisgah and obtained most of the other half before 1895, giving him ownership of 30,000 acres there, which included almost the entire mountain. He had crews build a rustic hunting lodge near Pisgah.[1]

---

[1] He continued to purchase land and in 1905 the estate reached its maximum of more than 130,000 acres, extending westward farther than the eye could see, from Biltmore House to Lake Toxaway, forty miles away.

This 1893 photo shows walls up at the Biltmore House.

Slowly the house began to take shape, and even the workers admired its beauty and the monstrosity of the job they were doing. The house's winter garden, now the Palm Court, measured sixty feet square; the main salon was forty feet in length; the banquet hall seventy-two by forty-two feet with a seventy-five-foot ceiling; the living hall was sixty by thirty feet; and the swimming pool was also sixty by thirty. The beautiful tapestry gallery measured seventy-five feet in length, and the library, sixty by forty feet.

The library terrace, thirty-feet wide, led to a South Terrace, more than three hundred feet long. Stables made of stone would accommodate about forty horses.

The entire world was impressed by the size and magnificence of the building, and Vanderbilt spared not a dollar in building the home he had dreamed of for many years.

As the house neared completion, construction of the village of Biltmore was well underway. Vanderbilt had hurried construction of the Biltmore Railway Station, and the area's designation of Asheville Junction faded from use. The estate office in Biltmore and the Plaza office structure both were finished, and work was moving along on All Souls Episcopal Church.

Vanderbilt was grieved that summer in the loss of two of his closest friends. Baron Eugene d'Allenger, the estate's farm supervisor, died July 28, and Richard M. Hunt, his architect and counselor, died a bit later. During that summer the house moved swiftly toward completion.

Vanderbilt opened the house a month before the scheduled formal opening with a dinner on November 4, 1895, and invited Richard H. Hunt and his wife. Hunt was the son of the architect and close friend of Vanderbilt's.

Biltmore House nears completion.

The formal opening was a society event. Vanderbilt invited about forty persons for a Christmas-New Year's holiday house party. He arranged for passenger coaches on his spur line to bring guests from Biltmore Station to the house. A private telegraph line was strung from Biltmore Station to the mansion. His mother arrived on December 20 to supervise arrangements.

Several relatives came for the holiday festivities. On the day of the party Vanderbilt invited the permanent estate employees with their wives and children, 250 in all, and distributed gifts from a huge tree in the banquet hall, and then the employees and their families enjoyed a bountiful Christmas Eve dinner.

It was on New Year's Eve that the real gala was held. Among the guests were many young friends of Vanderbilt from New York and various other locations.

Writing in the *Citizen-Times* years later, Doug Reed described the party thusly:

GAY SCENES were presented by the guest party at Biltmore House during the hours that bade farewell to '95 and ushered in the snowy New Year morning.

The festivities began with dinner in the banquet hall at 8 o'clock. The hall was magnificent in its elaborate appointments of statuary, tapestries, and oaken furniture, and the heavy hanging crimson velvet curtains embroidered in gold that draped the arches of the entrance ways.

Tables extended the length of the apartment and were brightly illuminated and tastefully dressed with flowers. Three huge log fires glowed in the western end of the room and at the opposite wall in the organ gallery the Imperial Trio of Kenilworth Inn played their finest selections during the feasting.

At 9 o'clock the gathering repaired to the tapestry gallery where the time was spent in cards and chess and the melodies of the Meistersinger, Paglacci and Cavaleria Rusticana. After 11, the call to dancing returned the guests to the banquet hall where mirth reigned until the hour of 12 was suddenly announced by the Imperial Trio, who broke from a Strauss waltz into Auld Lang Syne.

A loving cup was quaffed and a toast was offered to "our host."

When the musical honors stilled, there was a short response by Vanderbilt and the dancing resumed. The last dance, a Virginia reel, was led by Vanderbilt and Mrs. Charles McNamee.

Vanderbilt married Edith Stuyvesant Dresser and to them was born one child, a daughter, Cornelia.

Biltmore House became the center of many great social occasions, duly reported in the New York newspapers.

Often, for months at a time the house would be a quiet abode peopled only by servants, for the Vanderbilts traveled often, both in the United States and abroad, and would sometimes be gone for months.

Doug Reed reported one early viewer, upon seeing it, described it thusly: "Biltmore House is grand and imposing in

Huge banquet hall, completed in 1895.

Stonemasons pose before their work at the Biltmore House in 1892.

its proportions. Its solid battlements and stone towers can be seen at great distances from the country roads about the Vanderbilt property. Having an extensive knowledge of architecture, Mr. Vanderbilt has given his designers full power, restricting them in nothing to make it the most noble residence owned by a private individual in the country, or perhaps the world."

After a century, it is still the most noble, and is now peopled with wall to wall tourists, who come by the thousands to view the splendor.

Vanderbilt lived nineteen years after opening the house, carrying on his amazing work in forestry, horticulture, dairying, development of Biltmore Village, Biltmore Hospital, Biltmore Industries, and his vast collection of art treasures.

Biltmore House, finished in 1895.

24

THE FIRST SCHOOL OF FORESTRY

While the Biltmore House was Vanderbilt's masterpiece, a project that proved to be worth much to the American people was his reforestation and development of the land. With his own wealth and foresight and the assistance of Gifford Pinchot and Dr. Carl A. Schenck, whose technical knowledge of forestry was endless, Vanderbilt wrote the first chapter in the story of forestry in America.

Olmstead, who was in charge of landscaping the estate, insisted that Vanderbilt install a planned forestry program and that he hire Pinchot as forester. Pinchot was newly returned from training at the Forestry Academy at Nancy, France. He hired as a field assistant Henry Solon Groves, who would later succeed Pinchot as chief forester of the United States.

The hiring of Pinchot set in motion the first venture in technical forestry ever attempted on a large scale in the United States. At a time when there was not a single American forest school and when Pinchot was the only technically educated forester, Vanderbilt made Biltmore forestry a going concern.

Pinchot cleared, drained, and beautified bottomland along the French Broad River, planted eroded land in white pines (some of which border Interstate 40 just west of Biltmore today), built miles of trails and roads, burned out pine needles, once destroyed every infested tree in a 5,500-acre tract to stop the spread of beetles, and planted hardwoods but discovered they grew best when they regenerated themselves. Biltmore became the nation's first tree farm fifty years before the American Tree Farm System was organized.

Pinchot left Biltmore Estate in 1895 to become head of the Division of Forestry in the United States Department of Agriculture and suggested that Vanderbilt replace him with the imperial forester of Germany, Dr. Carl Alwin Schenck.

Schenck was a rather thin, mustachioed man who stood ramrod straight. Some thought he looked like Kaiser Wilhelm.

Schenck planted half a million white pine seedlings on the estate in 1897, and built 200 miles of trails for his surveyors, loggers, and fire rangers.

Forestry students take break at Biltmore School, circa 1900.

Noting that all the erosion on the estate had not been conquered and that huge gullies dotted the land, he had work crews build rough wickerworks at the head of gullies. These were built by weaving strong brush through several poles placed deep in the ground to stop the surging runoff. Within five years, the gullies were gone and in their place the forest was thriving again.

In 1896 Schenck had five or six assistants who worked without pay in order to learn forestry under the German master. This plan evolved in 1898 into the idea of starting a School of Forestry through which Biltmore Estate would educate its own foresters, but which also would turn out foresters for other woodland areas.

The Biltmore Forest School opened that fall ahead of a similar school at Cornell University, and for years Biltmore, as a school that specialized in teaching technical forestry, was the only school of that kind.

Cost of attending the school was about a thousand dollars, and each student had to have a riding horse since mobility was essential on the sprawling estate. The school had no trouble filling its quotas; there were plenty of applicants and most of the time the school had a waiting list for admission. Half of the school's profits went to Vanderbilt.

The curriculum consisted of morning lectures and afternoon rides to areas where students observed forestry work in progress.

The school remained in session throughout the year. Each session was a year and a half long with the first twelve months devoted to extensive study and the last six to practical experience. Successful completion of the course led to a bachelor's degree in forestry and forest engineering. Winter classes were held on Biltmore Estate. In the spring, classes moved to lower Davidson River, and in summer the students were quartered at a lodge in the Pink Beds. In September or October, depending on the weather, classes were returned to the estate headquarters.

In the sixteen years of school operation, 367 students were graduated by Dr. Schenck's school. Many became outstanding foresters and timbermen.

Two events in 1908 spread the word of the school's work like nothing else. The first came in May when President Theodore Roosevelt called the first Conference of Governors, and at Vanderbilt's invitation, held it on the Biltmore Estate. The theme was natural resources conservation, for which Roosevelt had been battling since taking office in 1901. The conference was one of the keys that led to passage of the Weeks Law in 1911 under which the National Forest System was established. The first tract of land for a federal forest was bought on the Biltmore Estate.

The second event came on Thanksgiving weekend when Dr. Schenck insisted on a tenth anniversary of the school's founding with German pomp and circumstance. The Biltmore Forest Festival was attended by senators, congressmen, other public officials, bankers, lumbermen, editors. Recreation and entertainment featured carriage tours of the estate, dinner at the Battery Park Hotel, lunch in the

Ready for a day's ride at the Bilmore School of Forestry, circa 1900.

woods, a possum hunt, fishing trips, and various projects to show Biltmore's foresters in action. That weekend undoubtedly contributed heavily toward passage of the Weeks Law.

One of Schenck's faults was his German hardheadedness. He had trouble getting along with almost everyone but his students, who worshipped him not only for teaching them forestry but also for the fact that he roughed it with them.

Schenck had hard words with many on and off the estate, and once came to blows with C. D. Beadle, head of Biltmore landscaping department and nurseries, and wound up in court.

Finally fired by Vanderbilt in 1911, when he left the estate he took the school with him, but it was already in decline and continued a downhill slide until he discontinued it in 1913 and returned to Germany to serve with his homeland forces in the first World War. Commissioned a colonel in the German army, he was wounded in action and spent the rest of his life at Darmstadt and Lindenfels, Hessen, near the Rhine River.

But his school had opened America's eyes to the need of proper management of its forests, and had showed the nation how to do it.

He died in Germany in 1955.

In 1912, Vanderbilt sold all the timber on Biltmore Estate for a million dollars, a tidy sum when you remember that his reforestation program had begun only two decades earlier with scrub trees, a lot of brush, and wide gullies.

Vanderbilt died in 1914 and his legacies were twofold:

One of the nation's finest and most productive forests, a haven for wildlife, profitable for managed timbercutters, and a huge attraction for tourists who drive through it to view the beautiful forestlands, waterfalls, and wildlife. And the Biltmore House, the nation's largest private home, and what remains of the estate's 130,000 acres have become a location for movies and one of the nation's top attractions of its kind for tourism.

25

CENTENNIAL

A sheville celebrated its centennial on January 27, 1898, a hundred years from the date the city became a municipal corporation by vote of the city commissioners. It had been incorporated by the state legislature in November 1797, the date the city chose to observe its bicentennial in 1997.

By that time, it had been determined that Asheville lay on an elevated plateau 250 feet above the French Broad River at a mean elevation above the sea of 2,389 feet. The downtown was safe from floods, and the city was protected from tornado-force storms by the mountains around it.

It was a jewel of a small city, with property evaluation of $4,820,690 and a tax levy of $101,784.74. High in the hills, it lay 272 miles west of Raleigh, 495 miles south of Washington, and 297 miles northeast of Charleston.

Seven small towns adjoining Asheville were absorbed by the city proper between 1905 and 1929. These were Biltmore, Montford, Victoria, West Asheville, Kenilworth, South Biltmore, and Woolsey, originally known by the biblical name of Ramoth. All had been incorporated individually.

Three short descriptive paragraphs, one from the centennial edition of *The Asheville Daily Citizen* of Saturday, February 5, 1898, another from Sondley's writings, and a third from the Asheville City Directory of 1896-97, give us a small insight on the city's early inhabitants, terrain, and the structure of the city after a hundred years.

The Citizen spoke of the people:

WE HAVE reaped, for the most part in peace, where these early pioneers sowed in peril . . . . They builded broad and deep; and fair structures, social, material, and political, have been reared on the foundations they prepared. How they built, what they built, what they built with, and what manner of men they were is the theme of our centenary . . . . One thing we find they seemed to know from the beginning— that they wanted true liberty and would have that at any cost. Had we been with them, the work had not perhaps seemed so great. But at this distance they loom as veritable giants in the work they accomplished.

Sondley wrote of the land:

WE HAVE endeavored to collect from imperfect and indefinite records, and vague and uncertain traditions a little of the history of Asheville. The very physical features of the place are no longer recognizable even to people yet living who had known it years ago. The streams have ceased to rise and flow where they once rose and flowed. On the west side of Water Street (Lexington Avenue) immediately north of Walnut Street once stood a famous spring called for in the old deeds, but now not to be found. Below it, on both sides of the street, springs have disappeared in the last quarter of a century. Even subsequent to the late war (the Civil War) horses have been seen to mire up to the body in the blue mud of Water Street just south of Woodfin Street. Almost the same state of affairs has existed, and the same changes taken place in Central Avenue since 1865, when it was a narrow lane ending at a private residence now opposite the entrance of Orange Street. And I am informed by Mr. R. B. Justice that at the time of his first visit to Asheville in 1846, a spring of good water, much used, existed on the spot where now stands the post office (Pritchard Park).

The editor of the City Directory had this to say about the city:

WITH HER miles of paved streets, four banks (two Nationals), churches, fine public school system, well-equipped private schools, business college, elegant hotels accommo- dating 1,200-1,500 people, miles of street railway, morning and afternoon daily papers, library, Opera House (finest in the state), water works and sewer system, electric and gas lighting, telephone exchange, fire department, associations and clubs of various kinds, factories, splendid business houses, Federal Building, City Hall with fine market accommodations, Asheville takes rank as a city which for push and pluck is not anywhere surpassed. For its size, the city is perhaps the most cosmopolitan in the United States. This is not surprising to those who meet here people from every point of the compass. Stagnation in such an atmosphere is impossible.

There were imperfections in the jewel, like the raft of saloons and fly-breeding livery stables on streets leading from the square, like the Pest House on Riverside Drive where folks with smallpox and diphtheria suffered, like Hell's Half Acre along Sycamore and Valley streets, and a few other dens of iniquity scattered around the town, but all in all, Ashevilleans were proud of their city—and they should have been.

They had as fine a City Market as could be found in the state. Each morning hotel chefs, housewives, and cafe owners flocked to the market to buy fresh produce in the stalls in the basement of the City Building on Court Square.

Fresh fish and oysters were brought in daily by rail; carcasses of freshly-killed beefs, sheep, and game hung from hooks in the butchers' stalls; and fruits and vegetables could be bought in quantity or in meal-sized portions. This was the busiest place in town—and on hot days, the coolest.

The city post office was located in the Federal Building, built in 1892 on a triangle of land between Patton Avenue, Haywood Street, and College Street. The post office served the

Post office became Pritchard Park.

city forty years until it was removed in 1932 and the land, deeded to the city, became known as Pritchard Park, a public park named for Jeter C. Pritchard of Asheville, former U. S. senator and senior judge of the U.S. Circuit Court of Appeals.

Citizens no longer had to bury relatives in church or family plots, or in Newton Academy graveyard, oldest burial ground in town. Riverside Cemetery had been established in 1885 and was in 1897 the preferred place of burial.

Newton was the oldest graveyard in town, but the oldest graves were Indian graves on Patton Avenue, immediately west of the intersection with Lexington. The city's first burial ground was at the southeast corner of Eagle and Market streets, but that land long ago was taken over for businesses. Methodists established a burying ground in 1865 just below Central Methodist Church, and there were some burials in the churchyard of Trinity Episcopal and on a lot adjoining First Presbyterian Church. Sondley claimed the oldest burying ground in the county was the old Shawano Indian plot on the east bank of the French Broad River a mile north of the mouth of the Swannanoa, and that the oldest white graveyard was the Robert Patton burying ground near the town of Swannanoa.

Folks no longer had to saddle up to ride to town. Three electric railway systems served almost every point in the city, and it cost only a nickel to ride to town in comfort and style, entertained by the clanging bells of the trolley cars and the constant change of passengers.

It was in this centenary year that the blow was struck that eventually served as the death knell for the Asheville Street Railway System. It came in the form of a four-wheeled horseless carriage grinding along, snorting, tooting, and backfiring at every turn. On its side for all to see was a sign that read "Octagon Soap." Clarence Sawyer, who owned a grocery, rode in the thing and seemed to be guiding it.

It was a one-cylinder Locomobile Steamer, the first automobile anyone ever saw in Asheville. The Octagon Soap Company sent it to Asheville on a rail car and hired Sawyer to drive it around town, advertising soap.

It sent horses into fits, startled people on the street, and, of course, captivated those who were not afraid of it.

Clarence Sawyer's brother, Eugene, who owned the Asheville Cycle Company, built his own automobile two years later, in 1900, using a two-cylinder Brennan motor and spare parts with chain drive to build a machine that met with limited success. The next year Sawyer purchased a single-seat Locomobile Steamer that gave Asheville its first long look at a real automobile.

J. P. Coston and Ernest Alexander bought a two-cylinder Locomobile steam surrey, J. E. Rumbough got a Centaur Electric,

George and Edith Vanderbilt decorated the car for May Day Parade, circa 1910.

and in 1902 Tench Coxe bought a one-cylinder Cadillac for $950, and the following year he purchased a White Steamer in Philadelphia for $2,750, and before long Ashevilleans became accustomed to automobiles.

Eugene Sawyer opened an automobile agency in Asheville in 1901 and had the market cornered for six years or so until motorcars really began to catch on and others opened agencies. The first Ford arrived in Asheville in 1905 and by 1906 there were about thirty-five motorcars in the city. The town of Woolsey, on the northern outskirts of Asheville, was first to impose a speed limit on its macadamized streets, limiting cars to twelve miles an hour on straight streets and five miles an hour on curves.

One of the largest machines on the streets in the early days was a four-cylinder, thirty- to fifty-horsepower Pope-Toledo belonging to Dr. E. W. Grove, to whom many referred as "the Asheville capitalist," and driven by his chauffeur, H. McDonald. This powerful machine was one of the fastest and best American autos of the day.

Clarence Sawyer bought a 1906 delivery truck to carry parcels, and it was driven on errands around town for fifteen years by Alonzo McCoy, a Negro driver. Outside Asheville there were no roads fit for automobiles. A trip to Burnsville consumed nineteen grueling hours of bouncing, slipping, and tire-changing, and a drive to Hendersonville, only twenty miles away, required all day. Few drivers, regardless of how daring, ventured beyond the end of

William Jennings Bryan and motorcade of friends on a country drive near Asheville in the teens.

pavement, which extended about a mile from the square in every direction. A trip of twenty miles was worthy of being reported in the paper.

John B. Rumbough of 41 Zillacoa Street, established a record in 1905 when he drove a Peerless-Mercedes from Asheville to New York in only fourteen days. He was also the first to take an automobile over the Appalachian Mountains, performing that remarkable feat in October 1911 in a Model 10-D Speedwell, manufactured in Dayton, Ohio.

Dr. Grove and his chauffeur drove the Pope-Toledo from Asheville to St. Louis and back and described the trip as "five hundred miles of nothing but mud and rock with the exception of fifteen miles of fair traveling."

A good story, apocryphal as many good stories are, made the rounds here later about a man who ventured into the countryside in his horseless carriage and when it came struggling up a hill, roaring and snorting, an old mountaineer, frightened out of his mind, took a shot at the thing with his squirrel rifle, the ball striking the steering wheel, and the driver bailed out and scampered to safety.

The hillbilly's wife came to the door and said, "What was that, Pa?"

"Dunno what that thing was, Ma," answered Pa, "but I shore made it turn that man loose!"

A person with a toothache had no problem getting the tooth attended. The Asheville Dental Parlors on Patton Avenue advertised a new painless method of extracting teeth. The charge: 25 cents.

Or, if the tooth didn't need pulling, he could get a cement filling for 50 cents, an amalgam filling for 75 cents, a silver filling for a dollar, and a gold filling from one to two dollars.

Folks had to admit, the prices were all right. Bridge work was done for $4, a porcelain crown for $4, a crown of 22 karat gold was $5, a full set of false teeth cost $6, and the best teeth made were $8.

Those were the days of bargains—and five-cent hourly wages.

The dentists were highly qualified, too. Dr. Fisher, whose offices were in the Drhumor Block on Patton Avenue, advertised himself as "former demonstrator of operative dentistry at Pennsylvania College of Dental Surgery, Philadelphia. Nitrous oxide gas administered."

Advertising in the *Asheville Daily Citizen*'s centennial edition, the city's businesses gave an insight into local commerce. T. S. Morrison's, which is still in business on Lexington Avenue, the oldest retail store in town, sold Silver King buggies. Ray's Book Store had lace valentines from a penny up. Vacation spots in Florida and the Caribbean advertised family vacations in Miami, Nassau, Key West, Palm Beach, Ormond, and St. Augustine. And the cheapest firewood for sale was through all coal dealers and all grocery stores "which have a phone."

The Baltimore, a mercantile on Patton Avenue, advertised a "great rebuilding sale," in which everything would be sold at cost or less and two and a half percent would be given away! "We shall give 2 1/2 per cent of this sale to the poor of Asheville," the ad read. "The same shall be paid into the hands of J. E. Rankin, cashier of the Battery Park Bank, who will dispose of the same." There were good bargains in that sale: 10¢ ladies hose 5¢; $4 jackets $1.50; $10 capes $6.50; cotton toweling 3¢ a yard; calico shirting 3¢ a yard; $3 ladies shoes $1.98; $5 gents shoes $2.98.

Bonanza Wine & Liquor Company advertized Schlitz, the beer that made Milwaukee famous; the Asheville Ice and Coal Company's ad read: "A good natured maid is what you will always have when you burn Jellico coal. She doesn't have to keep up a wearisome trot in replenishing fires all day." Eugene Sawyer of the Asheville Cycle Company advertised: "Bicycling is a pleasure . . . if you have a good wheel. We sell only high grade wheels."

The new Grill Room at the Battery Park Hotel had just opened. Situated under the Palm Parlor, it had entrances from every direction, and "Every delicacy that can be obtained in a metropolitan cafe is on the bill of fare."

Brown, Northup & Company: "Stand Firm . . . . Even in slippery places you can maintain your uprightness by using our ice creepers, easily applied and easily paid for."

One firm apparently wanted to be rid of a partner, thus this advertisement:

"The firm of H. Redwood & Co., Asheville, N. C., expires this day by limitation. Signed: Henry Redwood, Claudius H. Miller, Annie C. Pressly, John W. Neely.

"The undersigned have this day formed a copartnership under style of H. Redwood & Co., for the transaction of a business in general merchandise in the city of Asheville, N. C. Signed: Henry Redwood, Claudius H. Miller, John W. Neely."

The public library in Asheville was a going thing when the city celebrated its centennial. It began in 1870 as a circulating library, the idea of a few public-spirited women. Rounding up all the books they could find, fifty or sixty, they began circulating them.

One of the first contributors of books was Judge Edward J. Aston, for whom Aston Park was named. He was a literate man, a native of Tennessee who came here as a druggist and bookseller in 1850 and opened a drug store and stationery shop. He donated several books and helped the women find a place to house the library.

Aston, whose title of Judge was honorary, immediately became perhaps Asheville's greatest booster. It was he who first suggested use of the slogan "Variety Vacationland" to describe the Asheville area, and it was he who was responsible for persuading thousands of visitors to vacation in Asheville.

With a good income from his drug store and an insurance agency, Aston, Rawls and Company, which he formed in 1871, he had time to pursue the thing he liked most: extolling Asheville's virtues to the world.

At his desk in his drug store at the corner of Patton Avenue and the square, he used more writing materials out of his stationery store than he sold, penning thousands of letters and mailing hundreds of thousands of pamphlets he published. They described the greatness of Asheville and Buncombe County—the climate, scenery, agricultural resources, mineral wealth—and were read around the world. At this task, he worked tirelessly.

It was he who influenced the Reverend L. M. Pease to establish Pease School for Girls, which later became Asheville Normal School.

Asheville City Auditorium, constructed in 1904.

He induced George W. Pack to move here, a man who became known as Asheville's greatest benefactor. He persuaded the Gatchell Brothers to open the first sanitarium in Asheville, a move that started the push that made the city world-renowned as a health spa. He resolved to make Asheville the "sanitarium of the nation" for pulmonary diseases, a move that failed to thrill many Ashevilleans after several other sanitariums went up.

Aston kept records of temperatures and rainfall which he used in his self-imposed promotional task.

His work did not go unnoticed by Asheville's citizens, who thrice elected him mayor and once chairman of the Buncombe County board of commissioners.

Cordelia L. Gilliand was his wife. She was a granddaughter of pioneer settler Col. John Patton, and she encouraged her husband in his campaign to promote Asheville as a tourist and resort town.

Aston helped locate the public library in several places, moving it from the basement of the courthouse on the square to rooms over a store and then to the YMCA. The Asheville Library Association was formed with Aston a member and managed to borrow $2,000 with which it erected a small library building on Church Street. That remained its home until 1890 when George W. Pack gave a building to the association that had been the First National Bank on the south side of the square, and the library moved there a few months later. Asheville's citizens are, and always have been, very literary, and the library has become one of the city's most necessary and most used institutions.

Edward Aston's death in 1893 removed one of Asheville's greatest boosters. The City Directory's editor wrote of him: "However much others labored for building of the city, no one will dispute that Aston's untiring persistence in advertising Asheville and vicinity, his sturdy devotion to her interests, and his splendid example as a noble, upright citizen, should forever enshrine him in the affections and memory of the people."

He was, indeed, one of the city's giants.

The number of newspapers published in Asheville, today and in times gone by, is proof enough of Asheville's hunger for the written word. *The Highland Messenger*, started in 1840, was the first. Zeb Vance bought it in 1853 and changed its name to *The Asheville Spectator*.

The Asheville News was born in 1849, and in 1867, as the city recovered from the Civil War, a periodical called *The News and Farmer* began publication. It lasted only three years, folding February 3, 1870, and its machinery was purchased by Randolph Shotwell, who founded *The North Carolina Citizen*, ancestor of today's *Asheville Citizen-Times*.

There were others. In 1879, *The Weekly Pioneer*, established in 1867, became the *Asheville Semi-Weekly Journal*. Then came in 1885 *The Asheville Daily Advance*; 1886, *The Town Topic*; 1889, *The Asheville Evening Journal*; 1890, *The Asheville Advertiser*; 1893, *The Asheville Saturday Register*; 1895, *The Asheville News and Hotel Reporter*. Not any of those lasted many years, but in 1896, some serious newspapering began in town.

On March 15, 1896, the *Asheville Daily Gazette* brought out its first issue, followed in the spring of 1903 by *The Asheville Evening News*. At that time it billed itself as "the only morning newspaper in Western North Carolina." *The Citizen* was an afternoon publication.

The *Daily Gazette* and *Evening News* merged on New Year's Day 1904, as the *Asheville Gazette-News*, publishing in the afternoon, and *The Citizen* switched to morning publication. The *Gazette-News* was forerunner of *The Asheville Times*. On its ear the paper proclaimed it was "the only Asheville paper sold on railroad trains and circulated in all mountain towns."

Competition became a dog-eat-dog affair as the *Gazette-News* and *The Asheville Daily Citizen* hustled for scoops. They were the big boys

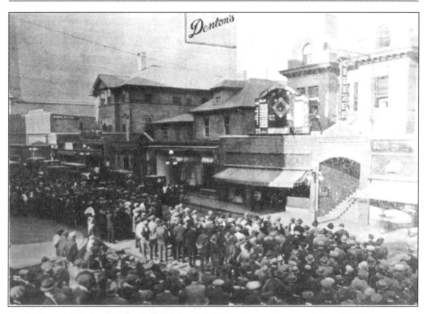

A large crowd watches the World Series on The Asheville Citizen's *Playograph on* The Citizen *building on Haywood Street in the 1920s.*

on the block, cornering the news market, although there were still a few weeklys in publication.

The *Gazette-News* changed its name to *The Asheville Times* on February 19, 1916.

Finally in 1930, *The Citizen* and *The Times* merged into one company, calling its publications *The Asheville Citizen* (morning), *The Asheville Times* (afternoon), and the *Asheville Citizen-Times* (Sunday).

In the 1980s, the afternoon *Times* was discontinued, a victim of dwindled street sales, which was the lifeblood of afternoon papers, and the daily and Sunday publications became simply the *Asheville Citizen-Times.*

Asheville has been a haven for writers—not just news writers but literary artists also. Glenn Tucker of Flat Rock, an historian who wrote extensively on the Civil War, complained about the lack of street recognition given these learned men. In an article in the *Citizen-Times* he wrote:

"On the approach to Asheville, where the Stoneman raid (of the Civil War) is celebrated by an official plaque, an official marker might inform that in this city and the territory

around, renowned authors have lived or written: Thomas Wolfe,
O. Henry, John Fox, Jr., author of the beautiful story 'The Little
Shepherd of Kingdom Come,' DuBose Heyward, Sidney Lanier,
Bill Nye, Carl Sandburg, F. Scott Fitzgerald, and many more.
Few cities the size of Asheville have a literary heritage so rich.
It is more worthy of being cherished than the momentary and
searing passage of a side eddy of war."

Circus elephants plod around Pack Square, 1910.

26

TO BENEFIT THE PEOPLE

George Willis Pack was also a giant—one of the tallest. Writing in the *Asheville Citizen-Times's* 90th Anniversary Edition of Sunday, July 17, 1960, Doug Reed described Pack's contributions to Asheville:

> PACK SQUARE bears his name. Pack Memorial Public Library stands in his memory. He was largely responsible for the Vance Monument. The Buncombe County courthouse stands today on property he gave for its predecessor. Children and adults enjoy three parks donated to the city. Mission Hospital and the YMCA are greatly in his debt. The public schools will find his work in early kindergartens. . . . Pack was a man of great foresight. He perceived those things that would serve, and supplied them. In bestowing his charities, he did not grant them as favors. Thus, he never robbed the city of its stalwart pride, matching a charity of the purse with a charity of the mind.

A New Yorker by birth, the fifty-three-year-old Pack came to Asheville in the spring of 1884 because physicians advised him to try the North Carolina mountain climate for his wife's fragile health. He had made a fortune in the lumber business in Cleveland, Michigan, New York, and the American Northwest, operating at one time seven huge lumber companies.

When he reached Asheville and his wife sampled the climate and liked it, he built a home on Merrimon Avenue and named it "Manyoaks." They lived there sixteen years until Pack, then sixty-nine and in

George W. Pack bought this building on Court Square and gave it to the Asheville Public Library in February 1899.

failing health, was forced by his physicians to move to New York and live as near sea level as possible.

Pack was a quiet and retiring man who shunned the public and avoided the spotlight of public praise. Though extremely generous, especially toward the city and people of Asheville, he usually made his gifts either through the mail or through an intermediary, seeking happiness in service without applause. On many occasions, when his gifts were announced, he made it a point to be out of town.

His philanthropy was first noticed soon after he came to Asheville when it became known that he was quietly providing funds for a number of widows and orphans, both white and colored. He contributed to the Flower Mission to provide for the poor, and even when far from home he found time to send money for food and fuel for the needy.

To Pack, money was a means of accomplishing worthwhile things, and he kept the public in mind. He had more funds than he would ever need and used them to benefit his neighbors.

His first major benefaction for the public came in 1892 when he built the Sarah Garrison Kindergarten for the Asheville Free Kindergarten Association at a cost of about $3,000. For the remainder of his life, he paid the salary of one of the kindergarten's teachers and provided one-fourth the cost of operating the school annually. The kindergarten prepared less fortunate children for further education.

When Pack came to town, he must have envisioned the square as something more than the commercial center of the city. In 1890 he confided to a friend that the square should be deeded to the people of Asheville in perpetuity. The friend, George S. Powell, a prominent citizen, replied that he was a member of a movement to build a monument somewhere in the city for Zebulon Vance, the Civil War governor from Asheville, and when Vance died the next year, an association to promote construction of a Vance monument was formed.

On May 30, 1896, Pack wrote a note to the county commissioners: "Gentlemen: If the County of Buncombe will give the land in front of the courthouse for a site for a monument in honor of Zebulon B. Vance, I will give $2,000 towards the erection of such a monument. Your obedient servant, Geo. W. Pack."

Pack promised enough money to insure the construction, but gave only about half of what the monument would cost, leaving the remainder to be donated by the citizenry. In that way, everyone could have a hand in building it. Designed by Richard Sharp Smith, the monument's cornerstone was laid December 22, 1897, and the capstone, weighing nearly a ton, was put in place on Friday, March 11, 1898, completing the job.

The Swannanoa hunts were finely conducted fox hunts but had no ruling body. They were widely recognized as one of the Carolinas' major winter sports. The famous Meadow Brook Hunt Club of New York held a special meeting on December 29, 1891, to decide whether its Master of Fox Hounds, Thomas Hitchcock, Sr., should bring the whole or only half of its pack of fox hounds to Asheville for the winter season.

George Pack was a proud member of the Swannanoa Hunt Club, forerunner to the Country Club of Asheville.

Two days later the Swannanoa hunt members agreed to organize because the territory demanded a well-managed hunting organization. So it was that in 1893 the Swannanoa Hunt Club was born, and Pack, who was a member, was proud of it. It was the predecessor of the Country Club of Asheville.

On Christmas Eve 1898, Pack finished giving enough ground to the Swannanoa Hunt Club to build an eighteen-hole golf course. This became the Country Club of Asheville where golf, which had already been played in Hot Springs, was spawned in Asheville.

Pack learned that year that Asheville boys of the First North Carolina Regiment, fighting in the Spanish-American War, needed money to tide them over till the government payday and sent them $500. They later insisted on repaying the entire amount, a gesture that moved Pack to tears.

More often than not, there was no advance notice of Pack's philanthropies. When the president of the Asheville Library Association, Haywood Parker, opened his mail on February 1, 1899, he was astonished to read a note from George W. Pack:

"Dear Sir: I offer to purchase from its present owner the Palmetto Building, formerly the First National Bank building, with the land appertaining thereto and give it to the Asheville Library, with the understanding that the Library shall be installed in the large room formerly occupied by the bank, and that the corporation shall be free from debt when it receives the conveyance of the property.

"I will remove the bank vault and do the necessary work to prepare for the library, but will not supply furniture or lighting fixtures. The property to be conveyed and possession given on or before April 1, 1899. Yours respectfully, Geo. W. Pack."

Pack purchased the property from Miss Ida Forman for a sum between $20,000 and $30,000. He arranged for the income from other offices within the building to go to the library association and requested that library services be provided free to the public. This was done.

Now Pack faced his other, perhaps his biggest concern, turning Court Square into a public park for all time to come. The county commissioners, on July 7, 1896, decided to advertise for proposals for a courthouse site, either by outright purchase or in exchange for the land on the square on which the courthouse stood. The question was kicked about for more than three years, and at the end of 1900 the county had liabilities of $40,000, which concerned citizens so much that a public meeting was called in the courthouse on January 2, 1901, to discuss county finances.

Courthouse built on College Street property donated by George W. Pack in exchange for the promise that Asheville's public square would belong to the people forever.

During that meeting, a businessman, W. B. Gwyn, who often spoke for Pack, gained the floor.

"Mr. Chairman," he said, "I have a letter to read. . . .

"To the Commissioners of the County of Buncombe: I offer to give to the county, to be used for a site for a courthouse and county offices, the land on College Street in Asheville which I purchased from Col. A. T. Davidson, provided that the county will dedicate the square to the public, forever, to be used for the purposes of a public square, so-called, in Asheville, the present courthouse to be removed therefrom prior to such date as you may agree upon with Judge Merrimon and Mr. Gwyn, acting for me. December 31, 1900. Geo. W. Pack."

Pack was by then living on Long Island for health reasons, but his heart still resided in Asheville.

Just as he had done before, he did not give the entire project to the county, but left considerable work for the county to do in order to build the new courthouse. His offer of the tract of land, which lay on the south side of College Street, fronting 210 feet on the street and extending to a depth of more than 400 feet, was the most generous he had made to the public so far. The land covered most of what is today City-County Plaza and was an extremely valuable property then. As he did when he left half of the expense of the Vance Monument to the public, and the library to be furnished and lighted, this offer, too, not only aided the public but challenged it deeply. The commissioners estimated it would require between $50,000 and $100,000 to build the courthouse. There was much work to be done, but Pack had given them incentive to do it.

The county accepted Pack's offer on January 8, 1901. In the transactions necessary to accept the land from Pack, the county deeded its land on Court Square to the city, which placed it in the public trust in perpituity, to be used only as a public park.

The courthouse was completed and the county moved in. On Christmas Eve, 1902, county commissioners carried out the final part of their contract with Pack, selling the old courthouse on the square for $1,000 to John A. Campbell and C. T. Rawls, to be removed in its entirety by May 15, 1903. There were 1,200,000 bricks in the old courthouse, which probably helped Campbell and Rawls turn a neat profit on the deal. Court Square was then renamed Pack Square, a designation it carries today.

Until his death, Pack continued to bestow gifts upon Asheville. He gave the YMCA $1,000 to help build a new building. He gave land for three city parks, Aston Park, Montford Park, and another at the corner of Flint and Magnolia.

Pack died August 31, 1906, at the age of seventy-five.

The Asheville Daily Citizen eulogized him elegantly: "No grief is too deep, no eulogy too extravagant, no memorial shaft too costly to do justice to him in whose heart the city of Asheville was enshrined."

27

TO ARMS AGAIN

B efore the century turned, Asheville went to war again. From the time of the War Between the States, almost every generation of American people went to war in one place or another—the Spanish-American War, the Mexican War, the World War, World War II, Korea, Vietnam, the Persian Gulf.

When Cuban nationalists revolted against the rule of Spain in 1895, the "yellow press" blew accounts of alleged Spanish atrocities in Cuba to enormous proportions, and helped raise American resentment against Spain to warlike heights.

Up to February 15, 1898, America stayed out of hostilities, but on that date, mysterious explosions within the U.S.S. Battleship Maine, anchored in Havana Harbor, sank the ship and took the lives of 260 American sailors. The ship had been sent to Havana in December of 1897 to protect American citizens and property against riots in the Cuban capital. The sinking of the battleship was the straw that broke the camel's back. Certain American newspapers seized the opportunity to trumpet a new slogan, "Remember the Maine; to hell with Spain!" Armed intervention by the United States followed in April. Spain declared war on April 24, and America returned the favor the following day.

As usual, Asheville was quick to respond. The Asheville Light Infantry, organized eleven years earlier, had anticipated the outbreak of hostilities and had been training diligently for several weeks. Three days after the declaration of war, the company was called into federal service as Company F, First North Carolina Volunteers.

When the call for 125,000 volunteers came from President William McKinley, *The Asheville Daily Citizen* did not wait for its next scheduled edition to announce the notification, but had an "Extra!" on the streets at 4:35 p.m., thirty-five minutes after the call was received.

The call came as an order from Adjutant General A. D. Cowles of the North Carolina State Guard to Captain Thomas W. Bookhart, a dentist who practiced on Patton Avenue and was at that time commanding officer of the Asheville Light Infantry.

The order directed Capt. Bookhart to move his company to camp in Raleigh on May 2, precipitating feverish activity by members of the unit. That Monday, May 2, was an exciting time. It always was when a military unit marched off to war, banners flying in the breeze, Old Glory waving at the head of the column, tough sergeants barking marching orders, and stiff-backed officers leading the march down the avenue.

A *Citizen* reporter described the scene: "Three streets and side-walks were packed with pedestrians, men on horseback, bicyclists, and people in carriages, while every available window held a group of watchers."

The troops entrained at the station in Biltmore at 9:05 a.m. and arrived in Raleigh at 6 p.m., reporting with a strength of three officers, five non-commissioned officers, and 113 privates.

The smoke of the train had not melted into the morning sky when Captain John A. Wagner set about raising a company known as the Asheville Guards, which left for Raleigh May 23 and was mustered in the next day as Company H, Second North Carolina Volunteers. This company was made up mainly of Asheville men but with others from elsewhere in Western North Carolina on the roster.

A third company, composed of black soldiers from Asheville, was mustered in June 23 and designated Company K, Third North Carolina Volunteers.

When this company departed the city, more than 300 men had marched out of Asheville, Enfield rifles shouldered, stepping smartly down South Main Street on their way to war.

Other companies were mustered around the mountain area and joined the three North Carolina regiments.

The shooting part of the war for the United States ended so quickly, on August 12, 1898, four months after it began, that only one Asheville company, the Light Infantry, went overseas, and it did not embark until the shooting stopped. The Western North Carolinians felt right at home in their regiment which was attached to the 7th Army Corps, commanded by General Fitzhugh

Lee, a nephew of Robert E. Lee. Fitzhugh had been a brigade commander in the Civil War.

On December 11, the regiment arrived in Havana and moved into garrison duty near Mariaoa, seven miles from Havana. Capt. Wagner, who had taken the Asheville Guards of the Second North Carolina Regiment into service, had been transferred to the First Regiment and wound up in Cuba with the Asheville Light Infantry. Wagner became acting provost marshal of the First Regiment and in that capacity was required to make a detail as the guard of honor for lowering the flag of Spain and raising American colors over Morro Castle at noon, January 1, 1899.

He made up the detail of ten men from the Asheville Light Infantry, under command of Second Lieutenant Robert O. Patterson of Asheville. The detail included Charles A. Reynolds, Archibald A. Miller, Oscar O. Burnett, John E. Sigg, Augustus L. Whitaker, Archie Miller, David C. Ledford, James Payne, and Jesse M. Patton.

The Spanish-American War brought Theodore Roosevelt to fame as leader of the 1st Volunteer Cavalry, the "Rough Riders," who stormed the heights of San Juan Hill on July 1, breaking the back of Spanish resistance and bringing the war to an end. The Rough Riders, recruited by Roosevelt and composed of cowboys, miners, law enforcers, and college athletes, was as colorful an American army unit as ever existed. Unorthodox in its methods, it succeeded in its charge up San Juan Hill by sheer guts and superior sharpshooting. Roosevelt, who led the charge, had resigned as assistant secretary of the navy to become second in command of the Rough Riders. Their commander was Colonel Leonard Wood, who himself had resigned as White House physician to get into combat.

As a result of combat in Cuba and the Philippine Islands, Spain ceded Guam, Puerto Rico, and the Philippines to the United States, and Teddy Roosevelt won the White House.

Turn of the century weavers at work on a porch of an Asheville home.

Fire wagon and members of the Asheville Volunteer Fire Department in December 1906.

28

TURN OF THE CENTURY

Asheville passed its centennial and entered the 20th century on an icy Monday of blowing snow and arctic temperature. Big Ivy River, which rarely froze hard, was iced solidly from bank to bank and the French Broad was frozen along its banks. Pungent coal smoke, mingled with the lighter smoke of wood fires, hovered over the city beneath lowered clouds, and most folks chose to remain at home to celebrate the New Year's holiday in warmth and quiet.

In the last twenty years, Buncombe County had doubled in size to 44,288 citizens, and Asheville, expanding greatly since the coming of the railroads, had sextupled to 14,694 and was becoming quite a city.

There were two distinct groups of citizens, who mixed and mingled freely and got along with rapport. One group was composed of rough and ready countrymen—sidehill farmers, loggers, miners, and moonshiners—many of whom carried .38 revolvers in their hip pockets and came to town on Saturday to let their hair down and celebrate their week's work. Most of the larger farmers were stalwart, cultured citizens. The second group of citizens was made up of genteel people, schooled in the classics and arts, who conducted the city's commerce by day and attended plays and musicals in the Grand Opera House by night.

Built in 1888 at 41-43 Patton Avenue at the North Lexington Avenue corner, the opera house was considered the finest in the state. It occupied the top three floors of a four-story building. At street level, the building housed the home furnishings business of Taylor, Bouis & Brotherton on the west side of the opera house entrance, and on the other side was T. W. Thrash & Company, which dealt in china, glass, crockery, and lamps. Inside the Patton Avenue entrance to the opera house was a broad stairway of polished mahogany leading to the beautiful three-tiered theater. A huge crystal chandelier hung from the center of the ceiling. Above the main floor was a horseshoe balcony, and above that, a second balcony of nose-bleed seats that stretched across the rear of the theater.

Into this elegant house came roadshows featuring the latest comedies, dramas, and musicals. In the theater Ashevilleans thrilled to the beat of John Philip Sousa's band playing rousing martial airs, to the dramas and beauty of Sarah Bernhardt, to A. G. Field's Minstrels, and to blackface comedians Lee Lasses White,[1] Slim Vermont, Bert Swor, and Billy Beard. Madame Schumann-Heink sang to a house so packed that onlookers sat in rows of chairs on stage. Madame Galli-Curci's soprano delighted a packed house, and Calvin Coolidge, when a vice presidential nominee, spoke from the Grand Opera House stage against entry into the League of Nations.

When Sousa came to town, he marched his band up and down Patton Avenue and around the Square in the afternoons, playing lively tunes to advertise the evening's show in the opera house. A turn-of-the-century joke about Sousa went this way: "Did you hear that Sousa was drowned the other day?" "No. How did it happen?" "He was playing 'On the Banks of the Wabash' and fell in."

Crowds larger than those in the opera house often turned up at the depot when Miss Bernhardt came in on the train. They delighted in seeing her entourage of twenty or more persons lugging trunks of dresses and costumes, and one white-painted, teakwood casket. Miss Bernhardt had purchased the casket because she liked it and, wanting to be buried in it, took it with her wherever she went. It was usually packed with costumes, too.

Sarah Bernhardt was the one star that everyone in Asheville wanted to see. She had no trouble selling out the house. She was a beautiful woman and Asheville's womenfolk loved to see her act. She wore such sparkling low-cut gowns that the women had no trouble coaxing their menfolk to attend, and they sat breathlessly waiting for Miss Bernhardt to take her final bow.

William S. Hart, the first great star of silent-screen western movies, coached Asheville's first little theater in the Grand Opera House in the mid-1890s, and Asheville followed his later career with

---

[1] Lee Lasses White went on to Hollywood and became one of the famous cowboy sidekicks of western movies.

great interest. Thus it was that *The Daily Citizen* carried a front-page story near the turn of the century on Hart:

W. S. HART began a week's engagement at the People's Theater in New York in "The Man in the Iron Mask." Asheville friends of the young actor will read with interest the following taken from the *Dramatic Mirror:* "Of Mr. Hart's acting in the principal part, or rather parts, nothing but words of praise can be said. In the first act he was the boys, tender and passionate by turns. In the scene with the father of Marie he moved the audience deeply by his portrayal of the various emotions, and when the curtain fell it had to be raised several times in response to genuine applause. So it was throughout the play, recall followed recall. He avoided all tendency to overact, and his performance was characterized throughout by refinement and intelligence."

Asheville didn't have to be told. The city's theater set knew William S. Hart was destined for greatness on the stage. They didn't yet know how popular he would become in the movies.

Over at the Battery Park Hotel, folks learned the latest dance steps from a young man from New York named Arthur Murray.

At the Berkeley Hotel on South Main Street, in a room off the lobby, people watched kinetoscopes, the forerunners of movies.

President Theodore Roosevelt spoke at Vance Monument in 1902.

Democratic presidential candidate William Jennings Bryan's Parade down Patton Avenue in 1898.

Large cabinets were arranged in the room and for a nickel, a person could peer inside and listen by earphones to an Edison kinetoscope, a short reel of pictures with a synchronized phonograph record providing music. The kinetoscopes lasted about a minute and repeated as often as nickels went into the slot.

Asheville turned out in force to hear the famed orators of the day. More than 10,000 gathered on Pack Square in 1902 to hear President Theodore Roosevelt make a bully of a speech.[2] Upon seeing the magnificent mountains, Roosevelt exclaimed in delight, "Oh, this is indeed a most magnificent country—the grandest east of the Rockies!"

William Jennings Bryan, Democratic and Populist leader in the United States, visited Asheville during his three unsuccesful campaigns for the presidency, 1896 and 1900 when defeated by William McKinley and 1908 when defeated by William Howard Taft, and eventually built a home on Edwin Place and moved here. He was a good citizen who taught Sunday school at the First Presbyterian Church and made friends by the hundreds.

On one of Bryan's political forays into Asheville, he was invited to come to Reems Creek and speak to a gathering of farm people who

---

[2] For text of Roosevelt's speech see Bob Terrell's *Grandpa's Town,* published by WorldComm.

City Hall behind fountain on Pack Square about 1905. Police and fire departments were behind the arches.

could not come to town. Readily accepting the invitation, Bryan arrived on the scene and found the people gathered in a field. He asked for a podium or something on which he could stand to view the crowd, and the only thing available was a nearby manure spreader, upon which he climbed and announced to the crowd: "Ladies and gentlemen, this is the first time I have ever made a speech from a Republican platform."

(In 1925 Bryan helped prosecute John T. Scopes, the Dayton, Tennessee, school teacher charged with violating state law by teaching the theory of evolution, and upon Scopes's conviction July 21, 1925, Bryan was so exhausted that he died five days later.)

Pack Square was still dominated by the old courthouse with the imposing obelisk monument to Zeb Vance in front of it and City Hall and the City Market behind it.

Asheville's doctors, disturbed at the continuance of dreaded diseases, launched a program of free vaccinations designed to curb the spread of illnesses. Where persons showed a willingness to be vaccinated, physicians often went to a neighborhood and administered vaccines on the spot.

However, many people had a decided antipathy to having to endure a great throbbing sore on their arm and preferred to take a chance of escaping disease without vaccination, and physicians often encountered them on their rounds.

On one fine spring day a doctor on his rounds struck a neighborhood in which there were a number of people who had not been vaccinated. While arguing the merits of vaccination with the obstinate crowd, the doctor saw another physician approaching. The first doctor asked the second if he had yet been vaccinated and was told that he had not. The first doctor asked the other to have his vaccination on the spot to show the crowd that it was a simple and painless operation. The doctor consented, drew his coat and rolled up his sleeve, and the knife was applied. At sight of the first drop of his blood, Doctor No. 2 fell over in a dead faint—and the crowd of objectors fled in a stampede, leaving the first doctor to resuscitate his fellow physician as best he could.

On the other side of the cultural coin were the rowdies who hitched their mules along Water Street (then affectionately called Mule Alley and today known as Lexington Avenue) and made for the red light district around Carolina Lane and Saloon Row on South Main Street.

Life became so rough along Saloon Row in the early 1900s that seventeen men were violently killed on that street in the ten years preceding prohibition, which was authorized by vote in 1907.

Classic among the memories of old-timers of yesteryear were the sights, sounds, and particularly the smells of the old general merchandise store.

Things came in barrels, boxes, sacks, and kegs. The things people bought they either took home or had them delivered in brown paper "pokes." Most of the Asheville general stores had their own delivery services and housewives knew when they telephoned an order that they would receive exactly what they ordered and that it would be fresh and good.

The general store smelled of kerosene oil, leather harness, sweet chewing tobacco and Arbuckle's best coffee. Coffee came in bushel sacks of beans and the hand-operated coffee grinder always livened the scents in the store. Sweet Apple and Brown's Mule were the favored chewing tobaccos, and Reyno and Piedmont cigarettes were the popular brands. Most smoking tobacco, however, came in small sacks, and each brand produced a different smelling and tasting smoke. Bruton's Scotch Snuff was the ladies' favorite, but in many homes could be found Grandma's small jack knife and a plug of chewing tobacco behind a picture on the mantle. Grandpa carried his plug in a pocket of his overalls.

Boys learned to smoke and chew before their adolescent years, and almost all men used tobacco.

One of the choice items in the general store were yellow bone-handled Barlow knives, fifteen cents for a one-blader and a quarter for a two-blader. Men used one blade for whittling and the other for slicing plugs of tobacco.

Every house had a big bottle of liniment, and Sloan's was the popular brand. Liniment was used for almost every ailment, sprains, bruises, headaches, toothaches, rheumatism, lumbago, you name it. Onion poltices would break up chest congestion overnight, and foul-smelling asafetida, which had been in use since the 14th century, would either prevent or cure an ailment, and to be sure it would render any ailment noncontageous for no one would venture close enough to the user to catch the disease. To the utter consternation of teachers, schoolkids wore bags of asafetida tied around their necks to ward off germs at school.

Most men, especially those who lived and worked in the country, wore high brogan shoes, and a good pair would run a customer a dollar and a half. Women and girls bought high-topped, button shoes, and with each pair came a new buttonhook.

Usually someone in each family could make music, and one of the most popular instruments around was the cigar-box banjo with a cured-poplar handle, seasoned oak pegs, and store-bought strings.

Suppertime marked the end of the day's work, and between supper and darkness, those who could play and sing made music on their front porches and neighbors gathered in the yard to listen. Often musicmakers would know neighbors were listening by seeing the glow of cigarettes under trees by the edge of the yard. Sometimes the music was better than toe-tapping and families danced a reel or two in the yard.

This was the Asheville that Thomas Wolfe was born into on October 3, 1900. He was christened Thomas Clayton Wolfe by his parents, stonecutter William Oliver (W. C.) Wolfe and Julia Elizabeth Westall Wolfe. His genius was detected early in life, but no one suspected that the tall, gangly, awkward, unathletic boy would grow up to drop on his hometown the biggest bombshell Asheville ever saw.

By the turn of the century, Asheville had had its own city police force for a number of years. Headquartered in part of City Hall on the square, the force numbered perhaps fifteen men, including a couple of captains and a chief. Physical power was required of those who applied for work on the force but was not such a necessity as it was in the earlier days of the force when officers were required to weigh more than 190 pounds, have a visible paunch, and a handlebar moustache, the more vicious-looking the better, and carry no firearms. They were armed with clubs and for formal dress with swords bearing their names embossed on the blades.

Officers wore long blue coats with brass buttons and shields, good walking shoes, and English bobby helmets. Until 1906 the police department did not possess a rifle, shotgun, pistol, or a mechanized vehicle of any sort. The swords were used for such duties as escorting famous persons, like the many presidents of the United States who visited Asheville. They were evident in September of 1902 when Teddy Roosevelt came to town and was escorted from the depot to Pack Square by marching officers and city dignitaries.

The first police vehicle was a bicycle the city purchased in 1906 for $32.50, and this extravagance with city funds cost the mayor and some aldermen their jobs in the next election. Officers thought the bicycle necessary because some had to walk a mile or more to their beats, and then walk back to the stationhouse at the end of a twelve-hour shift.

The first decade of the 20th century was marked by several measures of progress. In 1904 the Asheville Electric Company built and opened Riverside Park beside the French Broad River at the foot of Montford Hill, and Asheville had a playground worthy of notice.

It was a place where thousands gathered on the Fourth of July to watch fireworks displays, and where hundreds came on normal days and evenings to enjoy picnics, and the merry-go-round and other rides. The huge park had a self-contained lake where young men spooned their girls in canoes, and in the center of the lake was a man-made island on which an outdoor movie screen was erected. People sat in comfortable seats across the water from the island and enjoyed outdoor movies.

There was also a baseball park within Riverside Park, and the Asheville professional team played there. The outfield fences were short. It was written that a good fungo to right field would land in the river.

Asheville had its first professional team in 1897. It wore purple uniforms and was aptly named the Moonshiners. They played only twenty-one games, and then Asheville had no professional ball until 1909 when S. A. (Diamond) Lynch organized and managed a team called the Asheville Red Birds in the Western North Carolina League, playing its games at Riverside Park. From that time on, with brief times-out for wars and depression, Asheville has been represented in professional baseball.

Baseball was first played in Asheville in 1866. Men coming home from the Civil War had learned the game, some in Yankee prisons, others elsewhere, and they played on Smith's 118-acre tract located somewhere off Grove Street. A Currier & Ives greeting card depicted a baseball scene in Asheville in 1866.

Asheville residents objected to the slightest hint of extravagance by city fathers. On several occasions Asheville officials lost their positions in subsequent elections because of expenditures of public funds that the citizens considered unnecessary.

It took the murder of five good men to jerk the city from its lethargy. Not any of the city police officers were armed except with weapons they purchased for themselves. Most of those were pistols and many, purchased as cheaply as possible because of the low pay of city patrolmen, were underpowered.

The city was quick to vote in laws to stem crime, but law alone will not tame a town. There must be someone tough enough and willing enough to enforce the law, and he must be properly trained and equipped.

Asheville's darkest hour came near midnight on the cold evening of November 13, 1906, when a crazed, escaped felon from Charlotte named Will Harris shot up the town in a drunken rage, killing three Negro men and two white police officers.

His rampage began at the corner of Eagle and Valley Streets where he slew the first policeman, Charles R. Blackstock, and wounded Captain John R. Page with a shot through the arm. The killer continued up Eagle Street where with deadly accuracy he murdered an elderly black storekeeper and woodyard owner named Benjamin F. Addison; a younger black man, Walter (Jakko) Corpening, who was walking home from work in Gross's Alley; and a fellow named Tom Neil, a young black man who had been talking with friends and failed to run with the rest when he saw Harris approaching, thinking Harris was playing a joke or having a little drunken fun.

Turning the corner, Harris started up South Main Street, shot at several persons who ventured onto the street, and finally, in an exchange of shots, killed Patrolman James W. Bailey with a well-placed, steel-jacketed round that went through a twelve-inch telephone pole, entered Bailey's mouth, and exploded out the back of his head. The bullet ricocheted off the Vance Monument and into a store on the north side of the square.

Bailey had been armed with a .32-caliber revolver which did not have the firing power to accurately reach Harris down the street.

By mid-morning of the next day, more than a thousand men from Asheville and Buncombe County, directed by Chief of Police Silas G. Bernard, were armed and in the field, searching the county for the murderer.

James H. Caine, editor of *The Citizen*, indicated the trend of the times when in a front-page editorial he exhorted frontier justice. He wrote: "If Harris is caught and brought to Asheville he will be tried immediately in Superior Court and sentenced to be hung in short order. . . ." Harris then put his .38 in his hip pocket, took his horse out of the livery stable, and rode south to join the manhunters.

All that day the posses had no luck, but on the following day, three posses led by former police chief Frank M. Jordan, a veteran manhunter, cornered Harris in a laurel thicket on the Westfeldt estate at the Henderson County line and fired more than five hundred rounds into the thicket. More than a hundred of them struck Harris, knocking him out of one of his shoes. He died on the spot and his body was taken to Asheville in the bed of a wagon. Hundreds lined the streets in silence to watch the wagon and the posses troop by.[3]

James H. Caine had taken the first shot at Harris—and missed.

Three days after the shootings, Asheville's board of aldermen authorized the police committee to purchase twenty-five rifles and ten shotguns and 100 rounds of ammunition each "for use only in cases of emergency or at the discretion of the chief of police."Immediately the committee ordered the latest model Winchester repeating rifles and repeating, double-barreled riot shotguns that would fire buckshot. Steel-jacket ammunition was purchased for the rifles.

From that time on, city policemen have been able to counter the firepower of opponents of the law.

The Manor, a rambling English Tudor inn, opened on Charlotte Street in 1900, and in West Asheville the Asheville School for Boys started its first class that fall. The school attracted students from all over the world, including many who came from the nation's wealthiest families. Captain Eddie Rickenbacker, one of the United States's flying aces in World War I, received a portion of his education at the Asheville School.

*   *   *   *

---

[3] For a more detailed description of these incidents see Bob Terrell's "The Will Harris Murders," published by WorldComm of Alexander, N. C.

Richard Smith Howland moved to Asheville early in the century. He bought property and built a fine residence at the foot of Sunset Mountain. A quick-minded man who loved a challenge, he had been a newspaper executive in Providence, Rhode Island, and had built a railway in California before he came here.

He was one of the area's first aerial-minded men and at one time owned a glider. He built an interurban railway from Asheville to Weaverville and called it the Asheville and East Tennessee Railroad, which would indicate that he might have harbored plans of extending the line farther.

Sticking to rails, he built a scenic streetcar line to Overlook Park in the Craggies where he opened a music and dance hall. Because of the interest and use of his car line, the city granted him permission to operate his cars from Pack Square.

Born July 12, 1847 in New Bedford, Massachusetts, he was a graduate of Brown University in 1871 and then studied a year at Berlin University.

He particularly liked to dig into international problems. As a newspaperman, he went to Venezuela when public attention centered on disturbed relations there. He went to Cuba during the Spanish-American War and made similar excursions to Algiers and Mexico, sending eyewitness reports back to the *Providence Evening Bulletin* and *The Providence Journal.*

While his children remained in Asheville, Howland lived his last few years in Milledgeville, Georgia, died there and was buried on July 12, 1930, his eighty-third birthday.

The year 1902 was a milestone for Asheville. The last two legal hangings took place that year. Frank Johnson and Ben Foster were dropped to their deaths at the end of ropes in the old city jail on Marjorie Street. Their crime had been robbing the Emma Post Office in West Asheville and wounding—not killing—the postmaster. Hidden from view of a crowd that gathered, the men strangled to death, John-son requiring eighteen minutes and Foster, twenty-four. Both were buried that same afternoon in Riverside Cemetery's pauper's plot.

Asheville built a city auditorium on Haywood Street at the head of Flint Street in 1902, and the 2,500-seat auditorium, constructed of wood, burned in 1903. Undaunted, the city immediately built another auditorium of the same size in the same place and used it until it was replaced in 1939 by the WPA. That government organization fouled up its paper work and wrote the mayor of Asheville a letter in 1943 notifying him that the government would be unable to build an auditorium in Asheville. But by that time Asheville had been using the auditorium for four years.

Colorful characters continued to move to Asheville. In 1905, Dr. Lewis M. McCormick moved to town and became the city's first bacteriologist. Disturbed over the downtown location of at least a dozen livery stables with their huge piles of horse manure and millions of house flies, Dr. McCormick in 1906 started a campaign he called "Swat That Fly." Arming the city's children with fly swatters, he dispatched them in all directions in the summer months. They went door to door, offering to kill all flies in the house for ten cents. In the more affluent sections of the city, they raised their prices to twenty-five cents.

Miraculously, the campaign lowered the number of flies in Asheville by millions. Dr. McCormick became known as "the Fly Man" and his campaign attracted nationwide attention in the press. Delegations came to Asheville from many cities, including one from San Francisco, to study Dr. McCormick's methods so they could apply them in their home cities.

McCormick lived in Asheville until his death in 1923 and the city's new baseball park, then under construction, was named McCormick Field for its opening in the spring of 1924.

Asheville continued to grow. From a population of 14,694 in 1900, the city swelled to 18,672 in 1910, and then increased to 28,504 in 1920.

Census figures for Asheville and Buncombe County show the growth of the two from inception to the last census in 1990:

YEAR	CITY	COUNTY
1800	—	5812
1810	—	9277
1820	—	10542
1830	350	12281
1840	500	10084
1850	800	13425
1860	1100	12650
1870	1450	15412
1880	2610	21909

The Atkins Street bridge over Valley Street, 1906.

YEAR	CITY	COUNTY
1890	10235	35266
1900	14694	44288
1910	18672	49798
1920	28504	64148
1930	50193	97937
1940	51310	108755
1950	53000	124403
1960	60192	130074
1970	57681	145056
1980	53583	160934
1990	61607	175493

Crowd enjoys tennis match at the Country Club of Asheville, 1910.

29

WHIPPING
JOHN BARLEYCORN

P eople will only take kicks in the teeth for so long before they are compelled to rise and fight. Many women and children in Asheville suffered because of drunken husbands and fathers. There were those men who preferred to drink up their wages rather than care for their families. Neighbors noticed these shortcomings and sympathized with the embattled women and children. So it was that a great groundswell surged through Asheville in the early 1900s in favor of closing down saloons and grog shops and putting legal whiskey-makers out of business. Prohibition was sweeping the country and the good ladies of Asheville saw their chance for salvation.

As long as those saloons remained on South Main Street and others just off the square, and as long as city aldermen were so free in issuing liquor licenses, the unrest of the non-drinking public increased. South Main in the evenings was a rip-roaring street.

In 1902, Asheville contained six restaurants and fourteen saloons, and most of the bars were on South Main Street—the Acme, the Bonanza, Carr's, the Club, the White Man's Saloon, the Buffalo, the Laurel Valley, the Swannanoa Hotel bar.

But by 1906, the city had sixteen saloons and fifteen restaurants. There were also eighteen livery stables and twenty churches.

Probably the incident that propelled the city's prohibitionists into serious action was the wild shooting spree of Will Harris in November of 1906 when he killed five men on and near the square after consuming most of a quart of whiskey he had purchased in the Buffalo Saloon.

Through the early months of 1907 prohibitionists organized in force, circulated petitions to be signed by registered voters, and on

Giant parade by prohibition forces on date of successful prohibition vote, 1907.

August 16 W. R. Whitson presented petitions to the city signed by 759 voters requesting the issue be brought to the polls. The number of signatures was sufficient to call the matter to a vote and two issues were put on the ballot:

1. Whether intoxicating liquors should be manufactured in Asheville.

2. Whether barrooms or saloons should be maintained in Asheville.

Both sides girded for battle. Those favoring whiskey began rounding up support from prominent men, including Silas G. Bernard, the chief of police, and Dr. S. Westray Battle, one of the town's social leaders.

But political power fell heavily on the side of the prohibitionists, who counted among their numbers Locke Craig, who would become governor of North Carolina five years later, Judge Jeter C. Pritchard, Judge James G. Merrimon, Judge H. A. Gudger, and others of notable strength.

In addition, the "drys" called in one of the nation's most powerful prohibitionists, the Rev. Dr. Mordecai F. Ham of Kentucky, a fiery evangelist who twenty-seven years later, in 1934, would help Billy Graham to the altar of a 5,000-seat tabernacle in Charlotte especially constructed for Ham's eleven-week revival.

Ham was labeled a "professional prohibitionist" by those favoring retention of liquor sales in Asheville. He pitched into battle with evangelistic fervor.

The drys held nightly meetings, mass rallies, and camp meetings, mostly in the city auditorium, at which great orations were delivered and faithfully reprinted the following day in *The Asheville Daily Citizen.*

The wets retaliated with a daily colum in *The Citizen* entitled "Plain Facts," in which they hammered the point that to outlaw saloons was to curtail individual freedom. Matching the drys meeting for meeting, the wets held their sessions in the Grand Opera House.

The issue split the city but with little bitterness. Neighbors on opposite sides still got along as neighbors. Husbands and wives found themselves at odds over the issue but remained husbands and wives.

On occasion, the drys would encounter stout resistance as a group of women did when they made earnest appeal to an old fellow known for his love of purified spirits.

Listening respectfully to their pleas, the old fellow, with chin whiskers bobbing, replied, "I would like to accommodate you the best in the world, but I just can't bring m'self to vote against m'daily rations."

Dr. Ham spoke several times a day for more than a month without inserting enough fire to anger the other side, but nearing the eve of the election, he took note of a long list of prominent Asheville men who were listed in the newspaper as supporting liquor, and at the auditorium that night, he shouted, "I would prefer to be listed in the rogues' gallery with thieves and blackguards than to be in the ranks of that company."

That removed the kid gloves from the campaign, and the remark even drew indignation from some who were on Mordecai's side. The next day in the newspaper column, the wets countered with a reference to "that Ham, who by tolerance is called a clergyman."

On the morning of the election—October 8, 1907—crowds of drys flocked to each of the city's eight polling places, one in the courthouse on College Street, two in livery stables, four in stores, and one in an empty store building. Women and children came out in force in an effort to persuade the voters to "vote right."

They struck an extremely fortunate stroke when they encountered saloon owner John O'Donnell. Their argument was so compellingly that O'Donnell went straight to the polls and voted himself out of business.

The drys wore white arm bands that day, and the wets wore red bands. Drys taunted and shamed red-banded voters to the extent that some left the area without casting a vote. Many a man staggered to the polls and voted dry.

By 9 a.m. an observer noted, "Only a blind man, deaf and mute, could fail to see the outcome of this election."

He was right. The vote wound up 1,274 to 405 against operation of distilleries, which put the wholesalers out of business, and 1,274 to 426 against operation of barrooms and saloons.

So the whiskey peddlers were sent packing, and the whiskey-makers driven deep into the woods.

That evening the drys staged a victory march to the auditorium where Locke Craig declared, "This is perhaps the greatest day in Asheville's history!"

Dr. Ham was carried into the auditorium in a white chair. The governor of North Carolina sent a congratulatory telegram, and word reached the Asheville rally that women in Winston-Salem had met on the square there and prayed much of the day for the women of Asheville.

One reporter wrote, "The drys were magnanimous in victory and the wets were peaceful and submissive in defeat.

Dr. Ham, his duties done, left that night for his home in Kentucky.

The reverend was not the only one to leave Asheville at that time. John A. Roebling, grandson and namesake of the man who designed the Brooklyn Bridge and son of the man who built it, had lived in Asheville twelve years when prohibition was voted in. Apparently a man who liked a nip but didn't like to hide to take it, Roebling packed up his family and moved away, never to return.

30

O. HENRY

In 1905, a noted American author came to Asheville to be married. William Sidney Porter, whose short stories under the pen name of O. Henry captivated American readers, married Sara Lindsay Coleman of Weaverville and Asheville.

Weaverville was the Coleman family's home, but roads were so bad in the country that the family closed the Weaverville home and rented a house on Victoria Road in Asheville in winter.

Born in Greensboro September 11, 1862, Will Porter had worked as a cowhand in Texas, spent a little time in a Texas prison, and found that his creative juices flowed best in New York, so he made his home there and sold stories to newspapers and magazines, most of which have become classics in American literature.

He and Sara Lindsay Coleman had been classmates at Lina Porter's private school in Greensboro in the 1870s and Porter had gone to work either at the age of fifteen or seventeen (historians differ there) and four years later went to Texas "for his health."

In 1905 Sara's mother visited Greensboro and came home to tell her daughter, "Your old friend Will Porter is a writer. He lives in New York and writes under the name of O. Henry."

Sara had read much of O. Henry's literary output without knowing who he was, and at the moment her mother told her of him, she had one of his stories, "Bo-Peep of the Ranches," in her desk drawer. She, too, was a published writer, and on impulse she penned a note to O. Henry, ending it with an invitation for him to write to her, but adding that "if you are not Will Porter don't bother to answer."

From that point, the two became reacquainted and moved quickly to the altar.

After the wedding, the Porters made their home in New York and came often to Asheville for visits. In late summer of 1909, however, Porter was ill and he and Sara decided to come to Asheville for change and rest and possible medical treatment. He rented a small office in the American National Bank Building at the corner of Patton Avenue and Church Street, where he hoped to continue his writing. The office was sparsely furnished with a table, one chair, a basin with running weater, a yellow pad of foolscap, some pencils, the World Almanac, and a small dictionary.

His physician was William Pinckney Herbert, who had almost daily contact with him. Later, Dr. Herbert wrote of his association with Porter:

". . . during his stay here I never heard him referred to, or introduced as 'O. Henry' or as an author.

"Yet his personality was such that I can recall his appearance vividly. I can almost hear his low, rather deep voice talking of all the many ailments from which he suffered. . . . He was, I think, the first real patient who had come my way, he was frank as to his habits– 'I know I smoke too much, keep late hours, and drink too much, but that's about all.'"

Dr. Herbert did not agree with a New York diagnosis of neuresthenia, but found no serious organic disease, merely evidence of impairment of the function of several organs.

During his stay here Porter could not find inspiration to write. He spent most of his time hanging out his office window, watching traffic on Patton Avenue below. The mountains closed in on him, and in the months he was here he apparently wrote only one story, "Let Me Feel Your Pulse."

He enjoyed life at the Coleman place, with sprightly conversation and the gracious but intense life in a flourishing household with growing children.

The Porters returned to New York hoping O. Henry could get his creative juices flowing again, but in early summer 1910 his condition became grave and on June 4 he was taken to Polyclinic Hospital. The following day he said to his nurse, "Pull up the shades; I don't want to go home in the dark."

Funeral services were held on the 7th at the Church of the Transfiguration–the Little Church Around the Corner–so his New York friends could attend, and then his body was brought by overnight train to Asheville and on the 8th Dr. Robert Campbell did a simple service at the First Presbyterian Church. His pallbearers were Dr. Herbert, Judge Thomas A. Jones, Major R. T. Grinnan, Col. Robert Bingham, Dr. F. T. Merriwether, and Edwin L. Ray. He was interred in Riverside Cemetery on a gentle slope and his grave is marked only by a low, flat stone.

O. Henry's association with Asheville, up to 1910, coincided with the strange "visit" of another character, a fellow who arrived in Biltmore on the train one day, dressed in a natty gray suit and sporting a neatly trimmed Vandyke. He took a room on Montford Avenue and gave his name as Charles J. Asquith, better known as the debonair Lord Beresford, social favorite of half a dozen countries and member of British royalty.

He had been in Asheville only a short time when in November he died of a mysterious malady. Undertakers cabled England for information on Lord Beresford and instructions as to what to do with his body, and the following day word came back that no one knew a Lord Beresford. Try as they might, the funeral people could find no record of Lord Beresford. So they embalmed his body—actually mummified it—and put him on third floor in the Noland-Brown mortuary on Church Street.

The body lay unclaimed as days turned into weeks, weeks into months, and months into years. On lazy days, some of the guys who worked at the funeral parlor, would go up to third floor and play bridge or poker, and when there were only three, they would take the Dook from his box, prop him in a chair at the table, and let him be the "fourth" in the game.

Before long, one of the men got the wild idea of taking the Dook for a ride in the funeral home's surrey, propping him stiffly against the rear seat. The fellow drove the Dook up Patton Avenue, around Pack Square, down South Main Street, and back to the funeral home, and folks got such a kick of it that the ride was repeated a couple of times a year to the delight of onlookers. It was the best advertising any funeral home could have wished.

This continued until May 8, 1910, when the Dook's sister-in-law, Mrs. T. J. Summerfield, of Washington, D. C., came to Asheville to identify and claim the body of Lord Beresford.

She told the story of his life, that he was born Sidney Lascelles in England, left that country after he lost his job in a bank because of a great propensity for betting on the horses, and came to America. He wandered the world for a few years, assuming the identity of the imagined Lord Beresford, and turned into a notorious con man. He worked the east coast of America for years.

Once in Burma he had been cursed for shooting a Burmese guide with whom he had trouble, and since doctors had not been able to determine what had killed the Dook, word spread that he had died of a mysterious curse placed upon him by a Burmese jungle tribe.

He was taken to Washington and hopefully buried where he has rested in peace for all these many years.[1]

Asheville continued to grow, both in size and in attractiveness. With suitable hostelry for those who insisted on going first class, wealthy and prominent people chose the Land of the Sky as a vacation oasis. In 1906, looking for a place to hide for a while, three men of national and international fame, Henry Ford, Harvey Firestone, and Thomas A. Edison, checked into the Battery Park Hotel for a spell of relaxation. Ford had brought out his first automobile, which would revolutionize the automotive world, only two years before, and was by this time a harried man; Firestone was producing a good part of the nation's automobile tires from his plant in Akron, Ohio; and Edison? Well, he was probably delighted to see how well his Edison System lighted the Battery Park.

These same three drove a Ford to Asheville and spent most of the summer in the plushness of Grove Park Inn in 1918, bringing with them the famed naturalist, John Burroughs. Weary of the war effort, they relaxed and had a good time.

It was on this trip that they, walking along a hiking path through the woods, encountered a young boy throwing rocks lefthanded at a squirrel. Approaching him just as he knocked a squirrel off a limb with a hard, accurate throw, one of the three commented, "Young man, do you play baseball?"

"No, sir," the kid replied. "I ain't got much time."

"But you have time to come up here and throw at squirrels."

"I'm agittin' supper."

"Supper?"

"Yes, sir, I come up here every day I can and get some squirrels for supper."

"Well, there would be a great future in baseball for a young man like you, who can throw that well and who is lefthanded."

"Oh, I ain't lefthanded," the boy said. "I'm righthanded."

"Then why don't you throw righthanded?"

---

[1] For full details of this story, see Bob Terrell's Grandpa's Town.

"Ma told me not to."

"Why, for goodness sake?"

"She said I mangles the squirrels too bad when I hits 'em righthanded."

Asheville and Buncombe continued to struggle with poor roads and city streets. To beat the muddy roads running north, Richard Howland built his eight-mile electric urban railway to Weaverville in 1909.

In the early part of the 20th century, Asheville was a wonderland at Christmas. Long strings of variously colored, low-watt lights radiated out from the top of the Vance Monuments to buildings around the square. Four groceries were on the square, Smathers and Young, Pat McIntyre's, Edwin C. Jarrett, and Stradley and Luther. Midway in the line of buildings on the north side was the bright lights and musical sounds of the Gaiety Theater. Behind the monument were the public fountain and a huge Christmas tree, also sporting many colored bulbs. *The Citizen* office, W. O. Wolfe's tombstone and monument shop, the public library, the Asheville Hardware, Smith's Drug Store, French Dry-Cleaning, and other businesses ringed three sides of the square, but on the east stood the imposing City Hall with big, arched double doors of the fire department, the police department, and in the basement the City Market.

Riverside Park was in full swing with its huge exposition pavilion to the right, the boathouse to the left, a fortune teller's hut, the Penny Arcade, various rides, the outdoor movie theater, the canoe lake, and baseball park. Fourth of July fireworks were usually ignited by a wrestler, Big Mack McIntosh. What a delightful place for Ashevilleans and visitors!

Wrestling matches were bigtime with real slamming and banging and were featured in a tobacco warehouse on Valley Street.

In 1909 construction was completed on Asheville's most beautiful building—then and now—the Roman Catholic Church of St. Lawrence on Haywood Street across Flint Street from the Civic Center.

George Vanderbilt brought in the world's finest engineers, architects, masons, and foresters, including designer-builder Rafael Guastavino, to build the Biltmore House. Guastavino was a Spanish architect world famous for his resurrection of a lost Moorish construction secret that involved combining tile and cement in dome

Perhaps Asheville's most beautiful building, St. Lawrence Catholic Church, completed in 1908.

constructions capable of supporting enormous weights without the use of other supports.

He had come to America in 1881 to use Portland cement, which he thought suited his needs better than other cements. Retained by the architectural firm of McKim, Mead, and White, Guastavino was the contractor for many of that firm's major public buildings, including the Boston Public Library and Pennsylvania Station in New York City. Guastavino applied his system of cohesive construction to more than a thousand structures in America.

When he concluded his work at the Biltmore House, Guastavino, who enjoyed Asheville and the surrounding countryside very much, took residence in Black Mountain. His intention was to build a private chapel there at the same time that St. Lawrence's parish was attempting to build a new edifice for the city's Catholic population, so upon request he turned his attention to the St. Lawrence parish instead and launched into design and construction of a church that would be a monument to his work. He gave his time and money to the edifice that will stand as long and as proudly as the great European cathedrals.

He built the fifty-eight by eighty-two-foot elliptical dome by the Moorish methods he had rediscovered. It is made up of three layers of tile laid so that no two joints coincide. The floor and spiral staircases rest on thin tile arches.

Frederick Miles carved the limestone statues of St. Lawrence, St. Stephen, and St. Aloysius Gonzaga above the entrance. St. Lawrence, the patron saint of one of the missionary priests who built the first Catholic Church in Asheville in 1840, was broiled to death and Miles sculpted him holding the grill upon which he was martyred.

The church was not completed when Guastavino died in 1908. He was buried in a crypt in the church, a fitting resting place for one so talented and so devoted. His son, Rafael, Jr., completed the church.

By 1912 automobile races were being held in town, and the finish line for the hill climb was in Mud Cut where streetcars rumbled through on their way to the depot. Stripped-down, fenderless automobiles, piloted by goggled drivers, roared up the mile-long course, racing against the clock rather than each other. That year, Clarence Sawyer won—remember him who drove that Octagon Soap automobile around

Oates Park, home of the Asheville Royal Giants, about 1910. This was the park the Asheville Tourists used in 1916 after the flood washed away Riverside Park. The Royal Giants were the city's black baseball team.

town in 1898?—and said to his friends that he wouldn't be surprised if the automobile didn't replace the horse and buggy some day.

Theater was becoming big business by 1914. On Patton Avenue, where Government (College) Street split off, stood the Dreamland Theater which attempted to bring Edison Talking Pictures to town, but each time the film broke, which was often, the talking machine went right on talking to the crowd in the darkened theater. The Classic Theater stood diagonally across Patton from the Dreamland. An electric piano was in use there, accompanying silent movies with excellent music. Two doors away was a building with no top in which an open air theater played only on dry evenings in the summertime.

In 1915 the Asheville Tourists baseball team won its first pennant ever in the Class D North Carolina State League, under the guidance of Manager Jack Corbett by beating the Durham Bulls by five and a half games. The team played some games in Riverside Park and others in Oates Park in the triangle formed by Southside, McDowell, and Choctaw streets, and Thomas Wolfe often was the batboy. Dr. Joe Sevier was the official scorekeeper; it was he who later told the young Charlie Justice that he should never attempt to play football because of his fragile health—and Justice became the greatest-heralded All-American ever at the University of North Carolina.

Wealthy folks drove huge touring cars through a gate in left field and parked along the foul lines. The team: Ernie Burke or Al Bum played first, Rabbit Bradshaw second (tied teammate Jim Hickman for the league lead with 127 hits), Corbett shortstop, Earl Bitting third, Jim Hickman in left field (led the league with 95 runs and 14 home runs, and tied for the league lead with 127 hits), Doc Fenton in center, and Al McCoy (Wofford College coach) in right. Olin Perritt and Gary Fortune were pitchers, and Larry Woodall caught. The latter was an Asheville man just graduated by the University of North Carolina.

31

THE AGE OF FLIGHT

Two Ohio bicyclemakers, Wilbur and Orville Wright, changed the world on the cold, windy morning of December 17, 1903, by flying a heavier-than-air craft four different times on the coastal sands beside Kill Devil Hill, North Carolina.

Many in Asheville were not actually stunned by the news, because many figured the Wright brothers would accomplish powered flight sooner or later. They had been at the task for so long and had made such strides toward accomplishing their goal that it seemed to be only a matter of time. Others, however, were dumbfounded, repeating that old phrase, "If God had meant for man to fly He would have put wings on his back." Soon they came to the realization that God had also given man a brain and the knowledge of how to use it.

They said, though, that it would be a long time before anyone could fly into these high mountains, and, comparatively speaking, they were right.

The lazy, hazy days of summer were still a couple of months away when Lincoln Beachy, a daring barnstormer for Curtis Exhibition Company, came to Asheville on April 18, 1911, to make three exhibition flights sponsored by the Board of Trade, forerunner of the Asheville Area Chamber of Commerce. His aircraft was shipped in on a railroad flat car, hauled out to Baird Meadows[1] and put together there. He made all three of his scheduled flights and a bug-eyed throng of 2,000 watched. They had been cocked and primed for days with newspaper stories and posters tacked to telephone poles and were ready to make the occasion a gala one.

---

[1] Now covered by Beaver Lake.

Boys in knickers and knee high stockings, caps pulled firmly down on their foreheads, girls in pigtails and ribbons, women in long starched dresses, bustles, and bonnets, and men in suits, felt hats, and bow ties gathered to watch the exciting exhibition.

Aeroplane bodies had not been developed by 1911; therefore Beachy's craft consisted of two wings, one over the other, with small airfoils fore and aft to stabilize the machine, and the body of the plane was made up of two shafts on each side stretching front to rear. Beachy sat in a seat on the lower wing between the shafts.

Two stories in *The Asheville Daily Citizen* described the occasion so well that they are printed here in their entirety. The first was published in the morning paper the day of the scheduled flights, Tuesday, April 18, 1911:

AVIATION FLIGHTS
ARE THIS AFTERNOON

EVERYBODY WILL SEE WONDER-
FUL EXHIBITION

Lincoln Beachy Will This Afternoon
Demonstrate Wonders of Navi-
gating the Air.

THE AVIATION exhibition which will be given this afternoon from the Baird meadows will be one of the most thrilling sights which the people of Asheville have ever had the opportunity to witness. Lincoln Beachy, who will make the flights in a modern type of the Curtiss aeroplane, has won an enviable reputation for his daring in the air, and this afternoon the people of this city and the surrounding towns will be able to see the conquest of the air demonstrated by a man who is a master of the art. At the numbers of places at which Beachy has made flights he has given exhibitions fully worth witnessing, and the one here today will be no exception.

The weather bureau promises fair and warmer weather for today and if the winds are not too strong Beachy will be able to do all sorts of stunts up in the air. The site selected for the flights gives a sufficient amount of open space for him to work well, and also to accommodate the crowds which will be present. The Baird meadows are situated just beyond

Grace. A number of special cars will be operated by the Asheville Electric company over the lines of the Weaverville company direct to the grounds, the first cars to leave the square about two o'clock.

The first series of flights will be made about three thirty and after a short intermission of about an hour, a second series will be given. This is in order to allow all of the people an opportunity of witnessing the flights, those witnessing the first being expected to make way for the crowds for the second. The flights will consist of a series of high elevation flights, short curves, precipitous dives and swift dashes. Previous to the ascensions Mr. Beachy will give a lucid explanation of the workings of the air craft, showing how the machine is worked, and all of the particulars of the heavier than air machine.

Only those wearing "aviation tags" will be admitted to the enclosure of the grounds. The tags have been selling rapidly and by this afternoon everybody is expected to be wearing a tag. The price is only one dollar with special tags for the children at fifty cents. Everybody will naturally want to get as near the wonderful machine as possible, and to do so a tag is necessary. The sale will continue at the various stores in the city where they have been placed on sale up to two o'clock this afternoon, and on the grounds after that. A portion of the proceeds will go to the benefit of the children of Balfour orphanage, the sale of the tags having been partially taken in charge yesterday by the young ladies of the Young Women's Missionary society of the First Presbyterian Church. One thousand dollars is the amount which the aviator will get, the balance being distributed here.

If by any mischance the weather today should prove such as to make the flights impossible, they will be postponed until Wednesday, or if rendered impossible altogether the price paid for the admission tags will be refunded, the general sale having been in charge of the board of trade which is holding itself responsible for the funds.

On Wednesday, April 19, *The Citizen* described the thrilling event, the likes of which, indeed, had never been seen here before. Its headline read:

THOUSANDS THRILLED BY DARING
FLIGHTS OF BEACHY IN BIPLANE

Aviator Makes Series of Three Flights in Curtiss Machine Showing Perfect Conquest of Air by Man.

Thousands Gazed in Wonder

THE AVIATION exhibition given yesterday by Mr. Lincoln Beachy with a Curtis bi-plane was a great success and the afternoon of thrilling enjoyment was not marred by a single untoward incident. The weather during the first flight was very favorable, but grew squally before the last two ascensions. The three flights were witnessed by one of the largest crowds ever assembled in this section.

Although the first ascension was not made until four o'clock, a flowing stream of people began to make its way to Baird's meadow beyond Grace early in the afternoon in order to be on the grounds at the opening of the exhibition.

Before making the first flight one of the mechanicians gave a lucid and most interesting lecture on the machinery and the art of handling the machine. In his explanation of the bi-plane he first called attention to the eight-cylinder, sixty horsepower engine, which weighs 225 pounds and drives a seven and one-half foot propeller 1,200 revolutions per minute. The entire machine weighs 650 pounds and its dimensions are about 25 by 30 feet. The running gear of the machine is all in easy reach of the operator and wires connected to the steering wheel and the front wheel gear regulated the different motions of the rudders, while the tilting of the machine sidewise is regulated by the movement of the shoulders against levers that controlled the side rudders.

First Ascension

All was in readiness for the first ascension at four o'clock. The field was thronged with curious spectators who kept close to the machine to learn its every detail. Afar off on the hillsides were to be seen numbers of people who could not enjoy the privilege of examining the simplicity of this wonderful invention but who had a clear vision of the sensational flights.

As the machine, under perfect control of Mr. Beachy, gracefully glided upon the ground for several feet, then soared swiftly into the heavens, there were loud cheers from thousands of throats. The aviator turned his course across the mountain and passed over the field several hundred feet into the air. For about twelve minutes he circled high and low, covering an estimated distance of ten miles in his swift flight. Having satisfied the people that he had his machine under perfect control he safely landed within a few feet from where he made his ascension.

Again the curious crowd gathered around the aeroplane, but Mr. Beachy in his desire to avoid the rush quietly stole himself away. The second flight was fully as good as the first, but he remained in the air for only about four minutes. The third and last flight was just as interesting as the first and lasted for about six minutes. During the flights Mr. Beachy demonstrated his full control of the machine by giving both high and low flights, sharp curves and sudden dashes, once gliding along over the field about fifteen feet high, then ascending into the air at a height of about 1,000 feet or more and making a speed of about 60 miles an hour.

Wind Rises

After the first flight the winds began to rise gradually, and during the last two, a rising wind was noticeable. Mr. Beachy said it was squally at the elevations to which he rose, so much so that the last flights were much more difficult than the first.

Field glasses were much in evidence at times, when the machine was so far distant that the form of a man could hardly be recognized by the naked eye. Photographers were also much in evidence, and were making good use of their opportunities of taking snap shots of the machine in motion.

Frightened the Cows

An interesting incident during the first flight was the frantic running of a herd of cattle on a far-off hill as the roaring machine passed over them. Those having field glasses declared that the cattle plunged through a wire fence as if it had been built of paper.

What came near being a serious accident when the first ascension was made was the falling of a lady and child from a carriage as the frightened horse attempted to bolt. The lady fell on one side of the carriage while the child fell on the other. Neither was hurt, but barely they escaped being trampled upon by the frightened animals.

The attendance at the exhibition was estimated at about 2,000. Many people witnessed the flight from Asheville, as the machine was seen by many who remained in the city. People from the surrounding country and near-by towns attended the exhibition in large numbers.

Proving the dangers of early flight, the daring Mr. Beachy was killed in March, 1915, when his plane malfunctioned and crashed while he was flying over the Golden Gate Bridge in San Francisco.

It would be another eight years before Ashevilleans again saw an aeroplane flying above their city.

Beachy had found the air currents over Asheville so tricky that no one attempted to fly an airplane over the mountains and into Asheville until Henry Westall did in 1919. He was lucky, though, for another man would have beaten him to the accomplishment had it not been for an accident.

Lieutenant General K. B. Wolfe, then a young flying officer with the United States Army, decided in the summer of 1919 to fly from Americus, Georgia, to Asheville to visit friends here. However, engine trouble forced him to make an emergency landing in a cotton field near Augusta, Georgia.

Gen. Wolfe and a sergeant flying with him were badly shaken up when upon landing the aircraft flipped upside down. When they rested up, they took the train to Spartanburg and thence to Asheville.

So in June of 1919, Henry Westall, who later became operator of Beaver Lake Golf Course, made a talk about flying to the Rotary Club of Asheville. No other plane had reached the city since Lincoln Beachy flew around Baird Meadows in 1911. That afternoon the Rotarians took stock in an airplane venture that turned out to be historic. No one was allowed to subscribe to more than $100 worth of stock so no one would be drastically hurt if the venture failed. The sale of stock brought in $3,000, enough to do the job.

Westall took the money and rode the train to Toronto, Canada, where he bought a surplus training plane that had been used by the Canadian army. He got the plane for $2,000 and used the remainder to pay his expenses and buy spare parts for the plane.

He shipped the plane to Asheville by rail and assembled it. The craft was a World War Jenny with a powerful eight-cylinder OX5 engine.

Westall and other mechanics put the aircraft together at Baird Meadows and Westall, who had been trained to fly in the army, took the plane barnstorming to several places–to Morganton first, where he was paid $500 to put on a flying show for a soldiers' homecoming celebration. The following day he determined he would fly the airplane into Asheville.

However, he needed a better grade of fuel than that available, and he went to see Dr. McCampbell at the North Carolina State Insane Asylum who offered him some high-powered fuel that was used as a cleaning fluid in the hospital.

When Westall offered to pay, Dr. McCampbell laughed. "There won't be any charge. Just fly around the hospital a time or two so some of my patients can see that there are a lot of people running loose who are nuttier than they are."

In an hour's time, Westall brought the Jenny up over the mountains that had required years of back-breaking work and often death from those who pushed the railroad over the ridge. Reaching Asheville, he gave downtown a good buzzing–there were no laws then covering flight altitude over the city. Flying on to Baird Bottoms, he put the Jenny down slick as a whistle.

For a while, beginning June 19, Westall took passengers aloft, soared them around Asheville and back to Baird. His first passenger was his mechanic, Henry Crowell, and the second was Scott Dillingham, who was thrilled with flying. He took up another few passengers for $5 each, and then quit before someone got hurt.

He flew the Jenny to Winston-Salem and Greensboro in midsummer of 1919 for exhibitions, and on to Pope Field, which later became Pope Air Force Base at Fort Bragg. In September he flew out of town again, crossing the Smokies to Knoxville to take part in the Southeastern Appalachian exposition. For three weeks he based himself there, flying out of Knoxville to Rome, Georgia, and on to Dalton where he encountered such bad weather he stored the plane there until the following spring, and came home on the train.

When he went back the next year to fly the plane to Asheville, he flew by way of Milledgeville, Athens, Anderson, and Greenville, and from Greenville, with one cylinder gone bad, he flew over Saluda Mountain and soared into Asheville. His intention was to buzz the town, but hitting only on seven cylinders, he decided against it.

When he arrived over Baird Meadow, there were so many cows grazing on the field that he had to fly in circles for two hours until his mother rounded up enough boys to drive the cattle off the field.

Finally on the ground, Westall got out of the plane and kissed its wing. That was the last time he flew an airplane, explaining that it was too expensive, too dangerous, and that he had had enough of it.

Scott Dillingham purchased a plane of his own, and his father leveled the tops of a couple of hills on his farm in Haw Creek to make Asheville's second airfield. Today Dillingham Road runs along the flat that was once that airport. When Dillingham was flying there, people came to watch, especially on Sunday afternoon when traffic would be backed up for a half-mile toward town.

32

WET SUNDAY

Toward the middle of July, 1916, a hurricane swept up the Gulf of Mexico and its far-flung umbrella of rain saturated the Blue Ridge Mountains. Hard on its heels came a second hurricane, this one whirling across Cape Hatteras, and it, too, dumped torrential rain upon the mountains until the land could absorb no more.

With no more warning than heavy rains, at four a.m. on Sunday, July 16, 1916, the Swannanoa River, normally a small, tranquil stream of excessive beauty, fed by cloudbursts in the hills, leaped its banks and smashed into Biltmore with such brute force that it overflowed the village in a matter of minutes and drove people from their homes into the hills. Within the village the river was a mile wide and rising.

As if the flooding of the Swannanoa were not enough, later in the morning the dams holding Kanuga and Osceola lakes in Henderson County burst, sending a lethal wall of water down Mud Creek into the French Broad River, and when it reached Asheville it struck the city a second hammer blow.

The broader French Broad River had contained the floodwaters of the Swannanoa fairly well until that wall of water came from Henderson County, and it was more than the city's riverfront could stand. Lumber yards, factories, great warehouses, oil storage tanks, freight yards, bridges and homes gave way. Timbers cracked like rifle shots, and the air was filled with a dull roaring hum. Floodwaters obliterated Asheville's favorite amusement center, Riverside Park, wiping it from the face of the earth.

Water rose so rapidly in Asheville that automobiles and street cars were abandoned and their occupants fled.

Devastating flood waters from 1916 were a mile wide in some places.

A huge section of Weaver Dam at Craggy, which fed Asheville's electricity, broke loose and was swept away, and the city was plunged into darkness. *The Citizen*, striving to inform the public of what great damage had been done, was published on small presses pulled by gasoline engines at Hackney & Moale Printing Company on North Lexington Avenue.

The river moved deceptively slow in the backwaters, but in the main channel it swept along like a runaway express, laying waste to all before it. An hour after it hit Biltmore, the Swannanoa was fifteen feet deep in the center of the village.

Probably no one thought of it at that moment, with so much else to occupy them, but the river would have obliterated downtown Asheville had the town been located where many wanted it to be in 1792, near Gum Spring. That saloonkeeper who dispensed free whiskey to the committee locating the town, had acted providentially.

Telegraph and telephone lines running in all directions from Asheville were down and the city was isolated from the outside world as much as it had been before the railroads came.

Railroad rails were twisted like pretzels, roadbeds and tracks washed away, grades and fills destroyed, and spare crossties washed down the river. Only the Murphy line of the Southern Railway was operable. Its tracks west of the Asheville Junction, two miles west of town, were untouched, and trains from Murphy brought in supplies for the counties that were so hard hit.

While the flood claimed six lives in Asheville, it also spawned feats of raw courage. Fred Gash and Everett Frady of the Asheville Fire Department, Andrew Line, a boilermaker, and plain clothes policeman Fred Jones, who had distinguished himself ten years earlier by tracking the murderer Will Harris and driving him into the posses that killed him, made many trips across the Biltmore floodwaters in a boat and rescued forty people marooned in the Hans Rees Sons Tannery. Another man who was never identified stripped off his clothing and swam into the current to rescue a man trapped on the roof of a floating house. Dozens of men manned other boats and rowed marooned persons to safety.

At the Glen Rock Hotel across the street from the main depot on Depot Street, Lonnie Trexler, a white man, and Luther Frazer, a black man, lost their lives while trying to row a boat laden with food to the hotel to feed guests trapped inside.

Captain J. C. Lipe, one of the first men hired by George Vanderbilt in construction of the Biltmore House twenty-five years earlier, and his daughter Nellie, along with two nurses from Biltmore Hospital, Charlotte Walker and Mabel Foister, and Charlotte Walker's fifteen-year-old sister, Marian, had made a dash for the hills when the floodwaters struck. Seeing they had no chance of making it to safety, they had climbed a tree, upon which the waters rose higher and higher during the hours they were trapped there.

One by one, Charlotte Walker, Mabel Foister, and Marian Walker were swept to their deaths. After eight hours, only Captain Lipe and Nellie remained in the tree. The captain felt his strength weakening, and taking his coat he lashed Nellie to the highest branch he could reach, and then he disappeared into the floodwaters. Nellie was rescued by boat later in the afternoon. As long as that tree stood, it was known as the "tree of death."

The French Broad crested at twenty-one feet above its standard level, and today those who wish to see how high the water was can see a flood mark on the corner of the RiverLink building on Lyman Street. A tree that had been marked at the height of the 1876 flood, the city's previous worst flood, showed the 1916 watermark to be six feet, eleven inches above the '76 mark.

Sixty Asheville homes were washed away, four hundred persons were homeless, six people dead, and twenty-five industrial plants totally or partially destroyed.

There were many acts of extreme courage that day that held the loss of life to six persons. Without those men who acted on the spur of the moment with disregard for their own safety, many others would have died in the flood.

The six people reported dead in Asheville were the *known* dead. Undoubtedly there were others across the length and breadth of the flood damaged area. The twenty-nine all told reported were those known to be dead.

The Asheville Citizen, on Monday, July 17, the day after the flood, tried to sum up the horror:

THE UNKNOWN dead will long remain a secret of that angry and turgid flood of foaming fury swirling a mile wide .... Men, women and children were seen on wreckage and buildings sweeping down the river by thousands of spectators helpless to aid.

Hundreds of families are today without homes.... All the reserve supplies of a great citry are stored in the midst of the waste of waters which has turned the busiest section of Asheville into a scene of desolation and havoc without a parallel in the history of this part of the state.

Hospitals, the sick, and the babies of the city will today begin to feel the horrors of the situation. There will be no ice, there will be a shortage of farm products. The supply of gasoline is nearly exhausted . . . The gas plant is ruined absolutely.

Last night, Asheville was a city of the dead. The floods from the heavens ceased to descend, but the city was a city of utter and complete darkness ....

Everywhere is a widespread waste of foaming waters, dotted here and there with floating homes. At one point above Biltmore a house was carried almost whole out into the river with two men clinging to the roof. The men were seen to crash through the shingles into the Swannanoa. An unknown man imprisoned by accident in Potts furniture store at the end of Smith's Bridge is reported to have gone insane before rescuers could reach him ... he was lost ... and a boy's body was discovered in the cellar.

Asheville was not the only town devastated by the flood. In Marshall, downriver a few miles, fifty-eight buildings were destroyed in the town that was wedged tightly between a mountain and the river, and two people lost their lives.

Rivers erupting from the mountains, some flowing into the Piedmont of North Carolina, wreaked so much damage that it could never be estimated.

Others died later of flood related injuries and illnesses, including Captain W. T. Weaver, who had constructed Weaver Dam across the French Broad in 1904. He had originally built a dam on the Ivy River in Madison County, and then built the dam at Craggy. Weaver died at fifty-eight on November 16, 1916, of complications of illness suffered trying to salvage his electric works during the flood.

The flood almost destroyed the railroad, and it was hardest hit on Saluda Mountain, where practically all of it was washed away. Crews started from the top of the mountain and the bottom, repairing damage.

It was August 3, eighteen days after the flood, before the first passenger train reached Asheville across the repaired lines.

The city made do with what it had left and with what was hauled in on the Murphy Branch of the railroad.

33

THE WAR TO END ALL WARS

I t had been nineteen years since Asheville sent troops off to war—
if you didn't count Asheville Troop B of cavalry that helped chase
the radical Pancho Villa in the late Mexican Border War. And,
of course, there were the Rockwell brothers, Paul and Kiffin, who had
volunteered on the third of August, 1914, to fight for France against
the Hun—the first Americans to enlist in the service of France. They
had left Asheville two days after war broke out in faraway Europe on
August 1, 1914, and Kiffin would never return.

Paul came back after being wounded in the Foreign Legion
trenches and spending the remainder of the war as a war correspondent. Kiffin, the first member of the elite Lafayette Escadrille to shoot
down an enemy plane, was himself shot out of the sky on September
23, 1916, hit in the chest by an illegal explosive shell fired from an
enemy aircraft. He spun down to crash behind French lines. The
Escadrille was a small collection of American flyers who fought their
way to glory under French leadership, and the commander was later
to say there was none greater than Kiffin Rockwell, who had shot
down more than ten enemy aircraft, although he did not receive
credit for all of them, some being unobserved from the ground or by
fellow flyers.

After their return from Mexico, the city's cavalry troopers
showed off their horsemanship on the Biltmore Green, doing daring
Cossack rides. The individual winner was Clarence (Cupie) Mace,
who received a silver cup from Mrs. George W. Vanderbilt, radiant
in a broadbrimmed hat and seated in her long, white Packard.

However, on Friday, April 6, 1917, the United States declared
war on Germany, pitching the entire country into a state of rapid

preparation for war. On that same day, Buncombe County Commissioners voted to purchase and have erected a flagpole on the courthouse in Asheville, from which the Stars and Stripes flew for the remainder of the war and beyond.

Rather than gearing up slowly, Asheville got in the spirit of war four days after the declaration with a rally in City Auditorium attended by 7,500 citizens, 4,000 of whom wedged themselves into the building, and 3,500 who stood outside while bands played and speakers moved from one crowd to the other, whipping men into battle frenzy. At the end of this meeting Asheville's public opinion had been crystalized behind a wave of genuine patriotism in preparation for an all-out effort.

Not only did Asheville prepare to send its young men to war, it also made extensive plans for working on the home front for the benefit of those who went to France to spill their blood in the name of freedom.

Attention focused quickly on Asheville's already organized military units, the cavalry troop, and infantry companies F and K of the North Carolina National Guard. There was also within the city a hospital unit and half a military band. Nearby Canton furnished the other half.

Immediately, living conditions began to change. The price of barbed wire, sorely needed for the war, skyrocketed, and so did other prices, even that of soda crackers. Anticipating immediate shortages of wheat, the city's bakers increased the price of a loaf of bread from five to six cents, making front-page news in Asheville newspapers.

Asheville's pioneer ham radio operators boxed up their spark gaps and coils and condensers and hauled down their antennas on April 14, making sure no one would reveal anything he shouldn't on the huge developing net of airwaves.

Edith Vanderbilt offered the sprawling Biltmore Estate to the government as a site for an army training camp.

The problem of growing food was quickly addressed and by July there were three times the usual number of home gardens growing in the city. Buncombe County announced on August 2 that 40,000 tin cans would be bought and sold to users at cost for canning food for the winter.

That spring, Judge J. Frazier Glenn of the Asheville city police court secured the use of vacant lots in the city and sentenced lawbreakers to spend hours farming potatoes and turnips, beets and onions where none had grown before.

On May 4, the government announced it was seeking a place in the mountains to house 2,700 German sailors. Lake Toxaway, the Davidson River area of Pisgah Forest, Kanuga Lake in Henderson County, all were considered and discarded, and on May 26 the camp was finally located in the Mountain Park Hotel in Hot Springs.

Congress passed a selective service act on May 23 and registration date of all males between the ages of twenty-one and thirty-one was scheduled June 5. A Buncombe County draft board was set up consisting of Buncombe County Sheriff E. M. Mitchell, city health officer Dr. D. E. Sevier, and clerk of superior court John H. Cathey. A total of 6,376 registered. Those eighteen through twenty-one and thirty-two through forty-five registered in September.

Mme. Rudricel, a French woman living in Asheville, started a class in conversational French at the YMCA in July, teaching young men how to ask in French for a drink of vin rouge or a date with a pretty mademoiselle, and, of course, other things.

On August 31 preparations became reality when in early morning with a soft rain falling, Asheville's Cavalry Troop B and companies F and K marched off to war. Company K, with Captain C. I. Bard in the lead, marched in cadence down Southside Avenue, and Company F, led by Captain Ed Jones, swung down French Broad Avenue and Bartlett Street to the train station where a thousand relatives and friends waited to see them off. In September, draftees began leaving in groups of up to 150.

Asheville was then heavily invested in the World War.

As summer turned to golden autumn and finally to winter, Asheville suffered two great blows.

The winter of 1917-18 was the coldest in memory of the city's oldest inhabitants. Through the United States blizzard after blizzard struck with fury. Fuel ran low. Coal was rationed. Early in 1918 the city found itself with only one carload of coal on hand. After borrowing twenty tons more from Grove Park Inn, the coal was placed in the city coal yard on Market Street and carefully rationed in 250-pound bags. Wood supplies also ran low and citizens took to the woods with axe and saw.

Coal dealers made no deliveries. Some citizens hefted their coal rations onto street cars and transported them home. For a fifteen-cent fee boys hauled coal to homes on snow sleds. They had no difficulty negotiating the city's icy streets, and when on a downgrade they sat upon the coal sack and rode to the bottom of the hill.

A five-day shutdown of all non-essential plants and businesses conserved fuel and gave coal mines and railroads a chance to catch up. Theaters and offices closed. Gradually, the crisis eased.

Late in November of 1917, Asheville felt the advancement of another enemy, a grim and silent shadow of things to come. Asheville men at Camp Sevier had been placed in quarantine for influenza. This was just a whisper of the silent scourge that would sweep the country in the winter months ahead, claiming lives at a greater rate than German arms.

The flu spread. It was a malignant, fast-spreading, virulent type called the Spanish influenza that left pneumonia in its wake. It struck down even the strongest.

Soup kitchens organized, food for the sick was prepared at central places and distributed, volunteer workers went door to door, braving the weather and the disease to bring aid to the suffering. Silently, without fanfare they came and went, day and night, shuffling along in rain and snow, bringing comfort that meant life itself to hundreds.

Schools were closed and schoolhouses turned into emergency stations filled with cots. Doctors and nurses worked to the point of exhaustion, and many fell ill themselves. Some died. Workers of today were patients of tomorrow, and through it all there was a warm glow of compassion and cohesiveness in the community as neighbors helped neighbors and then helped strangers who were unable to help themselves.

The city took all precautions it could. Churches were closed except for funerals, and attendance at those was limited.

Heavy winter snows during January and February hid the ground for six weeks and slowly the epidemic of influenza subsided.

Draftees were placed in the various arms of military service. Asheville's Troop B of cavalry became Company B of the 115th machine gun battalion. Soldiers of companies F and K of Asheville were distributed among the 119th and 120th infantry regiments. All were placed within the 30th Division, the Old Hickory Division, made up of North and South Carolina and Tennessee sharpshooters.

The 30th Division and the 27th Division, made up of New Yorkers, fought side by side through several campaigns and then came up to the impregnable Hindenburg Line and were assigned a 20,000-yard sector in the trenches.

Asked by a correspondent about fighting alongside a Yankee division, a grizzled veteran from Tennessee answered, "North and

South? Hell, there ain't none over here. It's all America now. No Yanks, no Johnny Rebs. All Americans."

Side by side these divisions hacked and hewed through the Hindenburg Line, each supporting the other. Men from North and South, of different temperament, of opposing mold, fought valiantly against the strongest embattlement the Germans had built.

From September 29 to October 30, 1918, the 30th captured ninety-eight German officers, 3,750 men, and in that same period lost three officers and twenty-four men as prisoners, forty-four officers and 1,011 men killed, and 113 officers and 4,823 men wounded or gassed. Total casualties of the 30th Division: 160 officers and 5,858 men. This was the toughest fighting of the war.

Old Hickory distinguished itself in its first combat. Flanked by the 27th New York on the right and the 14th British on the left, the southerners on August 31 and September 1 went over the top and assaulted the Hun hammer and tongs. All objectives were bagged: Lock No. 8, the Lankhof farm, and the city of Voormezeele. The division advanced the American thrust 1,500 yards and halted facing the Hindenburg Line. The 30th was pulled back in reserve to catch its breath from the 7th till the 17th, and then moved back on line for the big push against the line.

Up to then, the Hindenburg Line had repulsed all efforts to break through by the allied armies. The Germans thought it was impregnable. At the point where the 30th was placed, the line curved in front of the Tunnel St. Quentin and consisted of three main trench systems protected by vast fields of barbed wire entanglements skillfully placed. The heavy wire suffered little damage from heavy bombardments of artillery.

The domination of the line's trench system and its thick, concrete machine-gun emplacements enabled the Germans to bring devastating fire all along its front.

A large number of dugouts had been carved from the earth behind the line, linked with the trenches by tunnels. The dugouts were lined with mining timbers, with wooden steps leading down to an underground depth of thirty feet where small rooms were located, each capable of holding four to six soldiers. Many of the dugouts were lighted by electricity.

A main tunnel, through which a canal ran, was large enough to shelter a division of troops. The canal contained a number of barges for rapid transportation of troops.

A smaller tunnel led from this huge tunnel through the ground to a farmhouse in the rear, in which the German's maintained area headquarters.

This entire complex, hidden from the eyes of the enemy forces, formed a subterranean method of communication, reinforcing, and supplying troops in battle.

Finally, the order came down that the 30th had been waiting for. It was to attack the Hindenburg Line along a 3,000-yard front at 5:50 a.m. on September 29. The attack would be made in three waves, one following the other in a specified length of time. The 30th would be supported by the 27th on one side and the 46th British on the other, with an Australian regiment in reserve behind the 30th.

Early on September 9, the men of the 30th, including many of those who had marched off from Asheville, stood in their forward trench, nervous, fidgety, checking and rechecking their weapons and ammo, steel helmets in place, waiting the hour of 5:50.

Officers sat silently by, looking at their watches. Overhead, barrage after barrage of high explosive shells whistled down to blast the barbed wire and the Hindenburg trenches.

At 5:50 on the dot, the barrage lifted, and the 30th stormed over the top and into no-man's land, charging the enemy. Straight into the jaws of death they ran, a hurricane of machine gun bullets, deluges of light artillery shells, and accurate riflefire from the German trenches. Men fell in groups, but there was no faltering. Wave followed wave, grim-faced men intent on their target.

The first wave of the 30th went down in heaps. The second wave paid a heavy price, but the third wave leaped into the breach when a gap opened in the wave in front. All along the line of the three attacking divisions casualties were the heaviest of the war, but still the Americans and British came. They blew up the barbed wire posts with grenades and hand torpedoes and rushed through, concentrating on knocking out the machine-gun nests—and then they were in the Hindenburg trenches, fighting hand to hand with bayonets and small arms They fought tooth and nail, no quarter given, and suddenly the resistance broke and the remaining Germans swarmed into the tunnels, running to safety.

Up and down the trenches rang a clear, bonechilling Rebel yell, and then the 30th poured into the tunnels after the foe.

By the end of the first day, the 30th had captured the entire 3,000-yard stretch of trenches and tunnels and had emerged on the other side. From there they fanned out, taking the cities of Bellecourt, Nauroy, Riqueval, Varriers, Betrecourt, Guillaine, Ferme, and Ferme de Diqueval. They advanced 4,200 yards, smashing two enemy divisions, taking forty-seven officers and 1,434 men prisoners.

The 30th was relieved and regrouped to catch its breath, and then was quickly cast back into the fray. On October 8, 9, 10, and 11, the 30th attacked each day, and at the end of the 11th had pierced enemy territory by 17,500 yards, a full ten miles beyond what was left of the Hindenburg Line.

The advance continued for a month until the Armistice was signed at the 11th hour of the 11th day of the 11th month of 1918.

In its last advance, the 30th moved so fast it did not have time to gather up discarded booty from the enemy retreat. Best estimates by salvage troops of the Fourth British Army was that the 30th had caused the retreating Germans to abandon seventy-two field pieces, twenty-six trench mortars, 426 machine guns, and 1,792 rifles.

Old Hickory had run the Hun ragged.

Charles T. Smith, Jr. of Columbia, S. C., a first lieutenant with a machine gun squad of the 30th, wrote this poem about the breaking of the Hindenburg Line:

"Forward" the orders, and forward they went—
    That day the Hindenburg line was rent;
Streamings of light against the gray dawn
    Heralded this day to history born.
Then a shower of lead, an inferno of shell,
    And the boys of Old Hickory waded through hell.
"Forward" the orders, and forward they pressed
    To fight or to die for our Land of the West!
Crossing barbed wires and trenches of blood,
    Crossing through guns, and stenches and mud;
Then a sputter of fire, and the foe was met:
    Did the boys of Old Hickory falter a step?

"Forward" with bayonets, and man to man
    In death's last grapple, some hand to hand,
The point of a bayonet, the butt of a gun,
    A hand grenade, then a missing Hun.
Yea, the crimson mixed with sweat that day,
    And the foe still fought like brutes at bay.

"Halt" were the orders—a pause in the track!
    No heaven nor hell could have held them back.
Smoking the batteries blazed again,

Comrades fell in the crimson stain
And swore by the blood of their sacrifice
The Germans should pay the bitter price.

Why orders to men of such blood as that?
Inborn of a spirit of daring intact;
Wavering the Hindenburg line gave way;
The Prussian was thrown from his mighty sway.
Then a heritage—true as our fathers tell—
The battlefield rang with the Rebel Yell.

Your task is well done, your glory secure,
You did what for years no others could do.
Singing your fame in story and song,
Your homeland will ring all the ages along:
The laurel crown is your well-earned due,
Ye boys of Old Hickory, here's homage to you!

In the immediate aftermath of the war, northern historians recorded that the 27th New York had broken the Hindenburg Line, but General John J. Pershing, commander in chief of the American Expeditionary Forces, wrote a letter of commendation to Major General Edward M. Lewis, commander of the 30th Division, which settled the issue. It read:

France, Feb. 19, 1919
MAJOR General Edward M. Lewis, commander, 30th Division, A. E. F.
My dear General Lewis: It gives me much pleasure to extend to you and the officers and men of the Thirtieth division my sincere compliments upon their appearance and inspection on the 21st of January southwest of Toille, which was excellent and is just what would be expected in a command with such a splendid fighting record.
After its preliminary training the division entered the line July 16, where it remained almost continuously until the end of October. In that time it was in actual battle from the 30th of August and took part in the Ypres-Lys and Somme offensives. On September 29, the division broke through both the Hindenburg and the Le Catelet-Nauroy lines, capturing Bellicourt and Nauroy, an operation on which all

subsequent action of the Fourth British army depended. From October 1 to October 20, the division advanced twenty-three kilometers in a continued series of attacks, capturing 2,350 of the enemy. Brancourt, Premont, Busigny, and St. Bernin, St. Souplet and Escaufort, La Hale, Mineresse and Vaux Andigny are names which will live in the memories of those who fought in the Thirtieth division. But its especial glory will always be the honor you won by breaking the Hindenburg line on September 29. Such a record is one of which we are all proud. . . .

Very sincerely yours,

John J. Pershing

The question of who broke the Hindenburg Line was answered once and for all.

Back home in Asheville, the armistice was greeted with a great din, the ringing of the firebell in the tower of City Hall, whistles, singing and shouting all over town, and dancing in the streets.

Word of the armistice came in a flash by telegraph into *The Citizen's* office on Government Street at a few minutes before three a.m. and the news staff necessary to get out an Extra! was called from their homes.

D. Hiden Ramsey, then commissioner of Public Safety, awakened from a sound sleep, ordered the ringing of the fire bell. Everyone knew what the ringing meant, and in an incredibly short time Asheville's streets were filled with revelers of all ages and classes. Bonfires blazed on Pack Square, Haywood Street, and the lower part of Patton Avenue. Street dancing and singing filled the city.

Later that day, in an amusing way, at least one German continued to resist. At three o'clock in the afternoon of November 11, a dummy figure of Kaiser Wilhelm Hohenzollern was to be hanged in effigy on Pack Square. The scaffold was erected and a huge crowd gathered to watch, but hanging the Kaiser wasn't so easy. The rope broke. Three times! Finally, the hangers gave up, doused the old fellow with oil, and burned him.

Not all was riot and carnival, however, In many Asheville homes where sleep had been ended for the night, mothers, sisters, and wives knelt in earnest prayer to thank Almighty God that the curse of war had once again been removed from the earth.

The War-to-end-all-Wars was finished.

In fifty-six Buncombe County homes there was little to cheer about. Their boys lay in Flanders Field and other faroff places, never to return.

Excavating Battery Park Hill in 1924 after construction of the second Battery Park Hotel. The Grove Arcade building went up on this site.

34

CITY SHOWPIECE

Of all the wealthy, business-minded men who came to Asheville in its formative days to invest money and help the city grow, not any was more productive than Dr. E. W. Grove, the St. Louis patent medicine king. He probably changed the face of Asheville more than anyone else, even if he did it for profit more than philanthropy.

It was he who built the Grove Park Inn on the side of Sunset Mountain overlooking the city; it was he who developed the Grove Park residential section, in which William Jennings Bryan made his home when he moved to Asheville; it was he who bought and razed the old Battery Park Hotel and replaced it with the new Battery Park and the George Vanderbilt hotels; and it was he who built a part of the Grove Arcade, and in doing so moved Battery Park Hill and used the dirt and stone to fill in a huge ravine and create Coxe Avenue. That he built only a part of the Grove Arcade will be made clearer.

The one thing that set wealthy men like Grove, Vanderbilt, and Coxe apart from ordinary men was the vision and desire to build something beautiful, profitable, useable, and monumental and the wealth to do it without really denting the bank account. They envisioned a business or an improvement to a business, made it, and profited by it. Fortunately, many of their visionary projects added immensely to Asheville and to the city's growth. The thing that set George W. Pack on another plane was that his efforts to improve Asheville were solely for the benefit of the people.

Dr. Grove made a huge fortune in pharmaceuticals, beginning in Tennessee, then moving his headquarters to St. Louis, Missouri.

Realizing the climate and the beauty of both the mountains and the city made the place a mecca for living, Grove thought business opportunities in Asheville would be tremendous.

A summer resident at first, Grove, who developed Bromo Quinine into an internationally popular tonic and reaped a fortune, finally moved here for his wife's health, and, businessman that he was, immediately went to work. He first opened a chemical plant on South Main Street, holding to the work that had made him wealthy, and then, sensing a real estate boom in Asheville's immediate future, he began to buy developmental property.

He worked in the northern part of the city, building hotels, resorts, and neighborhoods between the downtown area and Beaver Lake. It was said that Grove and Vanderbilt divided the city, Grove's part being north and Vanderbilt's south, and that each stayed out of the other's territory. That, however, like many other stories of developing Asheville, was probably apocraphal. More likely each simply stayed out of the other's way.

Asheville residents thought it miraculous that Grove Park Inn was built in eleven months and twenty-seven days, but enough workmen were put on the project to do the job in good time. More than 400 men were employed. All stone used in the hotel was hauled off Sunset Mountain on stoneboats and put in place by expert masons, who fashioned the window-filled walls and huge lobby fireplaces with excellent craftsmanship.

The inn's walls are four and a half feet thick, backed with granite and cement. Work crews were instructed not to let a piece of stone be visible unless it showed the time-worn face of nature.

Working with those great boulders was a mean job. Some weighed as much as five tons, and all were put in place with lichen and moss on them, just as they were found on the mountain.

The great hall, which serves the hotel as lobby, measures 120 by 80 feet and can easily accommodate a thousand persons. Fireplaces at each end of the lobby burn twelve-foot logs, giving a cheery atmosphere on cold days and evenings.

Building the roofs of the inn was a massive job. All were based with five inches of concrete reinforced with forty-five tons of steel rods. On that surface was then laid five layers of asphalt interposed between three layers of asbestos felt. Finally, fifteen carloads of fireproof tile were applied with 3,000 pounds of coppered steel nails and twenty tons of fireproof roof cement.

That work crews answered each challenge the job put before

them was evident in the short time required to build the place.

The hotel has been the city's showpiece since its completion in July 1913. Perched on the side of the mountain, it commands an excellent view of the city, and gives the city a good view of itself.

Many prominent people stayed in Grove Park Inn at Grove's invitation. That's where the Firestones and Fords and Edisons and several presidents slept. At Grove's beckon, Firestone, Ford, and Edison spent most of a summer there.

To deliver the official opening address, Grove called upon William Jennings Bryan, then a resident of Grove Park, and Bryan, as usual, responded admirably.

Needing someone to oversee construction and also oversee the hotel while he performed other tasks, Grove brought in his son-in-law, Fred L. Seely, Sr., and Seely, who was adept at when and where to advertise, how to treat elite customers, and the general operation of the hotel, made it a hit from the start.

Thus, the huge red-roofed, gray-stone building on the side of the mountain became a monument to those two, Grove and Seely.

A stone cottage on the Inn's grounds became the second White House for President Woodrow Wilson.

Grove turned the rolling hillsides at the foot of Sunset Mountain into a sparkling community.

Finally, Grove turned his attention to building his downtown showpiece—the Grove Arcade. The Battery Park Hotel, perched atop the highest hill in town, was still a commanding structure, but the man for whom it was a monument, Col. Frank Coxe, had been dead for ten years when the Grove Park opened, and now Dr. Grove set out to buy it.

When the purchase was completed in 1921, Grove announced his plans to tear down the old hotel, level the hill, and build a new Battery Park Hotel and the Grove Arcade where the old Battery Park had stood. Asheville stood agog at such a downtown development and realized what a boon it would be to the city.

The first job was to demolish the hotel, and this was half-completed when one night in 1922 a watchman's shanty caught fire and destroyed the remainder of the hotel.

Grove's workers employed a steam shovel and mule-drawn scrapes to level the hill, cutting seventy-five feet off its top. The new Battery Park, an extremely serviceable hotel with an exterior that added immensely to asthetics in the city, was completed and opened in 1924. Its seventh floor was at about the height of the leveled hill. The George Vanderbilt Hotel, a stone's throw away on Haywood Street beside the City Auditorium, was finished that same year. Both hotels were beautifully decorated and both were convention centers that were also intended to host social events and provide the average tourist with affordable rooms.

Now it was time for Grove to turn his attention to his last venture, the Grove Arcade, which would cover a city block directly in front of the Battery Park Hotel.

The arcade was to be one of the most unusual buildings in America. It would be the forerunner of the huge shopping malls that fill American cities today. He had planned it carefully and Asheville was both surprised and thrilled at the extent of the plan and the value it would be to the city.

Grove intended to build a tourist center featuring a roof garden with band shell, a restaurant, and an assembly room that could be developed into a community center. Beneath that would be an arcade filled with shops housed under one roof, and he intended to have his architect, Charles N. Parker, design it as the most magnificent building in Asheville. On top of the arcade would be a fourteen-story tower housing office buildings, equal in size to the new Jackson Building on Pack Square.

When the final plans were made and construction began, no one doubted that Grove was a man ahead of his time. Nothing like this had been heard of before. Four large, arched entrances, one on each of its four sides, would keep people from having to walk around any portion of the arcade to gain entry. On the north side, facing the Battery Park Hotel across the street, would be two large gryphons heralding entry to a supernatural realm. Grotesque heads, in vogue at that time, would decorate an ornamental band around the building, and large windows would give the public viewing access to goods in the arcade's shops.

Inside the arcade would be spiral staircases, sloped floors, oak shopfronts, more shop windows, and mezzanines.

Work on the $1.5 million arcade began in 1927, and while construction was in progress, Grove moved into the Battery Park Hotel where he could be handy to watch his project progress.

Grove Park Inn was Grove's most magnificent monument, but his plans for developing downtown Asheville were his most ambitious. It was a pity that he died before the arcade was completed. His death came in 1927 before the tower had been built. Work was suspended for a year, and the project was sold to Walter P. Taylor and associates who in 1928 completed the job. The tower was never constructed, so the arcade rests today on perhaps the strongest foundation of any building in town, strong enough to hold up a fourteen-floor building.

What Grove did for Asheville in the years he spent here made the city more beautiful and attractive than it had ever been, which undoubtedly attracted other builders.

In the 1920s Asheville experienced a boom unlike anything it had ever known. The Roaring Twenties were exactly that. So great was the land rush of new citizens that real estate offices on Patton Avenue hired full orchestras to play at the front of their building to attract customers.

Sixty-five new buildings went up in the 1920s and the business district pushed down Patton Avenue and up Haywood Street.

Paul Roebling, brother of John A. Roebling, who moved away from Asheville after prohibition, constructed the Haywood Building on Haywood Street in 1917 and everyone called it "Roebling's Folly," wondering why he built such a large building so far from the center of town. But Roebling was a far-sighted man, for within six years construction was booming all around his building.

Florida experienced a real estate bust in 1923 that drove hoards of investors out of state, and a fair share of them moved their operations to Asheville.

In 1923 Grove built the Bon Marche building on the northwest corner of Haywood Street and Battery Park Avenue, placing it adjacent to Roebling's Folly.

L. B. Jackson, a young man with big ideas, tore down W. O. Wolfe's old marble shop on Pack Square in 1924 and built the city's first "skyscraper," a neo-Gothic tower he named the Jackson Building. To attract attention to Asheville he put a powerful searchlight on the roof of the Jackson Building, and at night when the light swept the sky in circles, it could be seen as far as thirty miles away in Haywood County on the west and in other counties in other directions.

Built of brick and terra cotta around a strong steel frame, the building rose thirteen stories on a twenty-seven by sixty-foot lot.

In Gothic expression, the Jackson Building went further than office towers in other cities. It was indeed a new idea in construction, one that Asheville was proud of. Huge windows in the Jackson Building overlooked various parts of town and gave the offices a flavor those who rented them enjoyed.

Asheville Tourists pose at brand-new McCormick Field in 1924.

A year after the Jackson Building went up, the Westall Building, several floors shorter, was built beside it, and the two buildings shared a common elevator. Still do.

The twenty-seven-year-old Jackson was a promoter all over the South. He erected signs reading simply "See L. B." and few had trouble learning who or where L. B. was. Jackson also took over management of the Grove Arcade building and made it a profitable shopping and professional center.

McCormick Field, the city's baseball park, opened in April of 1924 with the Detroit Tigers playing the Asheville team. Detroit lost, 18 to 14, with Ty Cobb managing and playing in the outfield.

With so much building going on, architects looked for any new method and found one called art deco in 1925 at the Exposition of Decorative Arts in Paris. Asheville architects adopted it and constructed several new buildings using this motif, which employed various colored tiles and the use of plastic.

One of the first structures with art deco detailing was the First Baptist Church, designed by Douglas D. Ellington in 1925 at the corner of Oak and Woodfin streets. The church has a copper lantern on top of the dome and various colors in the tile roof. Orange bricks, terra cotta molding, and pink marble were combined on the walls.

The Kresge building, constructed at the corner of Patton Avenue and Lexington in 1926-27, where the Grand Opera House once stood, was among the first art deco structures. Its beauty, though somewhat faded, remains today.

An exceptional year was 1926. The Flat Iron Building, patterned after the Flat Iron Building in New York City, went up that year on Battery Park Avenue. The city's first radio station, WWNC, was housed in the pent house. One of Asheville's quaint streets—Wall Street—stretched along the south side of the Flat Iron Building. The street was named for a high rock wall built before the turn of the century to retain a long, sloping hill leading up to the Battery Park Hotel. The Coxe brothers, sons of Col. Frank Coxe, erected a row of business buildings on Patton Avenue about the turn of the century, with their rears reaching within a narrow street's width of the wall. The Coxes spanned Zero Alley between their buildings and the wall with bridges over which coal was hauled to fireplaces. The Coxes recognized the potential for making a street over the alley and did so, then opened the second floors of their buildings with shops fronting on Wall Street. The alley, darkened by the street above, became known as Rat's Alley.

The S&W Cafeteria building, which went up in 1929 on Patton Avenue, is perhaps the finest example of the art deco style in North Carolina. Ellington designed it, too, and when he was given free rein by the S&W chain to do with it as he wished, he knocked himself out. The building is two stories of polychrome cream, blue, green, black, and gilt glazed terra cotta with Indian and classical motifs. Inside, it is divided into several dining rooms and mezzanines with art deco decorations of the finest quality.

Two more art deco buildings of significance went up in the late 1920s. One was the Public Service Building on Patton Avenue, constructed in 1929. It was an eight-story office building with lavish art deco on its first two and upper two stories. Built by the Coxe Estate, the building housed Carolina Power & Light Company for many years.

The second building was the new City Hall. Designed by Ellington, City Hall is a cubical brick form set on a pink Georgia marble base and covered with a pink-and-green-tiled octagonal ziggurat roof.

It was originally planned to be one of two matching art deco buildings, the other being the courthouse next door. However, when county officials thought the city fathers were moving too fast in planning City Hall, they pulled out of the agreement, hired another architect, and built the then-largest courthouse in North Carolina beside City Hall. The building stands seventeen stories tall.

In the ten years from 1920 to 1930 Asheville made its greatest physical changes, and the population swelled from 28,504 to 50,193, the largest leap of any decade in the city's history.

The twenties were a great, progressive time in Asheville. For one thing, the city became a golf mecca. Biltmore Forest Country Club opened in 1922, Municipal Golf Course in 1925, Beaver Lake Golf Course's first nine holes were put in play in 1925, Malvern Hills Golf Club opened in 1926. The Country Club of Asheville had been in existence since before the turn of the century and had a fine, rolling course just below the Grove Park Inn.

The Asheville Fire Department put its firefighters on a full-time basis in 1924. Biltmore Junior College, forerunner of the University of North Carolina-Asheville held its first classes in 1927, the same year that the American Enka Corporation purchased land in Hominy Valley upon which it would build the largest industry in Buncombe County.

But the best year for Asheville was 1928. Both city hall and the courthouse offices were moved into new buildings on City-County Plaza, Asheville Senior High School opened on McDowell Street, Beaucatcher Tunnel was completed and traffic began moving through the tunnel to the undeveloped land on the east side of the mountain, the Biltmore Viaduct was opened, the Rhododendron Festival began, and a site near Fletcher was selected for the Asheville-Hendersonville Airport.

In the following year, 1929, with everything looking so rosy as the New Year began, two great bomb blasts shook the city.

The bombs came one week apart in October.

First was the publication of native son Thomas Wolfe's *Look Homeward, Angel,* a roughly autobiographical look at Asheville and its people in his growing-up days.

Second, seven days later, was the crash of the stock market, plunging the nation into its deepest depression ever.

The Roarin' Twenties came to a distinct halt.

35

TINSELTOWN

In the spring of 1921 Asheville, especially the Pack Square area, underwent a complete metamorphosis. Business signs were changed, names of stores, hotels and churches were changed, and hundreds of citizens mobbed the square on specified days. The town was hardly recognizable.

That was the time the first Hollywood movie ever to be filmed here was shot on Pack Square. It was a silent film called "The Conquest of Canaan," a story by Booth Tarkington of a small-town lawyer who made good against great odds. Almost all of the filming occurred on the square, in the old City Hall on the east end of the square, in the courthouse on College Street, around the First Baptist Church at College and Spruce, and on Biltmore Avenue, Patton Avenue and Broadway leading away from the square.

The Swannanoa-Berkeley Hotel on Biltmore Avenue, later known as the Earle Hotel, became the Canaan City Hotel.

Sign-painting, or repainting, was probably the biggest job of the movie makers. Every business on and around the square became something else, and even the Asheville Electric Street Railway became the Canaan Rapid Transit Company, with cars relettered and polished to a high degree.

The picture featured Thomas Meighan and Doris Kenyon, great stars of the silent screen, with Cyril Ring and Diana Allen, and the director was William Roy Neal, who came fully equipped with megaphone and beret reversed on his head, a real touch of Hollywood in those bygone days.

Only about a dozen persons comprised the Hollywood part of the Meighan company. Stars and principals stayed at Grove Park Inn and the cast's technical workers were put in the Battery Park Hotel.

Those were the days when movie companies worked with a few stars (four in this case) and since there were no speaking parts, they depended on local folk to play minor roles and, of course, to fill the roles of extras.

Those in the movie company looked for local persons who would fit certain roles, and when they saw one they thought would do, they hailed her on the spot.

Mrs. Fitzhugh Teague landed the role of one of the leading extras when she stepped off the elevator in the Bon Marche store, located at the corner of Patton and Lexington. Two scouts happened to see her, smoked her over, introduced themselves to her, and asked if she would like a role in the movie. She said she would have to talk with her husband, who operated a drug store on the northeast side of the square, who agreed, and she accepted the part. She and her mother, Mrs.L.V. Stowe, and Mrs. Jeter Pritchard took part in scenes around the drug store and in front of the church.

Antiques dealer Bob Bunn was local contact man for the movie company. He served as assistant to the assistant director, Jack Scott. Part of his responsibility each day was coming up with a sufficient number of extras for the day's filming.

So excited was Asheville over the arrival of the movie crew that Bunn had no problem finding extras early in the shooting. At times he had so many volunteers that he had to turn some away. Later, however, the new wore off of movie-making and instead of enjoying a deep flush of glory, extras found themselves mired in drudgery, standing around much of the day filming retake after retake. Extras then became harder to find.

In order to induce local folks into the limelight, Bunn had to carry a pocketful of five-dollar bills with which he paid extras in advance. Before the shooting ended, even these paid extras were so bored with the routine that many quit and Bunn had to beat the bushes harder.

Elsewhere, "The Conquest of Canaan" was accepted less enthusiastically. It was classed only as a medium successful picture.

But one scene was described as a dilly: a mob scene filmed on the square with local extras. Following an impassioned pep talk by director Neal, the extras went through their paces with slam-bang effort and the scene was widely hailed as a realistic success of silent movie making.

While all this bragging over one scene was going on, Ashevilleans who had participated slowly returned to normal. After a bit of time, shop signs were repainted, streetcars were redone, and life settled back into its routine. But for a while the city was Tinseltown and proud of it.

36

THE WOLFES

William Oliver (W. O.) Wolf was a Pennsylvania Dutch Quaker, born near Gettysburg in 1851. At fourteen in 1865, he stood on the side of a dusty lane and watched butternut-clad Confederate legions march into Gettysburg. He became a good stonecutter and sought his fortune elsewhere.

In 1869 he went to Columbia, South Carolina, and wound up carving and placing the caps on the State House. A year later, 1870, he moved to Raleigh and did the same on the North Carolina State House and the state's insane asylum. There he added an "e" to the end of his name, making it Wolfe.

W. O. had three wives. The first, Hattie, divorced him in 1876, and the second, Cynthia Hill, died of tuberculosis in 1884 in Asheville where he had brought her in 1880 for the fresh air cure. He opened a stonecutter's shop at 22 Pack Square, on the southeast corner of the square, and at 92 Woodfin Street he built a two-story home with his own hands.

Julia Westall was born in 1860, the fourth of eleven children fathered by Thomas Casey Westall in a second marriage. He had eight children by his first wife. Julia was twenty-four when she married W. O. Wolfe in January of 1885. Their union produced eight children, in order, Leslie (died in infancy), Frank, Mabel, Effie, twins Ben and Grover (Grover died at the 1904 World's Fair in St. Louis and Ben died in 1918), Fred, and Tom.

They lived at 92 Woodfin, which the children called "Ninety-two," and the marriage was strong, except for W. O.'s excessive drinking. Julia was hard-working and sober-minded and had little truck with her husband's benders. But she put up with them.

Julia bought the Old Kentucky Home at 48 Spruce Street in 1906 and went into the boarding house business. She and the children lived there, but W. O. maintained his residence at Ninety-two.

One of the twins, Ben, was the most-envied boy in town for the October job he had at the *The Citizen* office on Haywood Street. He worked the huge baseball scoreboard mounted on an upper ledge, on which World Series games were diagrammed play by play. Ben took instructions from a telegrapher just inside a window. He moved men around the scoreboard to show developing plays. Opposing lineups appeared on both sides of the board and were changed as players were substituted. When batters became baserunners, their route around the bases was shown by moving the man's figure from base to base. Huge throngs crowded the street to watch these games.

Mabel, born in 1890, was an accomplished vocalist and pianist. She and Pearl Shope, billing themselves as "Wolfe and Shope: Singers from Rag-time to Opera," played a circuit of small vaudeville theaters around the Southeast. In the summer offseason, Mabel played piano for the silent movies at the Nickelodian Theater on the square.

Large, unathletic, and a bit awkward, Tom had friends scattered about with whom he associated at times, but mostly he was something of a loner, always devouring books. An industrious young man, he carried a newspaper and magazine route, which at one point dipped into Carolina Lane, the city's red-light district, and it was said that Wolfe often traded papers or magazines for young women's favors. He was a voracious reader, and some said that by the time he left for the University of North Carolina in 1916 he had read every book in the public library.

Wolfe's progression through the North State Fitting School in Asheville and the University of North Carolina stoked his retentive mind and set him on the road to literary fame. There was little secret about who the genuises were at the university. Had a vote been taken, the winners would have been Tom Wolfe and Joe Ervin, brother of Sam Ervin, later a United States senator who conducted the Watergate hearings that led to the resignation of President Richard M. Nixon.

Wolfe wrote and acted in several one-act plays at Chapel Hill, and after graduation went to Harvard to study in George Pierce Baker's 47 Workshop with full intention of becoming a playwright.

While he was at Harvard, in 1922, his father, W. O., died in June of prostate cancer.

After Wolfe left Harvard in 1923, he lived in New York and taught at Washington Square College of New York University, but it was not long before he realized his talents lay in prose and turned himself toward that release of his massive talents with a fervor. He wrote endlessly and in such volume that his manuscripts had to be excessively edited. But he was on the track.

His bombshell fell on Asheville in October 1929 with the publication of *Look Homeward, Angel.* Characters in the book were real Asheville people with their names changed, and Wolfe painted them true to life. Few enjoyed reading what he had to say about them, and it was not a difficult task to tell who the fictionalized characters were based on. The Asheville people in the novel wore their most unpleasant guises, and if anyone in town had been involved in any scandal, no matter how minute, Wolfe's photographic memory had filed it away and brought it forth in the pages of the book.

Walter S. Adams, who reviewed the book for *The Asheville Times,* wrote, "... it is the story, told with bitterness and without compassion, of many Asheville people."

Asheville in those days was a much closer-knit, neighborly, and sensitive town than it is today. No one rose in arms, but those who were hard-hit reacted with hurt, shock, anger, irritation, indignation, resentment, and disgust, and wondered why this nice, quiet boy had written so.

George W. McCoy, who had grown up with Wolfe and who became managing editor of *The Citizen,* wrote many years later of the typical reaction among Ashevilleans:

FOR DAYS and weeks and months the book was a lively topic on the streets, at club gatherings, bridge games, parties, and teas. Conversations were started and carried on with remarks similar to these:
"Well, have you read it?"
"Isn't it awful?"
"Such a terrible thing to write about his own people!"
"He's a mad genius."
"Did you recognize so-and-so?"
"Now that Tom mentions it, I remember very clearly that . . . ."

These were the remarks of people who saw the book as an almanac of gossip, a collection of scandal.

The greatest shock—caused both by the book and by the community's reaction to it—was felt in Tom's own family.

They had been proud of Tom. He had gone to two universities, was the best educated member of the family. They looked up to him, expected him to achieve distinction.

And now this! Their pride was hurt.

Then came resentment. Why should he do this to them?

And there was a brief period of bitterness.

It would be stretching a point to say that all of Asheville was upset over the book. Those who felt they had been maligned were the most vocal. Others, however, remained calm and looked at the book as what it really was, a great contribution to literature.

Wolfe himself did little to assuage the feelings of Asheville. He remained in New York; in fact, the next time he came home was more than seven years later.

The librarian at Pack Library read portions of the book, did not like what she read, and refused to put the book on the acquisition list. When readers called for the book at the circulation desk, they were told simply: "I'm sorry, we do not have it." No explanation was given.

Six years after the book's publication, the library still had not stocked it. The writer F. Scott Fitzgerald called for it at the library desk one day and when told the library did not have it, he went to a book store, purchased two copies, and presented them to the library. They were accepted and catalogued and placed in open circulation.

When Wolfe finally returned to Asheville early in May of 1937, apparently uncertain of the welcome he would receive, he found that he was neither cursed nor reviled, and no one expressed bitterness or scorn. With warmth and friendliness, Wolfe was acclaimed in Asheville as a famous author.

Before Wolfe returned to New York, George McCoy asked him to write an article for the *Asheville Citizen-Times*, describing his feelings upon returning. In the article Wolfe wrote:

I HAVE BEEN seven years from home, but now I have come back again. And what is there to say?

Where are the words I thought that I must say, the arguments I thought that I should make, the debates and demonstrations that so often, in those years of absence, memory, wandering, youth, and new discovery I had so hotly made to solitude, and to the ghostly audience of an absent fellowship, the thousand things that I would prove and show when I returned—where are they now?

For now I have come home again—and what is there to say? I think that there is nothing—save the silence of our speech. I think that there is nothing—save the knowledge of our glance. I think that there is nothing—save the silent and unspoken conscience in us now that needs no speech but silence, because we know what we know, we have what we have, we are what we are.

So what is there to say?

He returned to New York and then came back home to spend the summer writing in Max Whitson's cabin on a wooded hilltop near the Asheville Recreation Park. He spoke of returning to the hills to live in Yancey County, which he loved, and of writing a novel of the Confederate soldier.

But he didn't. Those dreams died with him the following year. In July 1938, he developed pneumonia on a tour of the Pacific Northwest. Complications forced his removal to Johns Hopkins Hospital in Baltimore, and he died there on September 15, 1938.

His giant body was brought home to Asheville for funeral services in First Presbyterian Church and burial in Riverside Cemetery. The pastor, Dr. C. Grier Davis, and pastor emeritus, Dr. Robert F. Campbell, who had been Tom's pastor in his growing-up years, conducted the services. In part, Dr. Campbell said this:

"The assembly of his fellow citizens is gathered to honor the memory and mourn the untimely death of one who went forth from us to literary fame . . . . He undoubtedly had within a flame of genius which shone forth brilliantly and gave promise of a star of the first magnitude, had he lived to reach the maturity of his powers. . . .

"I wish I had something definite to say about his religious life. As there was a restlessness and lack of definite form in his intellectual and emotional processes, it is natural to conclude that the same was true of his religious beliefs and aspirations. This seems to find illustration in the words that appear on the preface page of his latest novel, *Of Time and the River*:

"'Where shall the weary rest? When shall the lonely of heart come home? What doors are open for the wanderer? And which of us shall find his father, know his face, and in what place and in what time, and in what land? Where? Where the weary of heart can abide forever, where the weary of wandering can find peace, where the tumult, the fever, and the fret shall be forever stilled.'

"As Tom's friend and pastor, I shall always cherish the hope and the belief that in the yearning desire of his restless heart to find his rest, his home, his peace in the heavenly Father's presence, there was the pith and substance of the Christian faith. . . ."

Today, the Wolfe home at 48 Spruce Street stands as a memorial to the memory of both Thomas Wolfe and his family. It is filled with period furniture and decor and for those who truly admire Wolfe's writings, it is the same as a trip to Mecca to visit the home and then the grave of Thomas Wolfe.

Fred Wolfe said his mother, Julia, hoped to make enough money in real estate to build a sizeable estate for her children. For a while she made money in Asheville real estate, but then she invested heavily in the Florida land boom and lost her money when the boom burst. Among the Wolfe memorabilia is a $26,000 check Julia wrote for a down payment on Florida property during that time.

Unable to meet payments at Wachovia Bank where she had borrowed considerable sums for her land dealings, Julia felt the "Old Kentucky Home" slipping away. Her fears were justified in 1941. The mammoth, gabled house of twenty-nine rooms where her children had grown up, passed into the hands of Wachovia Bank and Trust Company, and it was a sad day for Julia Wolfe.

Now let us regress a moment. Harry Blomberg, son of Lewis Blomberg who had a tobacco shop on Patton Avenue in the 1880s, had leased some of the Wolfe property in 1926 to start a business which, among other ventures, helped him make money between that time and 1941.

When Tom Wolfe was a boy, his mother used the back half of the her property, that which fronted on Market Street, as a large garden, growing fruits and vegetables that appeared later on the dinner table of the boarding house.

Always a cagey woman with an eye on turning a profit, Julia Wolfe had leased that garden lot, measuring 115 by 90 feet to Blomberg, who already had a gasoline station on the northeast corner of Market and Walnut, adjoining the Wolfe property. As shrewd as Julia, Harry saw the need for a large building for storing automobiles and approached Mrs. Wolfe about buying or leasing the garden lot.

"We sat in the parlor in the Wolfe home during those cold days of December," Harry recalled later, "ironing out the details of the lease—and she kept the house so cold I darned near froze."

On December 21, 1926, Julia Wolfe and Harry Blomberg signed a lease for ten years at an annual rental of $2,000 for each of the first five years and $3,000 for each of the next five. Harry borrowed $4,000 from the Central Bank and Trust Company, which went broke in 1929, and used it to begin construction of an automobile storage garage on the property, and in the lease Mrs. Wolfe specified the size and strength of the structure. Her specifications called for a building with a basement and one floor, and stipulated that it be of sufficient strength to support an additional floor. The building backed only twenty-five feet from the Old Kentucky Home.

At the end of the ten years, on December 21, 1936, the property, including the building, would revert to Julia Wolfe. What she planned to do with the building never became known. When the ten-year period ended, the country was still mired in the depths of depression, and Mrs. Wolfe accepted Harry's offer to renew the lease. Harry's business had thrived during that decade. Mrs. Wolfe was happy to have the income; her fortunes were still going downhill.

When Wachovia became convinced that Mrs. Wolfe could not repay her indebtedness—not even the interest—the bank entered a foreclosure suit and named all of the family as defendants. Tom disassociated himself from the suit by relinquishing any claim to family inheritance, thus avoiding a day in court.

Foreclosure proceedings passed ownership of the Wolfe home from the family to Wachovia—and there Harry Blomberg came into the picture.

He heard that a man named West intended to purchase the property from the bank, tear down the house, and build a produce market on the place.

"I thought it should be preserved," Harry said. "I thought it was important to the city that the house be kept intact rather than destroyed so a produce market could be built." Harry also wanted to keep his automobile storage place, which had been a going concern for years.

So on December 22, 1941, Harry Blomberg bought the Old Kentucky Home for $18,000. He bought it street to street, the house, the garage, and all. He told Julia Wolfe she could continue to make her home in the house.

Business was not all that was on his mind that day. A big teddy bear, Harry had a streak of sentimentality a yard and a half wide running down his back, and that's what spurred him. The home was a masterpiece of gabled construction, and to tear it down and replace it with a produce market in the midst of a nice residential neighbor-hood was more than he could tolerate. He had grown up on Woodfin Street, around the corner from Spruce, and as kids, although he was four years younger, he and Tom Wolfe had been pals.

"We neighborhood boys used to gather at the Wolfe boarding house on Saturday afternoon," he said. "The girls who danced at the Majestic Theater would come for supper in costume. They wore short dresses, a novelty in those days, and while waiting for supper they would sit on the porch and prop their feet on the bannister. We boys would sit on the concrete wall by the sidewalk and sneak peeks at them and giggle. We learned a lot about womanhood that way."

Late in February 1942, Fred Wolfe, Tom's older brother, came to Harry and said, "I want to buy mama's place."

Harry was agreeable to selling the house to Fred, but said he would keep the back lot with his building on it. He said when they began to talk price, Fred said, "I ain't gonna let you hold me up."

"I tried to tell him I didn't intend to hold him up," Harry said, "but Fred wouldn't let me get a word in. He kept saying he wasn't going to let me rob him and things like that."

All this time Harry was thinking about charging him $4,000 for the house, and when Fred continued to tell him that the Wolfe family money was gone and he wouldn't let Harry overcharge him, Harry began to think about taking $3,500 for the house.

When Harry finally got his chance, he asked, "Fred, what do you want to pay for the house?"

"I won't pay you a dime over $7,000," Fred said.

Harry accepted and the papers were drawn, and on March 2, 1942, Blomberg deeded to Wolfe home back to the family for $7,000."

As they left the lawyer's office, Harry put his arm around Fred's shoulders and said, "Fred, if you'd kept your damned mouth shut, you could have bought the house for half that much."

Julia Wolfe lived in the house until she died in 1945, and the home was finally sold by the family in 1949 to the Thomas Wolfe Memorial Assoiciation, Inc., for $16,000. Primarily, the association was made up of citizens interested in seeing the home established as a memorial to Tom Wolfe. The association became unable to make the payments and on April 18, 1958, turned the property over to the city, which paid off the indebtedness and operated the home as a museum.

It was designated a National Historic Site in 1973 and on January 1, 1975, the city deeded the property to the state to be oprated as one of the historic sites of the Department of Cultural Resources.

In August 1981 Harry Blomberg sold the back lot, where his garage building had stood for fifty-four years, to the Department of Cultural Resources which razed the garage and built an auditorium on the property as part of the museum.

The sale price was $88,000.

Had it not been for the soft heart and philanthropy of Harry Blomberg, the Wolfe house would have been torn down more than a half-century ago—and there would have been no anchoring point when the Wolfe fans came to Mecca.

The second hammer blow fell on Asheville—and the nation— a week after Tom Wolfe's book came out. As the stock market crashed and depression swept the country, Asheville's Central Bank and Trust Company closed its doors and went out of business. Hundreds of Asheville and Buncombe County people lost their life's savings.

The city ran up large indebtedness that would require a half-century to repay. Long lines of people looked for work. Lines formed at soup kitchens. Hobo jungles went up along the railroad tracks, places where vagabonds riding the rods in and out of Asheville congregated to eat from a common pot, commiserate with each other, and swap exciting tales of travel on the iron rails.

A newspaper editor provoked a little thought in 1934 when he wrote: "Naive Nellie thinks Uncle Sam ought to borrow twenty billions from Europe and then default, thereby squaring the account. . . . A pleasant thought to aid your digestion: That $19,500,000,000 which we tossed down a rathole in Europe (in the World War) would have supplied each unemployed man in the United States with $5,000 worth of food and shelter."

People thought he made a good point for as the country came out of the depression, it had to whip Germany again, and this time the Japanese as well. As the depression drew to a close, the Second World War struck with fury on both sides of the globe, and America fought its way to victory through the hedgerows of Europe and the jungles of the Pacific. The world did not settle down, however, and five years later the United States was mired in a police-action war in Korea, then a war in Vietnam, and an action in the Persian Gulf. Asheville contributed to all of these wars, and its men stood as fast on the battlefronts as they had at Bull Run or the Hindenburg Line.

The city continued to expand and grew a bit in population, although most new residents sought homes in the county. The interstates came, air travel developed and Asheville soared into the jet age, and prosperity reigned.

Asheville concentrated on tourism, industry, and agriculture, and continued to grow stalwart men and women. Television came along and changed the city as well as the rest of the world, but living in Asheville continued to be good. The jewel of a city developed into a large gemstone for all to enjoy.

Chronicling that era would require another volume, and I will leave that to future historians. Suffice it to say Asheville has a more varied history, and one just as glorious, as any other city in the state. People keep coming, still attracted by an all-around fine climate and the progress the city has shown. The only difference is that where they once came on horseback and afoot across the mountains, they come now by automobile and air. But they find that the Land of Eden is just as alive and rich and palatable as it ever was.

AFTERWORD

So you think all that adventure you read in Western novels—the Indian fights, cattle drives, gunfights—is peculiar only to that part of the country?

Consider Asheville:

It was a frontier town settled by fearless, heavily-armed frontiersmen who rode horseback and shot straight.

It had Indian fights, shootouts, street brawls, hangings, and scalpings.

It saw cattle drives and wagon trains, and had sheepherders in the hills.

It had its share of whiskey-makers, saloons, tobacco-chewing women, and brothels.

It had fiery newspaper editors: "If caught today, he will be tried immediately and hung in short order. . . ."

So how far removed are we from Tombstone or El Paso?

Let me tell you how far:

In West Asheville there lives a clear-minded ninety-seven-year-old man named Thomas Young, who is a pleasure to talk with.

Tom Young went from here to fight in both world wars. A navy man, he was so eager to get into combat he almost jumped ship in Normandy on D-Day to join ground fighting forces invading Europe.

He grew up in western Arkansas and worked in Texas and Oklahoma before coming to Asheville.

He was a second cousin of John Wesley Hardin, the Texas outlaw who slew forty-two men (Tom's father, a frontier doctor, was Wes's first cousin). And Tom was an acquaintance of Uncle Billy Tilghman, one of the last of the frontier lawmen who replaced Wyatt Earp as marshal of Dodge City, Kansas.

That's how far removed we are from history–not very far.

Peering into Asheville's past is only looking into yesterday.